Bottom Time

The Adventures of a Commercial Diver

Norbert Weissinger

Bloomington, IN  Milton Keynes, UK
authorHOUSE®

AuthorHouse™
1663 Liberty Drive, Suite 200
Bloomington, IN 47403
www.authorhouse.com
Phone: 1-800-839-8640

AuthorHouse™ *UK Ltd.*
500 Avebury Boulevard
Central Milton Keynes, MK9 2BE
www.authorhouse.co.uk
Phone: 08001974150

© 2007 Norbert Weissinger. All rights reserved.

No part of this book may be reproduced, stored in a retrieval system, or transmitted by any means without the written permission of the author.

First published by AuthorHouse 2/28/2007

ISBN: 978-1-4259-6602-7 (sc)

Printed in the United States of America
Bloomington, Indiana

This book is printed on acid-free paper.

Contents

Acknowledgments vii
Introduction ix

I. Early Dives

Commercial Diving School 2
The Life of a Tender 11
Live-boating 13
Trash Collecting 17
Mixed-Gas Diving 24
Wheel Job in the Atchafalaya River 28
Frolich Mud Divers 35
Blue Water, Black Death 42

II. Mexico

Merida, Yucatan 66
My New Home 68
Pipelaying 73
Pontoon Check 77
Midnight Dive 80
Almost a Fight 83
Spiny Dive 86
Dos Bocas 88
Lee Gets Injured 95
A Barge Overturns 98
L-bends at Nohoch 103
Mr. Bill and the Riser 116
Dickie Breaks His Thumb 122
Beer Run 131
A Buckled Pipeline 140
The 1,000-Foot Club 143
Shark Talk 148

Mark Spears a Big Grouper 151
No Air! 154
Barracuda, Tarpon, and Bangsticks 158
A Brief Interlude on Land 163
A Mexican Loses His Hands 171
Wheel Job in Rough Seas 173
Tales from Vietnam 178
A Panic Attack 184
Craig Finds a Horse Conch 188
Cayos Arcas 196
I Escape a Man-Eating Pipe 204
Scuba Dive to 160 Feet 210
A Taste of Singapore 213
Coatzacoalcos 217
The Night Before Christmas 220
The Worst Storm 223
The Geyser at Tecozautla 228
Whale Shark 234
El Chichon Volcano Erupts 236
Land of the Lotus-Eaters 243
Cancun 249

III. Southeast Asia

Train to Bangkok 270
Pattaya—The Thai Riviera 274
Bangkok, Venice of the East 277
Buddhism 280
A Visit To Surin 282
Phuket 284
Festivals 286
Sanuk 287
Dream's End 288

Acknowledgments

I would like to thank the following people who made this book possible:

Craig Cooper, Richard Campbell, Mike Sands, Lee Hoskins, Larry Alley, Tony Imperato, Steve Kelly, Mark Callis, Joe Savino, Chuck Breidert, Juan Enriques, Santiago, Dave Dagnall, Buck Frolich, Charlie Dupree, B, Ted Hess, Andy Craig, John Bidmead, Marty Alfonso, Craig Rock, The "Alaskans," Bob Henderson, Charlie Hilt, Don Byrd, Pat Farrell, the crew of the *L. B. Meaders*, and the divers and supervisors at Taylor Diving and Salvage.

I would also like to thank Janet Weissinger for her support and patience and Bobbie Christmas for editing.

Introduction

bottom time : time spent under water; time spent breathing air from a tank or hose; time spent under pressure; time spent taking nothing for granted; time that seems to be concentrated; an alternate reality where one experiences life as a fish; time that is utter terror or sheer bliss, but never boring.

I plunged into frigid water and gasped as cold enveloped me. I grabbed the buoy line and descended toward the bottom of an abandoned stone quarry, where the depth was thirty feet. A lead weight belt overcame the buoyancy of my thick wetsuit, and I drifted down easily. I swallowed repeatedly to equalize the pressure on my ears. My previous underwater experience had been in comfortable swimming pools during my college scuba class, never deeper than twelve feet.

An alien world greeted me when my toes touched the soft bottom. My senses came alive. The hiss of air from my regulator was amplified as I breathed. Through hazy water, my eyes tried to focus on rocks and mud, the color of granite. I searched for the slightest trace of movement in this quiet, timeless cave, where visibility extended only twenty feet in any direction.

My instructor, hovering like a sinister figure in a dark wetsuit, approached. He pointed to my mask. I removed the mask. Icy water stung my face and blinded me. My teeth clamped tightly around the mouthpiece of the regulator, and I sucked in a breath of air. I put on the mask, exhaled through my nose, cleared the water out of the mask, and blurred shapes acquired edges again. My instructor pointed to my regulator. I removed the regulator from my mouth and held my breath. I inserted the regulator into my mouth again, pressed the purge valve, and took a careful breath. I gave the thumbs up signal to the instructor, indicating I was all right.

He seemed satisfied with my demonstration of two basic underwater skills, clearing the mask and regulator.

We glided a few yards along the bottom. Large rocks loomed in a gray mist. The featureless hole offered little to attract the eye. Any life was hibernating on the cold February day, but I was thrilled. I forgot about the cold. The wetsuit insulated me from the frigid water. Drifting weightless in the strange world fascinated me. Time remained a spectator on the surface, and nothing mattered, except breathing.

I ascended alone toward the light, and my instructor returned to the descent line to wait for the next student.

I had made my first open-water dive in Blue Hole Quarry, Pennsylvania, in the middle of winter. I was hundreds of miles from the sea, but I had experienced a few minutes of bottom time, and I wanted more. I was a certified diver.

✳ ✳ ✳

I graduated from college that year with little money and no job. I was desperate. When I found an ad at the back of Skin Diver magazine promising high pay, adventure, and travel for commercial divers, I decided to take a chance. Those three words were like siren calls to a young, impressionable man. I borrowed five hundred dollars, took my last five hundred in savings, and enrolled in a commercial diving course in Oakland, California.

Filled with youthful ambition and ignorance, I stumbled into a profession considered by insurance companies as the most dangerous in the world. Humility and luck helped me survive. I was fortunate to leave the business with unforgettable memories and my body intact. I never experienced decompression sickness, didn't lose any fingers, didn't lose my hearing, and didn't become paralyzed, as some in the business did.

This book describes my travels and adventures as a commercial diver, from the frustrating times as an apprentice, to the dream years living on a pipelaying barge in Mexico. Join me on my most memorable dives, my brushes with death, and encounters with marine life. From a novice with practically no underwater experience, I became a seasoned professional, logging more than 400 dives during my last eighteen months in Mexico. The work and search for work took me around the world. I spent eight months in the Far East, traveling and living in Thailand, Malaysia, and Singapore.

Nothing is glamorous about commercial diving. It is an industry dependent on the boom and bust cycles of the oil business. Offshore oilfields exist in remote regions of the world with extreme climates ranging from brutal cold to searing heat. Mail delivery sometimes takes six months. Entertainment is limited..

I lived on barges and boats for six years and explored foreign lands during my free time. Life at sea was a mixture of nonstop diving marathons followed by lazy days where the boredom became oppressive. The sea can drive a man crazy, and I fought the boredom with diversions. I collected insects on the barge, ran laps around the crane deck, read books, studied the stock market, and even invented a board game. Some divers developed their carpentry skills and paneled their cabins with wood from shipping crates. Others painted, lifted weights, or played poker. The boredom drove some to alcohol or marijuana.

Sometimes I wondered why I endured the abuse of the sea day after day, month after month. Life at sea was physically exhausting. Twenty minutes of bottom time was equivalent to the energy a person expended in an eight-hour day. The sea punished the eardrums and sinuses, with the constant change in pressure during descent and ascent. The resistance to movement that water posed made even simple tasks difficult. One time, the current was running so badly off the stern that I could not swim twenty yards from the barge to a platform. The current swept me away, and my tender hauled me back to the barge by my lifeline. Barges also worked twenty-four hours a day, and divers were expected to work any hour, day or night. I often slept only four hours a night until a job was finished. Somehow, though, the opportunity to jump into the water always renewed my energy. I could be in my bunk, exhausted, and if someone came in and said, "Do you want to make a dive?" I'd jump up and say, "Sure." I couldn't get enough bottom time. A few minutes under water always drove away the boredom and produced an adrenaline rush unlike anything in this world. I was addicted to bottom time.

Although the work was punishing, opportunities for fun and travel always existed. On free days, I chipped spiny oysters off the rigs or explored coral reefs, when they were nearby. What other profession offered a chance to play in the mud, hunt for treasure, and get paid for it?

People ask me, "What do you do down there?" Sport divers go down to watch fish, photograph, or explore wrecks. I go down as a glorified construction worker, and fish watch me work. I have salvaged, repaired, and inspected pipelines; cleared boat propellers; cut steel; dug trenches; helped set platforms; installed mooring systems; and searched for bodies. I have wrestled hundred-pound hydraulic impact wrenches while tightening huge flange bolts. I have been tangled in cables while my mind was under the influence of nitrogen narcosis. Sometimes the water was crystal clear and warm, sometimes pitch black and cold as ice. I have vivid memories of crawling along a three-hundred-yard long manifold in black water, with nothing but the picture of a blueprint in my mind to help me navigate. Death sometimes looked over my shoulder, but I cherished the experience of having lived in the realm of the gill breathers.

I hope these dive narratives will give you some idea of the work divers perform to build and maintain oilfields hundreds of miles from land. Meet some of the rugged individualists and eccentric characters that compose a small, unique industry. The commercial oilfield diving industry employs perhaps a few thousand divers around the world, and many died so that millions can enjoy the luxuries black gold brings. Fifty-eight divers lost their lives during the building of the oilfield in the North Sea. Dozens died in the Gulf of Mexico, Persian Gulf, South China Sea, and other remote places.

Although inaccuracies may exist, I have tried to reproduce dialogue from memory in the spirit of each situation. I also made some tape recordings of conversations about Vietnam and the saturation dive to 1,000 feet.

The life of a commercial diver is a lonely one. Long months spent at sea away from family and friends wear down the soul. The ocean became my mistress. I fell asleep to the sound of waves banging against the barge. I plunged into her depths like a primitive creature returning to my ancestral home. I was humbled by her power, drawn to her violence, lured by her beauty and seductive charms, until life on land became nothing more than an interlude between those times when I was really alive, experiencing bottom time.

I. Early Dives

Commercial Diving School

My new life began with a bus trip from Pennsylvania to Oakland, California. The three-day journey took me past the Appalachian Mountains, into the heartland of America, through Oklahoma, then dusty Texas. An owl hit the windshield one night in New Mexico and forced a short delay. I had never seen tumbleweeds before, and the desert stretched forever. The saguaro cactus looked like statues of people in the darkness, their arms pointed in many directions. I'll never forget the brilliant green hills on the approach into Oakland. Houses swarmed on the hillsides bare of trees.

I found Roper's Boarding House in Alameda without much trouble. The dive school had recommended it. The next night I returned to the bus station, because the bus line had misplaced my suitcase. An overzealous traffic cop gave me a ticket for jaywalking in the rain.

Though it was January, the climate in California was nice and warm, and I put away my winter coat. The dive school was situated along an estuary, near a bridge that connected Oakland with Alameda. The campus consisted of a warehouse; classroom; thirty-foot free-ascent tower; a number of water tanks, one with a sub-sea wellhead at the bottom; a dock by the estuary; and a mini-saturation diving system.

The warehouse contained strange underwater contraptions. Some had been used in the movies. A giant blue and yellow capsule with the words "Nelson Research" stood next to a robot diving suit. Diving bells, robots, chambers, sleds, and oilfield equipment crammed the warehouse.

Big Al, a stocky man missing an index finger, owned the school. He said he had kept his finger over the edge of a pipe too long in murky water, and the other end of the pipe had chopped off the first two joints. He often played as Ernest Borgnine's double in the movies. He always entertained us with his stories. He said that one time he had been pouring concrete under water and had accidentally covered his air hose with concrete. He had to cut himself out of his Mark V suit to escape.

Al ran his school with a minimum staff. He had a secretary and two instructors, Charlie and Don.

Charlie, one of the first saturation divers, had accumulated a fortune welding under water in the 1960s, and retired. He wore a red baseball cap and a permanent squint.

Don, a short man who wore glasses, did most of the instructing. A veteran commercial diver, he always wore a sweater, even in the balmy California climate, because he had made so many gas dives that the helium had permanently affected his metabolism. He always felt cold. Don had suffered the bends in the shoulder, and he didn't dive anymore. The bends is the term used in the industry for decompression sickness, where gas bubbles come out of solution in the body, often in the joints, and cause excruciating pain and sometimes permanent disabilities. Don was developing bone necrosis and arthritis.

Charlie never smiled. He scared us with tales of saturation divers, those fearless individuals who lived under pressure in chambers for months at a time and went to the bottom in diving bells.

"This guy jumped in with a shiny new Swindell helmet and when they pulled him up, there was nothing on the end but a wetsuit," Charlie told us one day in class. "He must have looked like a fishing lure with that shiny helmet." Charlie told us to beware of the police in Louisiana, who liked to arrest people from out of state. Louisiana was where the offshore oil industry had started, and most divers migrated to Louisiana, where they learned their trade in the warm waters of the Gulf of Mexico.

Don liked to read to us from a diving manual while we sat in class. He read slowly, and his booming voice commanded attention. "Nobody gets in the water until they have memorized the six gas laws verbatim. Nobody gets in the water until they have memorized line pull signals. . . ." All students had to master those two requirements before they could get near a water tank.

Commercial divers go under water attached to an umbilical, which consists of a safety line, air supply hose, communication cable, and pneumofathometer hose (a thin hose used for measuring depth). A tender, or diver trainee, tends the umbilical from the dive station and maintains the correct amount of tension on the umbilical. A good tender keeps enough slack in the water to allow the diver to work, but he also keeps it tight enough to respond to line pull signals, if regular communications fails. One tug by the diver means stop; two tugs means give me slack; three tugs means pull up my slack; and four tugs means get me the hell out of there.

If our instructors taught us one thing, it was the importance of common sense. Written on a wooden plaque above our heads in the classroom were the words "There are old divers and there are bold divers, but there are no old, bold divers." In less than a year, I would know what those words meant.

Being of cautious nature, I felt I could be a good diver. I would keep all my fingers, and I would not let my umbilical be fouled on anything. I would follow the dive tables and not get bent like Don.

I admired my instructors. They looked like ordinary men, but they had done extraordinary things. They were awe inspiring. They had survived a dangerous game and lived to tell about it. Did I have the right stuff to be a commercial diver? I didn't see why not. I was in good health, had made a few scuba dives, and I was comfortable in the water.

The class was made of eighty students, an unusual mix of vagabonds, college dropouts, ex-convicts, construction workers, former Army Rangers, sport divers looking for adventure, welders, and a group of pile drivers from Alaska who considered the three-month course a luxury vacation far from the cold and rugged lifestyle of Anchorage, where the port was frozen most of the year. I remember the Alaskans most vividly, especially Kenny, Brian, Joe Kool, and Superman. Kenny never studied for an exam. He almost didn't graduate, but then a vacation is supposed to be fun. He slept in class to recover from his all-night drinking excursions. Superman had a hard time opening a bank account, because the teller didn't believe that was his name, but a driver's license proved otherwise. One of the Alaskans walked with a limp. His leg had been severed when a piling had fallen on it, but doctors had sewn the two pieces together and installed a metal pin.

The class of '78 came from all over the world. Andy had dropped out of Colgate University. Marty, an ex-convict from Oakland, said he just wanted a job. He had been given the choice of various trade schools for rehabilitation. He had chosen commercial diving. He also slept in class. Sigurdur was a member of the Iceland search and rescue team. Greg was a carpenter in San Francisco. George came from Lake Charles, Louisiana. David came from North Carolina. A former army paratrooper, he acquired the name "Shiteater," because he said he would do anything for a hundred dollars, including eat dog turds. The rest came from Bermuda, Trinidad, Israel, England, Canada, and almost every state in the United States.

We spent one week training with U.S. Navy Mark V deep-sea diving gear. I don't know why we had to work with such clumsy suits, but I suppose the instructors thought if we could work in the Mark V, we could work with anything. Abalone divers still used the Mark V gear, but oilfield divers did not.

"This will separate the men from the boys," Al said on the first day we tried on the Mark V suits. "Everybody gets in the Mark V. If you don't, you fail the course."

I stood by a tank of black, slimy water in the warehouse and waited for my teammates to help me into the suit, while Don explained the procedure.

"All right, Red Crew," Don bellowed from the podium. "Sit your diver on the bench and listen to what I have to say. It takes two men to assist a diver to the ladder in Mark V gear. He cannot walk alone. Never let him climb on the ladder alone. He can catch a foot on a rung and fall backwards and snap a bone. I've seen it happen. Be careful when you put the breastplate on. You can nick his chin. When a diver comes out of the water, two men must assist him at all times. Is that understood?"

I listened attentively.

"The suit is made of vulcanized rubber with an outer cotton twill layer and an inner cotton drill layer," Don continued.

I slipped my feet into the suit and soaped my wrists so I could slide my hands through the narrow cuffs. Greg, a mellow carpenter from San Francisco helped me step into the lead boots, and he laced them. I strapped the heavy weight belt around my waist.

"The boots weigh thirty-five pounds. The weight belt weighs eighty-four pounds. The breastplate and helmet weigh fifty-four pounds," Don said. "In a few minutes you will have doubled your body weight, but don't worry. You'll weigh a lot less in the water."

Greg gently lowered the breastplate over my head and set it on my shoulders. He attached the twelve wing nuts to secure the breastplate to the suit.

The helmet came down over my head, and I took a deep breath.

"The helmet is made of spun copper with four glass heat-treated view ports." Don's voice faded to insignificance. "Interrupted bayonet threads on the breastplate allow the helmet to be attached. A chin button on the inside right allows a diver to vent the suit if it becomes overinflated. The Mark V is a dry suit, so there is the danger of accidental blowup and unwanted ascent to the surface."

Charlie opened the front viewport and looked in to judge my degree of panic. How could I describe being tightly enclosed in a body suit, weighed down by lead boots? It was like being in a cave, with the walls inches from my face. Wearing that suit could easily be a claustrophobic's worst nightmare.

Charlie closed the viewport door and screwed it shut. I became apprehensive.

Greg attached the air hose and communication cable to the back of the helmet.

"Now you're almost ready to go in the water," Don said. "Put the three-finger gloves on. Two of you get by his side and assist him in walking to the ladder."

My teammates helped me stand. They held my arms as I clumsily took one step at a time, like a baby learning to walk. A fall with the equipment on could have been tragic.

"You'll have a week of training in the black water tank," Don continued. "You'll practice your buoyancy control, tie knots with the three-finger gloves, and do a hose changeover."

I fumbled for the air control valve by my waist. Air hissed into the helmet. I tried the chin button to exhaust air from the helmet. Now I understood why Don had said some Navy divers had a nervous twitch, sometimes jerking their heads to the side. They were subconsciously hitting their chin buttons frequently, to vent the suit. Don had told us of an abalone diver who once ran out of air in a Mark V suit. He was working alone, so there was no one to help him. Luckily, the suit contains about three minutes of air, so he cut himself out and escaped.

I carefully stepped onto the ladder and descended into the black water. After a few seconds, I landed on the slimy bottom. I could see a few inches past my nose. Air hissed loudly into the helmet. I felt much lighter and had some freedom of movement. The tank was only ten feet deep, so I didn't have to worry about clearing my ears. Sometimes I have trouble clearing. I cannot descend head first.

I walked around the bottom for a few minutes, then tugged three times on my umbilical hose, the signal for my tender to haul me up.

My first experience in a Mark V suit proved that I could be dropped into black water with 150 pounds of lead strapped to me and not panic. Being a prisoner inside a clumsy suit was not a pleasant feeling, but I trusted my teammates.

After a week with the Mark V, I never used the gear again. For the rest of my underwater projects I used lightweight masks and wetsuits, the preferred gear in the industry. The Kirby Morgan mask is widely used for commercial work. It's a rugged mask with demand regulator and free-flow valve, large faceplate, good communications, and a rubber hood that fits snugly, secured by rubber straps around the head.

The underwater projects in black water challenged me. Imagine being a blind plumber working in a weightless medium where even the air you breathe cannot be taken for granted. Some projects required physical strength, but most simply required a perseverance seldom needed for any task on land. On one project, I hung upside down from a wooden plank and drilled a hole, inserted a dowel, and nailed a lead plate over it in pitch black darkness.

Being a contortionist may help in being a diver, because the positions divers find themselves in defy gravity. It is one thing to pound a nail, but try doing it upside down without seeing the nail, plus the water presents a great resistance to the hammer.

Another project challenged my mental ability. Go down in the black water tank with a bucket full of thirty assorted pieces of pipe and assemble them into one piece. The ability to visualize shapes in the mind and construct an image such as might be seen on a blueprint is a great advantage. Ingenuity and a calm state also help. The job is often simple, such as inserting a bolt into a flange, but when visibility is zero, the flange is oscillating wildly, the temperature is brutally cold, and the current is running at ten knots, things aren't as elementary.

One project called "wrestling the alligator" required the diver to make an eye in a two-inch-thick steel cable and secure the eye with Crosby clips. A Crosby clip is a U-shaped bolt with a saddle piece that allows two cables to be joined. I rolled in the oily slime at the bottom of the tank, bending the thick cable with my hands. The cable was ready to uncoil with tremendous force. I squirmed in the dirt and wrestled the invisible monster and finally tightened the nuts with a crescent wrench after almost an hour. I had absolutely no visibility and came up with a black face, because my mask leaked.

On another project, I had to enter a ten-foot tunnel at the bottom of a tank, remove a plate, and retrieve the gasket behind it. I completed the task, but my teammate, Andy, wasn't so lucky. While he was in the tunnel, his helmet popped off. Blinded, he scrambled out of the tunnel and shot to the surface. I had never seen Andy move so fast. The lack of air can be a tremendous motivator.

The road to becoming a commercial diver is like the process of natural selection. Not all survive the struggle. Those who do are stronger. There were always tests, mental tests, tests of physical skill, and tests that could not be prepared for. Fate sometimes decided who continued to the next crossroads and who did not. The oxygen tolerance test sometimes eliminated a candidate. One of the requirements to be qualified for commercial diving work was the ability to breathe pure oxygen for thirty minutes. Breathing 100-percent oxygen was the quickest way to eliminate nitrogen from the tissues, so divers breathed oxygen every day. Everyone in my class passed that test.

One day Don took groups of us down to 220 feet in a decompression chamber, where we took a written test to see how well we withstood nitrogen narcosis. The test consisted of simple arithmetic problems such as six plus two and eight times ten. I noticed the worried looks on some of my classmates during the ride down. A depth of 220 feet is equivalent to more than six atmospheres of pressure, an extreme depth for breathing air. The chamber quickly degenerated into a madhouse of laughing and giggling. I found it difficult to concentrate. I felt drunk. I don't remember finishing the test, and I had a runny nose. We returned to the surface after decompressing for forty-seven minutes.

Most commercial dives deeper than 160 feet are not made breathing air, but with a helium-oxygen mixture. Helium does not produce the narcotic effects that nitrogen does. Some individuals can tolerate the narcosis better than others, but everyone is affected, and a diver becomes a danger to himself at great depths, if he breathes air. Nitrogen narcosis has been compared to drinking a six pack of beer on an empty stomach, but the effects become more noticeable the deeper a diver goes. Tunnel vision, disorientation, giddiness, and loss of time sense are frequent symptoms.

Spring came, and I was eager to find work. While the Alaskans enjoyed themselves in the nearby bars, I wrote their research papers for a modest fee. I banged out seven reports on my manual typewriter. The reports were about various aspects of the commercial diving business.

I envisioned commercial diving not as a glamorous career, but as a grueling profession suitable only to strong-willed individuals who like to work alone in hazardous environments. The vast majority of divers worked in offshore oilfields in the Gulf of Mexico, the North Sea, and the Persian Gulf, but some divers also worked inland, on rivers. Some divers found their niche cleaning boat hulls. Some divers harvested abalone.

Greg and I did our research paper on the abalone-diving business. We drove to Half Moon Bay one day and interviewed an abalone diver.

A young man in his thirties, he used Mark V gear. He said in the 1970s there were more than three hundred abalone divers in California. Overfishing and the issuance of fewer permits had reduced that number. For every ten divers that dropped out of the business, the Fish and Game Commission issued only one permit by lottery. He said he sold his abalone meat for $9.50 a pound wholesale, cleaned and shelled. He could get $7.50 a pound with the shell. Each abalone weighs about one pound. Haliotus, the scientific name for the prized mollusk, is known for its delicate flavor. The shellfish settles on the ocean floor and attaches itself to rocks. A diver knocks the shell loose with a hammer and crowbar. Five species are harvested: red, pink, green, black, and white. They live in waters from Alaska to Mexico in depths up to two hundred feet. A dying business, abalone diving didn't seem profitable to me. I intended to migrate to the Gulf of Mexico when I finished the course. I would be an oilfield diver, whatever that meant.

During the last two weeks of school, I dived on a wreck in the estuary. The depth was about forty feet, and I salvaged a piston from the engine of the thirty-foot pleasure boat.

School ended, and the class dispersed to all corners of the world. Pat, Andy, Scott, and I drove to Louisiana in a pickup truck and began our search for work in the Gulf of Mexico, where a major portion of commercial diving work existed. Andy, a photography nut, gave me copies of his slides he had taken from class, especially the ones that showed us in Mark V gear. Pat, a construction worker from New York, brought along his revolver, because he had heard New Orleans was a tough town. One of the welders who lived in New Orleans invited us to stay at his place on the West Bank for a few days while we visited the dive companies.

Louisiana was like a foreign country where the people spoke a different language. People "made" groceries; the streets and rivers had Indian names, like Tchoupitoulas and Atchafalaya; and streetcars still rolled up St. Charles Avenue past huge mansions and oak trees adorned with Spanish moss. Santa Claus came to town riding a sleigh driven by alligators, and millions of people flocked to New Orleans during the Mardi Gras, around February. Louisiana was a great melting pot of French, Spanish, English, and Native Americans like Choctaw and Chitimacha. Even the legal system was different. Louisiana practiced Napoleonic Law, as opposed to English Common Law. Louisiana didn't have counties; it had parishes. In Acadiana Parish, west of New Orleans, live the Cajuns, descendants of French people that were exiled from Nova Scotia in the 1800s. Louisiana is famous for its food, and the Cajuns have many delicious recipes, such as crawfish etouffee and jambalaya.

Andy and I bought an old Buick in Marrero for $500 and drove the stretch of Highway 90 from New Orleans to Morgan City, where most of the dive companies were, such as McDermott, Santa Fe, Martech, Oceaneering, Subsea, and Solus. I was amazed when I saw a dozen gleaming decompression chambers in the sprawling complex of Taylor Diving and Salvage Company on Engineer Road in Belle Chasse. Taylor was one of the biggest companies, employing about 150 divers worldwide. Taylor was founded by Mark Banjavich and Edward Lee Taylor, former Navy divers, in 1957. The timing couldn't have been better. The offshore oil industry was moving into deeper water, and Taylor supplied the Mark DCL saturation diving system and closed-circuit breathing apparatus. Taylor divers such as Nick Zinkowski made record-breaking dives in the Gulf of Mexico in the 1960s. Oil platforms damaged by Hurricane Betsy in 1965 were salvaged using saturation diving techniques.

I submitted my application to half a dozen companies. Oceaneering hired me. I was disappointed Taylor Diving didn't make me an offer.

Andy and I found a trailer in Bayou Vista, west of Morgan City. The town had a supermarket, laundromat, and a bank. Swampland and cypress trees ruled south of Highway 90. In Morgan City, huge half-completed oil platforms lay on their sides in the fabrication yards of McDermott International. When completed, the platforms, some of them as tall as ten-story buildings, would be towed out to sea and anchored to the ocean floor with pilings driven into the hollow legs.

Morgan City was a working-class town. Welders, pipefitters, deck hands, roustabouts, engineers, and mechanics lived in the swamps among the alligators, herons, crawfish, and mosquitoes. The alligators liked to walk around peoples' backyards, and many pet dogs had disappeared. In Cajun country, I was close to my dream. Would I become a diver? Would I one day drop from the hatch of a diving bell and explore the bottom of the Gulf of Mexico? I had much hope, but nothing else.

The Buick broke down after two weeks. It had an oil leak I didn't know about, and the engine burned up. I was a prisoner of the bayou until I could earn enough money to buy a car. Luckily, Oceaneering was only a ten-minute walk from my trailer. Black Bayou was a little distance down the road. I don't know where Blue Bayou was, the place Linda Ronstadt sang about, but this place would be home for a while, until the wind changed direction and blew me someplace else.

The Life of a Tender

I was surprised to see Marty, the ex-convict from Oakland, in the work yard on my first day at Oceaneering. I helped him unload a truck of gas cylinders. The driver of the truck tried to pick a cylinder up from the top, and the cap snapped off and almost broke his jaw. Marty and I took him to the local hospital.

Marty lived in a trailer a few blocks down the road from me. He spent his free time hunting for psilocybin mushrooms in the cow pastures surrounding Bayou Vista. Ps. cubensis, a hallucinogen, is plentiful in Louisiana and grows in cow manure.

I couldn't dive immediately. All aspiring divers must first serve an apprenticeship. An apprentice diver is called a tender, one who tends the diver's umbilical while the diver works on the bottom. Tenders also do all surface work. Divers don't do anything out of the water.

I spent the summer months doing odd jobs at the Bayou Vista facility while I dreamt about going offshore. I built umbilicals, drove divers to the dock, swept floors, cleaned chambers, scraped paint, built storage sheds, and unloaded trucks for minimum wage. I was frustrated, but still hopeful.

While I fumed about not going offshore, my former classmates fared worse. One condition of employment was a complete spinal X-ray. My spine was normal, but Andy discovered he had a small growth on his spine, and Oceaneering wouldn't hire him. Insurance premiums were high in the industry. Commercial diving was considered one of the most dangerous professions, and companies hired only candidates in the best of health. I thought the dive school should have told us that valuable information, but all they wanted was our money. Andy made the best of a rotten deal. He found work at the local fabrication yard as a pipefitter's helper. He would return to college in the fall. Scott, a young man from Sacramento, slipped on a barge deck, hurt his back, and returned to California.

Pat didn't get along with people from the South. One day he burst into the trailer. "I'm tired of those damn coonasses!" He waved his revolver in the air, and we tried to settle him down. Pat returned to New York after a few months.

I felt sorry for Andy, but our problems were minor compared to some of the local people. I discovered life on the bayou was not as idyllic as it seemed. Andy met a girl who worked at the fabrication yard. He and I visited her in Morgan City one day. Her father owned a gas station, but he suffered from an incurable spine disease. Her mother stared out the window all day, stroked her white hair, and mourned for her son killed in Vietnam. The girl lived with her son in her parents' trailer. She had been married, but one day her husband had pointed a gun at her and told her to get lost. Her sister lived there, too, but she spent most of the time with friends all over town. I don't know why life treated some people so cruelly. After seeing these people, I didn't feel so bad.

One night Andy and I were playing tennis, and he noticed a girl in the bleachers, watching us. "Did you see that girl? She's got a black eye. Her husband probably beat her up."

Andy did his best to keep the local people amused. One time he put on his scuba mask and fins and paraded around the front yard as the neighbors across the street drove by. He had a way of attracting women. One night, he told me he was sitting alone at the kitchen table dressed in only a bath towel, and a girl he had never seen before walked into the trailer without knocking.

"Gosh, I was embarrassed," Andy said. "I was still wet from my shower, and she sits on my lap. She was drunk. God! She was too drunk to know what she was doing. She jumped off and ran out of the trailer. I never saw her again."

"Lucky you," I said.

Summer dragged on. I developed a hatred for Ace, the dispatcher. Why wouldn't he send me offshore? I was too proud to beg for work. Andy and I visited the bars in Morgan City to forget our problems. I had never been much of a drinker, but I slowly acquired a taste for beer. I fantasized about the curvaceous girls dancing on stage. Maybe I should take Ted Hess's advice, I thought. He was a dive supervisor who said, "If you want to find girls, join a Baptist church." I wasn't the church-going type, so I resigned myself to a lonely life. I wanted to go offshore. I wanted to spend eight months at sea, save all my money and buy a car, so I could have some freedom to travel and find a decent company to work for, not this pathetic company on the bayou that didn't want to give me any work.

Later I learned that the companies often hire too many tenders in anticipation of a busy summer season, then lay off most of them when the work doesn't materialize. I grew more cynical every day, and my idealized vision of deep-sea diving faded.

Live-boating

In June, I went offshore on my first job, to inspect a pipeline. Rick, the senior tender, looked like a California surfer, with powerful biceps and bleach blond hair. Chris, one of the divers, had a crooked finger on his right hand, where a pipe had almost crushed it. I lived on an aluminum-hulled crew boat for seven days and took Dramamine to overcome my seasickness. Almost everyone gets seasick their first days on the water. The boat rocked up and down constantly, and keeping my balance was difficult.

The term "live-boating" refers to the fact that the boat is moving, or "alive", while a diver is working in the water. Normally, divers don't work in areas where boats are operating, because of the danger in fouling an umbilical hose on propellers. Inspection jobs are the exception, requiring miles of pipelines to be traversed and inspected for damage. Sub-sea pipelines have a concrete coating, and sometimes boat anchors knock chunks of concrete off, or boat anchors crimp the pipelines themselves. Jet barges, or dredges, are employed to bury pipelines offshore, and a team of inspection divers usually precedes a burying operation, to ensure the pipeline is not damaged before being buried under twelve feet of mud.

Live-boating requires constant vigilance. As the diver moves along the pipe, the boat follows slowly. The tender must watch the diver's bubbles, so the boat doesn't get ahead of the diver. When the diver comes up, the boat must shut off its engines.

On June 13, I boarded the crew boat on a humid night and headed fifty miles into the Gulf of Mexico. I arose at 7:00 and didn't have time to eat breakfast. When I came on deck, a vast ocean surrounded me with a few platforms, a barge, and some boats in the distance. I checked the fuel in the air compressors chained to the stern deck and put a towel in the decompression chamber, then attached two Kirby-Morgan masks to the main and standby umbilicals at the bow.

We made buoy markers and positioned them where pipelines met. Chris entered the water later in the morning. He jumped off the bow into a calm sea, where the depth was about 100 feet. The sun scorched us all day. A few flying fish sailed by. I felt nauseated all morning.

Chris spent about forty minutes on the bottom, inspecting the pipeline. He tied off the buoy line, and I pulled him up. With a hundred feet of umbilical in the water and the boat rocking with the waves, Chris felt unbelievably heavy. I held the umbilical tightly with both hands and leaned against the railing. The boat rose with a wave, and I needed all my strength to keep my grip. I thought the railing would cut me in two. My back ached. Rick shouted at me. "You're gonna kill yourself doing it that way. Stand up straight."

I pulled with biceps and thighs and tried to maintain an erect posture. A few times the wet umbilical slipped, but I managed to pull Chris up. The optimal ascent rate was one foot every two seconds, but I had no idea how fast I was pulling him. My hands were red and raw. I knew I would develop a healthy set of biceps on the job, if I had to pull divers out of the water twice a day.

Chris surfaced, and I pulled him to the ladder. He stripped off all his gear, and spent twenty minutes in the decompression chamber.

I ate a light lunch, but my stomach felt unsettled. I hoped to be able to eat more in a few days, because the food was good. The cook offered us baked ham, rice, tossed salad, sweet potatoes, rolls, and corn. The freezer was full of ice cream and Popsicles.

Thursday June 15: The divers entered the water four times today. Each made two dives. They wore sneakers and jeans and a wetsuit top. Sometimes they went down with a bailout bottle, a small scuba tank that held emergency air. As the diver followed the pipeline on the bottom, the boat closely followed his bubbles. When the diver came up, the boat stopped its propellers, and the diver safely surfaced near the stern. I stripped him of his gear, and the diver entered the chamber nude. Usually we decompressed him at forty feet for fifteen to thirty minutes. The diver breathed oxygen in the chamber. I vented the chamber periodically to freshen the chamber atmosphere.

We had some free time in the afternoon, so we went snorkeling around the structure where the boat was tied off. Hundreds of fish followed us around. Fish love to congregate around structures, because it gives them a protected area within the perimeter of the legs. Visibility was at least 100 feet. The lavender seas were calm, and the swimming was a relief from the scorching sun. After work, we enjoyed a steak. Some of the crew did some fishing before dark.

Friday June 16: Arose at 6:30, ate a light breakfast, and set up for diving. Each diver made only one entry today. A fitting on the main compressor volume tank broke, so we went to a Brown and Root barge to find a replacement. Running the chamber is becoming routine. Sometimes when the depth reaches 150 feet, the divers have a few water stops at forty feet and thirty feet. Once again, we feasted on shrimp gumbo for lunch.

Saturday, June 17: A busy day, though we arose after seven o'clock The sea was running, and hauling the diver up at twenty-five feet a minute was exceedingly difficult. I rubbed my hands raw and bruised my arms. A problem occurred while I was running the chamber. The main dive compressor was shut down, and I forgot to turn on the standby air valve to the chamber, so while venting, the chamber pressure dropped to thirty-six feet. Chris yelled at me to open the valve. How stupid of me to forget to switch to the standby compressor. I went down with the diver in the chamber twice, but didn't equalize quickly enough, so I came up with nosebleeds. My sinuses are not clearing fast enough, so they fill with blood and mucous. At 5:00, when I thought we were done for the day, we made another dive. At sunset, we prepared for another dive, but the barge off our bow wouldn't let us approach, so we concluded for the day at 8:30. A quick supper, and I slipped into my bunk exhausted.

Sunday, June 18: Arose at 5:45, and the divers hit the water at 6:30. Hauling the diver out of the water was again extremely difficult. Rick made it look so easy. Luckily for me, we only made three dives and were done at three o'clock. We fished and swam. The main chamber compressor is leaking oil. We ate steaks tonight. The crew is happy, because the television works, but the picture is terrible, with constant interference and static noise.

Monday, June 19: Arose at 7:00, enjoyed a leisurely breakfast, and didn't set up to dive until ten o'clock. The boat was tied to a Brown and Root barge, and we made two dives under it to inspect a flange. Tonight we dined on shrimp and potatoes.

Tuesday, June 20: Made one dive at 7:00, then waited until 4:30 before heading toward shore. Expect to reach home around midnight.

When I stepped off the boat, I grabbed a pole to steady myself. I swayed with the motion of the sea. The sea stayed inside me for days afterward. I wasn't going to let seasickness dissuade me from my dream, but my first week offshore gave me a glimpse of the austere life and put calluses on my hands. The offshore life was a simple life. Only hard work amid stiff breezes, a burning sun, and spectacular scenery. One week at sea made me physically stronger. Pulling a diver up from 150 feet every day strengthened my biceps and back muscles. I still needed to acquire mental toughness; to be able to withstand the many hours of waiting, the endless waiting for orders, for the sea to calm, for a barge to move, or for a storm to pass.

Trash Collecting

The longest job of the summer took me to Eugene Island, Block 175, in the Gulf of Mexico, to an Atlantic Richfield platform where we picked debris off the bottom to reduce cathodic corrosion of the structure. Steel and other metals corrode, because of their tendency to return to the native oxide state. In other words, they rust. Zinc sacrificial anodes are placed on structures to reduce corrosion.

I couldn't believe the things oil companies threw in the water. Anything they didn't want, they tossed overboard, including grating, pipes, toolboxes, staircases, and other junk. I spent a month at sea, worked from dawn to dusk, with no breaks except for meals hastily eaten below deck. My stomach had settled, and I didn't experience seasickness.

I helped load equipment on the *Mr. Cliff*, a large workboat. We loaded a chamber, two compressors, twelve oxygen cylinders, underwater burning gear, masks, umbilicals, a welding machine, air-powered winches, and a mobile crane we called a cherry picker.

The boat arrived at the Eugene Island platform on August 1. The platform rose out of the sea to a height of a ten-story building.

Seas were restless. The dark blue water swirled and thrashed at the boat. I gazed into the depths from the stern. I could see perhaps forty feet down. The bottom was at ninety feet. I wanted to be down there. I wanted more bottom time. Surface time and bottom time were different as night and day. On the surface, I wasted time, wanted time to pass quickly. I slept, daydreamed, lamented the past, worried about the future, and endured the drudgery of tending. On the bottom, with senses electrified, I savored each precious second. I lived in the moment. There was no past, no future. Bottom time promised fascination, exploration, discovery, and adventure.

The next day, we arose at 5:00, ate a wholesome breakfast of eggs, bacon, toast, and juice, and crawled on deck before dawn. Starting the air compressors with a hand crank knocked the sleep from my mind. By the time the scorching sun stood above the horizon, we had already worked an hour. I stood on the stern and dutifully tended my diver's umbilical as he worked in the depths. I watched the radioman, who sat in the shade toward the bow, away from the noisy compressors and crane. The cherry picker was chained to the deck, but the crane block swung madly in rough seas.

The divers attached whatever they found to the crane line, the crane raised the debris, and deposited it on deck. At night, the crane from the platform lifted the debris to the top of the platform, where it would be decided what metal to salvage and what to take away by boat.

On Saturday, a thunderstorm entertained us at night. Lightning split the sky, but we never heard the thunder, because it was so far away.

Sunday brought bad weather. I tended in the rain, until the sun emerged in the afternoon. Many interesting life forms came up with the cables, tires, pipes, boat bumpers, and scrap metal. The debris crawled with shells, bristle worms, crabs, sea urchins, coral, barnacles, starfish, and lobsters. I found one strange creature that looked like a giant bug but had eight spidery legs and a long snout. The crabs camouflaged themselves well on the pipes. We didn't eat them.

On Monday, the first diver, Mark Norris, jumped in about 7:00. When he surfaced, he complained of pain in the left shoulder and elbow. He crawled into the decompression chamber, and I pressurized it to sixty feet.

I treated Mark on a Table Five, a short treatment schedule of two hours for pain-only bends, but his symptoms were not relieved within ten minutes, so I treated him on Table Six.

Mark had ascended too quickly from ninety feet, causing decompression sickness. He was reckless, always thinking he could break the rules. The ascent rate should have been twenty-five feet a minute. He came up in two minutes. Mark spent six hours breathing oxygen in the chamber.

Mark, who had served in the Army, frightened me with his energy. He dived into the water head first, and he walked on deck in a controlled rage. One day, he took the oxy-arc cutting torch and made a barbecue grill from pieces of pipe salvaged during the day. The grill featured a hinged steel top that must have weighed fifty pounds. He used half-inch-thick steel pipe. The entire grill would last a century, but it weighed at least five hundred pounds, and I didn't know how he would transport it home.

The other divers seemed like reasonable people. Randy was an easygoing cowboy. Dave, the supervisor, didn't impress me, but later, my attitude changed. The quiet, unassuming diver had almost been swallowed by a grouper at 500 feet in the Gulf of Mexico. Groupers are territorial, and they will defend their turf. Dave had been diving out of a bell to inspect a wellhead, and I can only imagine what the jaws had felt like as a grouper the size of a Volkswagen clamped around his waist. Perhaps the metallic taste of Stave's bailout bottle didn't agree with the grouper, and the fish spat him out. Such an experience would humble me and serve as a reminder that when I go under water, I am the prey.

Chuck, the image of a warrior, with jutting chin, massive brows, a powerful build, and tall frame, must have said three words to me the entire month. He was the only diver who stayed for the whole job.

We dived again at 2:00 in the afternoon. It rained for a few hours. Because of Mark's injury, we paid close attention to ascent rates for the divers. We brought up boat bumpers, cables, and assorted scrap metal. Mark and Randy brought up some coral at least a foot in diameter. Though the structure was used to produce oil, it attracted all sorts of marine life, including fish, shellfish, crustaceans, and coral. Coral grows only half an inch a year, so this platform may have been twenty-four years old.

The last diver was out of the chamber by 8:00. Tenders washed the deck, refueled compressors, and secured the dive station by 9:00.

After a week of making seven to eight dives a day, the grueling work showed its effect on the tenders. Bob Hangren seemed exceptionally grumpy on Tuesday. He looked haggard, with shaggy hair and unshaven face. Was the pace too much for him? The supervisor didn't like my performance and threatened to send me home, if I didn't improve. I didn't know what I was doing wrong. Standing by the stern under a hot sun, near rumbling machinery was boring. It was never easy to awake at 5:00, climb to a heaving wind-swept deck, start the compressors, and set up the dive station, but I had no great desire to see land again, so I worked harder and paid close attention to the diver at the radio station.

On Saturday, August 12, we made one dive, then rain came, and we stopped working. We were on the edge of a fierce storm, but it passed quickly. Harsh weather plagued us again the next day. Seas became rough within minutes, the wind stung our faces, and rain poured down. Tom, the crane operator, wanted to go home. He said he was sick of running the crane all day.

By Tuesday, August 14, our equipment was in ruins. The crane leaked hydraulic fluid on the deck, and one of our compressors pumped oil, so we decided to go to shore to replace the crane.

On Friday, we loaded a new crane and resumed work at the platform. Dave Stave didn't return to the job. I don't know why. Ted Hess was our new supervisor. Mark Norris complained about the situation of the unstable crane rolling with the seas while the hook swung inches from the diver's head. He was replaced by Steve Hall, who Ted Hess described as the Pillsbury doughboy who turned into the Hulk under water.

Ted Hess was short and balding, but he possessed such energy that he reminded me of the Tasmanian Devil. He whizzed about, shouted commands. He knocked my complacency loose, revealed my ignorance, and insulted me when I did a bad job. He stuck his tongue out at me when I looked in the chamber. He plunged his head into his mask like a hungry dog. He wore a red jumpsuit over his wetsuit. The divers said he got excited under water. "Slack me off! Slack me off!" he barked into the radio. In short, he was another maniac that liked diving. He inspired me. Perhaps the job was behind schedule, because Ted dived and supervised. He also lengthened our work hours. We awoke every day at 5:00 and worked past sunset.

Sunday, August 20: We made seven dives and finished at 8:00, before a storm forced us to move the boat away from the platform. The next day, we brought up a huge boat bumper, but the cable snapped, sending it to the bottom. Randy caught a forty-pound sea bass. He tied it to the starboard side. We pulled the rope up the next day, and only half the fish remained. A shark must have taken a bite, but didn't finish the meal.

Thursday, August 24: Randy was on the bottom salvaging debris when a tremendous brown bubble erupted on the surface. A few seconds later, a geyser of oil and air turned the water brown for hundreds of feet.

"Shut everything down!" Ted screamed.

We scrambled to shut down all machinery.

When the crane line came up, it had crimped a pipe on the bottom, creating a massive oil leak. Diving was suspended. Men on the platform sprayed detergent mixed with water on the oil slick. The air smelled ripe with oil fumes looking for a spark to create an explosion.

Ted made a dive to repair the leaking line two days later.

The weather report said a tropical storm with winds up to forty miles an hour was headed toward us. We picked up nine men from the platform, which was being evacuated, and we headed for home.

We went offshore again when the storm passed. I still remember September 6, a black day for me. I was tending Ted Hess from the stern. Communications failed, and I didn't recognize four pulls on the umbilical, a signal from Ted that I should pull him up immediately. The tugs had been too weak, and I didn't know if he had pulled on the umbilical twice or four times. He was not in any danger, so he patiently sat on the bottom and collected umbilical that I was happy to give him. When the radioman finally signaled to me to pull Ted up, I received a nasty shock. Ted emerged on the surface holding a huge clump of umbilical in his arms. He crawled up the ladder, dropped the pile of umbilical at my feet, threw his mask on deck, flung his gear in all directions, and hurled insults at me until the color of his face matched his red jumpsuit. I was speechless. Ted stomped off to the chamber, and Gary offered to run the chamber, so I could avoid the wrath of the angry diver. I think he enjoyed embarrassing tenders.

An offshore day always holds surprises with the ever changing moods of the sea, but the routine might go something like this: The deck hand wakes us at 5:00. We convince ourselves to leave our cozy bunks and dress. One by one, we float into the galley and order the way we want our eggs cooked. A few cans of refreshing cold apple juice, a small strip of bacon, a glass of chocolate milk, four pork sausages, a couple slices of toast with butter and marmalade complete the meal. We eat in slow silence trying to fight away a whole night of sleep in fifteen minutes.

We grab our tools and ascend to the deck where we prepare the dive station for a day of work. Bob sets up the radios and screws the hoods onto the masks. Gary checks the compressors that have been fueled the night before, and he starts them with a hand crank. I check the decompression chamber, place a dry towel in the outer lock, set up the radio to the chamber, and pressurize the chamber to seventy feet. John checks the crane and makes sure the slings are in good shape and throws them into the water.

Once the compressors are running, we blow the condensate out of the dive umbilicals, then connect the masks. Communication is checked, the ladder is lowered into the water by the stern, the air manifold is connected, and we're almost ready to go. We have oxygen to the chamber, the crane is running and waiting to pick up the first load. The compressors are rumbling, and communication is good.

We're all excited, as the sun comes up and turns the black, shimmering water into a deep translucent green surging force that rocks the boat effortlessly. It's harder to work when you have no firm surface to walk on, never a sure grip on the rails. The wet boat deck is always slippery. The boat is tied to the side of a platform, but the boat still jumps and tilts. The truck tires chained to the sides groan and screech each time the boat hits the side of the platform.

Finally, the divers emerge from below, and Randy dresses in his wetsuit. The lights on the platform fade, as sunlight bathes the deck. The sea swells three to four feet, not too bad, but still rough enough to shake loose the sleep from our bodies. The compressors are not too loud. We are ready.

It's seven o'clock. I help Randy put on the mask and weightbelt. The hose gets clipped to his harness, he slips his hands into cotton gloves and dives in, swimming to the crane line a few yards off the stern. He will descend down the cable and search for debris to salvage. The water is ninety feet deep. Bottom times and ascent rates are closely monitored to ensure safe diving.

On the murky, cold bottom, Randy gropes for pipes, cables, and scrap metal thrown off the platform years before. He hooks the crane line to a load and ascends to fifty feet, before the crane operator is told to lift the load on deck. While the crane deposits the load on the boat, Randy looks for coral and barnacles attached to the legs of the platform. If he finds some he likes, he brings it up at the end of his dive. Gary and Bob unhook the slings from the scrap metal gratings, pipes, old wire cables, and flanges. For some of the heavier pipes, we use an air winch, called a tugger.

Randy works for ninety minutes, the optimum bottom time for the depth, according to company decompression schedules. I pull him up at a slow pace, twenty-five feet a minute. He climbs up the ladder onto the wet deck, and I remove his mask, harness, and weight belt. Time is crucial. He must be in the chamber and blown down to forty feet within five minutes, otherwise bubbles start forming in his tissues.

Randy strips off the wetsuit and climbs into the outer lock with a tender. I am at the chamber controls. Randy opens a crossover valve, and air roars into the outer lock from the inner lock. When the pressure of the two locks equalizes, the hatch opens, and Randy crawls into the inner lock. He makes himself comfortable, then breathes oxygen. I bring the tender in the outer lock up to the surface. I ventilate the chamber every five minutes and maintain pressure equivalent to forty feet. Randy breathes oxygen for thirty minutes, then breathes air for five.

John washes the diver's gear with fresh water, and Gary cleans the mask. Chuck, the next diver, slips into his suit fifteen minutes before Randy is due to come out of the chamber. The tenders stay busy cutting sections of pipe and checking the slings for wear. As Gary hands Chuck the mask, Chuck says, "Are you ready?" Smiles all around as the comedian's head disappears in the mask. Chuck is a tall, bearded warrior who has been diving three years.

We make six dives. Lunch and dinner take place whenever someone can find fifteen minutes to hurry to the galley and gorge himself. The sun burns us without mercy. We consume gallons of water and soft drinks as the day progresses. The metal comes up covered with mud and sea growth. Our clothes become dirty and our feet wet from the seawater splashing on deck.

At the end of the day, we rig all the scrap so the crane on the platform can pick it up. Later, a workboat comes by and takes away the scrap from the platform.

I was working hard, developing my sea legs, rubbing shoulders with colorful personalities, growing accustomed to the offshore life, building muscles in my arms, but still not diving. I knew I might have to be a tender for perhaps two years, before "breaking out," or being promoted to diver.

What a difference commercial diving was, compared to sport diving! The sportsman goes under water to have fun. The commercial diver goes down and performs arduous tasks. He cuts steel, repairs pipelines, salvages boats and structures, and operates mechanical devices associated with the oil industry. He does all these things sometimes in complete darkness, where a vicious current impedes his movement and the cold saps his strength. He spends hours in the decompression chamber breathing oxygen, to remove inert gas dissolved in his tissues. He risks his life every day doing a thankless job. Who were the adventurers and individualists who loved to suffer abuse at the hands of the sea, to discover her secrets? They came from all walks of life. Military men, college graduates, criminals, doctors, construction workers, and artists slipped into wetsuits and tangled with the deep.

Mixed-Gas Diving

The 1900s saw many developments in diving technologies. Individuals, governments, and diving companies experimented with breathing mixtures using helium and hydrogen.

In 1919, Professor Elihu Thompson proposed that helium in breathing gases could eliminate nitrogen narcosis, allowing divers to remain clear-headed at extreme depths. Thompson, a successful inventor whose company merged with Thomas Edison's company to become General Electric, worked with the U.S. Navy and the Bureau of Mines to develop helium-oxygen breathing mixtures. Luckily, major supplies of helium had been discovered in Texas gas wells, and the cost of helium dropped significantly.

In 1937, Max Nohl set the world's depth record, 420 feet in Lake Michigan, using a helium-oxygen mixture. His unique diving helmet conserved the inert gas and absorbed carbon dioxide produced by the diver's metabolism.

In 1962, Swiss mathematician Hannes Keller made history by descending to 1,000 feet near Catalina Island, California. Keller and Peter Small, a British journalist, descended in a chamber, Atlantis, and used a secret breathing mixture. Keller planted the Swiss and American flags on the ocean bottom, but he became entangled in the flags and was forced to rush back to the chamber with only minutes of breathing gas left. Tragedy followed. Disoriented when he returned, Keller flooded the chamber with air, and his fin became stuck in the hatch, preventing a seal. Small died of embolism, but Keller survived.

Testing has been done with other gas mixtures. COMEX, the French deep-diving company, experimented with hydrogen during the 1980s, but found that hydrogen below 500 feet produced a narcotic effect similar to LSD, and consequently would not be useful for deep diving.

Helium-oxygen mixtures are typically used for commercial diving below 165 feet, because divers become useless at extreme depths, if they breathe compressed air. Nitrogen narcosis and oxygen poisoning are two inherent dangers of air under pressure. Air is twenty-one percent oxygen, seventy-eight percent nitrogen, with small amounts of carbon dioxide and other inert gases. Breathing that same mixture at 132 feet is equivalent to breathing pure oxygen on the surface.

Helium does not produce the narcotic effects that nitrogen does; consequently it is used for deep diving. Gas mixtures can be created to produce the optimum percentages of oxygen and helium. At an extreme depth of 1,000 feet, for example, the percentage of oxygen in a gas mixture can be as low as one percent and still maintain life.

Unfortunately, helium has some undesirable effects. It is an excellent conductor of heat, so it robs the diver of his body warmth. Divers breathing helium are also more susceptible to decompression sickness, because helium comes out of solution more quickly than nitrogen. Extremely long decompression times are required to completely eliminate inert gas from the body. Helium also affects the vocal cords, producing high-pitched speech. At depths below 500 feet, divers sometimes experience tremors, or high-pressure nervous syndrome.

✳ ✳ ✳

I went on a deep-water dive job in October. Much more equipment was required for mixed-gas diving. The entire stern deck of the workboat was covered with compressors, racks of helium and oxygen, a decompression chamber, an open-bottom bell, air winches, and a dive station with devices and instrumentation to mix gases.

An open-bottom bell consists of a hemispherical Plexiglas top connected to a platform where a diver can stand. Gas cylinders are attached to the bell, and the diver can breath without a mask in the small pocket of atmosphere under the Plexiglas dome.

I arrived at Cameron Block, somewhere off the Texas coast, at 9:00 in the morning. The water was dark blue and the depth was 190 feet. Again, I remained on the surface and refueled compressors, while the divers made their lucrative depth pay.

A tender usually accompanied a diver when he came out of the water and began his decompression in the chamber. If the diver experienced serious symptoms of decompression sickness, the tender would be able to give first aid. Once the pressure in the chamber reached forty feet, the diver entered the inner lock, closed the hatch, and the chamber operator released the pressure to the outer lock, allowing the tender to leave the chamber. I almost ruptured an eardrum, once, when a diver pressurized the chamber too quickly. I entered the chamber with one of the senior divers, Stan E., and he opened the intake valve all the way. Air rushed into the chamber, and my ears didn't clear quickly enough. I frantically blew air out of my nose, wiggled my jaws, and snorted, but my right ear didn't clear, and I was in severe pain for a few minutes, until the pressure was released in the outer lock. Luckily I didn't perforate my eardrum, or I would have been sent home.

A typical dive lasted thirty minutes. The diver breathed air until he reached forty feet, then he switched to a helium-oxygen mixture. After completing his work on the bottom, he ascended in the open-bottom bell. He breathed a fifty percent nitrogen fifty percent oxygen mixture from ninety feet to the surface for decompression. The diver made water stops at sixty, fifty, forty, and thirty feet for additional decompression, then spent forty minutes in the chamber breathing oxygen.

The gas manifold was not difficult to operate. Air, helium, and the decompression mix came into the manifold, where the correct mixture could be produced and delivered to the diver through his umbilical.

On the second day, we made four dives and finished at 11:00. I spent the night cleaning masks and reconnecting manifolds to fresh helium cylinders.

Friday, October 13, turned into an unlucky day. We continued work to repair a valve assembly on the bottom, but oil came to the surface from a leak. We spent all day tightening two flanges to stop the oil leak, but at 8:00, we were called to dive again. The boat had caught an anchor on a pipeline. Two dives later, the anchor remained caught, and the valve assembly had been pulled twenty feet off the sea floor. To free the boat, we cut the anchor cable and headed for Morgan City for repairs. We finished at midnight.

✳ ✳ ✳

On Sunday, October 15, I took another boat with five divers for a gas job in 290 feet of water. Our task was simply to open a valve, but things were never simple at sea.

On Monday, we waited all day for a survey boat to find the valve. On Tuesday, rough seas pounded the boat. We stayed below deck and played poker. The boat finally set anchor in the evening, and we made a dive at 8:00. The first diver found nothing. The survey marker had been misplaced. The diver had many lengthy water stops and decompressed for two hours in the chamber, and we shut down the compressors. The deck was secure by midnight.

The next day, the boat didn't set anchors until late in the afternoon. Another diver went to the bottom and found the valve two hundred feet from the original survey location. The valve stem had been damaged by an anchor cable. The next diver brought up the damaged valve stem. We secured the deck some time after midnight.

On Thursday, we made a dive at noon. The diver brought up the rest of the valve for us to repair. On Friday the job was canceled. We were told a barge called Sea Rigger would repair the valve.

Rough seas pounded the boat during the journey home. Although the compressors, chamber, and gas racks had been chained to the deck, the sea rearranged everything in the night. The sea had tossed a two-ton chamber halfway across the deck like a toy.

The dive supervisor chuckled. "Yeah, we had thirty-foot seas last night."

I hadn't felt a thing. I was too exhausted and had slept soundly.

Wheel Job in the Atchafalaya River

The winter brought less work, and I found myself spending too much time on land, a place I didn't want to be. The air grew colder on the bayou, and morning fog covered the bridges.

I accepted a week of work as a deck hand on a boat. I worked the night watch shift and spent my time in the wheelhouse of *Mr. Cliff*, watching the gulls bob on the waves. I wrote poems, walked around the deck, checked the hawsers that secured the boat to a structure, and gazed at the moon while the rest of the crew slept. I enjoyed the peace and solitude, but I belonged somewhere else.

On board, divers from James Dean Company were handjetting to uncover a buried pipeline in shallow water, a depth of twenty-eight feet. A handjet is a metal pipe in the shape of a "T" connected to a fire hose. Water under pressure shoots out the ends. The tool blasts mud loose on the ocean bottom and digs holes. Because the water comes out both ends, the tool remains balanced, torque is eliminated, and the diver is not thrown around by the force of the water.

I slept in the day, sat in the wheelhouse at night, and contemplated my lonely existence. The boat rose and fell with the ground swells, and the hawsers groaned. The gulls floated on the water in groups. Were they asleep? The platform, with its blue lights flashing on and off, cast a friendly glow in the desolate night. The water glistened like silver and sloshed against the hull. I stared at the full moon like a lover. I forgot my troubles for a week, or was it two?

✳ ✳ ✳

My frustration with the company grew, because I was not diving and I spent too much time on land. After a busy summer, the work slowed to a trickle in November. I recalled the jobs I worked the previous months, and they were pitifully few.

In September I received a phone call late at night and took a helicopter to *Sarita*, a Norwegian crane ship. In the helicopter we bumped along at midnight above the water, then I jumped onto a windswept helideck on a huge ship in the Gulf of Mexico. The adrenaline surge was short-lived. The job lasted only two days. I was impressed with the cleanliness of the quarters, though. The ship was setting a platform in forty feet of water. Steam hammers pounded pilings into the hollow platform legs. A 2,000-ton crane held the platform. The crane operator was perched two stories above the deck in a small booth. The divers handjetted the bottom to allow the platform to rest evenly.

In December I drove to the Grand Chenier dock for a live-boating job. Grand Chenier is about the most remote place in Louisiana. It's a six-hour drive from Morgan City through mostly uninhabited swampland. While I was there, I saw a sixteen-foot alligator on his back by the side of the road. The mosquitoes swarmed so thickly around my pickup truck that when I opened the door for one second, dozens flew in and pestered me.

That winter I also helped recover the body of a welder off the coast of Texas. He had been killed when a piece of metal fell from above and struck him on the head as he worked on a lower level of a platform. The diver found him at sixty feet sprawled on a diagonal. Sharks and barracuda cruised around the perimeter of the structure. The depth of the water was 230 feet. We didn't know where the welder was at first, so the company sent both air-diving and gas-diving equipment to the structure. The air-diving equipment arrived first, and we found the welder early in the morning. The boat with the gas gear arrived later. Too bad! We found him. Turn around and bring the gear back. It's only a sixteen-hour boat ride. April Fool!

I went on a few other jobs that winter. I lived on a drilling rig for a week and enjoyed good food. We set a Christmas tree, a subsea wellhead assembly. The deck of the rig stood about seventy feet above the water. A crane lowered the diver to the water with a small metal cage. Holding the umbilical from the great height required strong biceps and forearms, but I managed.

✳ ✳ ✳

One lonely night I was relaxing on the couch while Andy made hash pipes on the kitchen table with high-pressure stainless-steel tubing and fittings he had scavenged at the McDermott fabrication yard.

"Why are you always lying around?" Andy asked.

"I'm conserving my energy. I never know when I'll need all of it."

"What do you think you are, a Delco battery?"

I laughed.

The phone rang. I picked it up.

"Ya'll be at the shop in ten minutes. I got a wheel job for you."

I recognized Ace's voice. "Okay."

Ace Leray was the company dispatcher I hated. He never gave me enough offshore work.

I put the phone down and trotted to the bedroom. I collected my toolbox and boots and wondered what else I needed.

"Where are you going? It's ten o'clock." Andy asked.

"I'm going on a job." My adrenaline was flowing.

I left the trailer and walked the mile and a half to the Oceaneering site along Highway 90.

I cut through the field and reached the back of the company shop in little time. I was excited. Would I get a chance to jump in the water? It might be only shallow water, but anything was better than the daily grind at the warehouse.

I found Gary, another tender, loading a pickup truck with umbilicals and masks.

"You going on this job?" I asked.

He nodded. "Go find some burning rods. They got a big workboat with cable wrapped around the wheel at the Berry Brothers dock. We got to take along a welding machine and a cutting torch."

I threw my dive bag and toolbox in the back of the truck and walked into the shop to search for Broco rods, tubular steel electrodes used for underwater cutting.

After almost a year of work, I was still a tender, an apprentice who did all the menial work for two to four years until somebody thought he was ready to be promoted to diver. Only divers worked under water. When they came on land, they became lazy and worthless. A tender works twice as hard as a diver and gets paid half as much. He washes the diver's wet suit, tends the umbilical hose while the diver works under water, operates the decompression chamber, fuels the compressors, maintains the diving masks, and is responsible for all surface work on a job at sea. When there is no job offshore, he reports to the company shop and builds umbilicals, cleans trucks, drives divers to the airport, delivers mail, paints supervisors' houses, sweeps the floor, loads gas cylinders on trucks, builds storage sheds, and mows the lawn, all for minimum wage.

I found a box of rods and a canvas pouch and walked back to the truck. Gary had loaded a cutting torch and knife switch.

I didn't like working with Gary. I thought he was lazy. He would rather tell people what to do than take the initiative and do the work. I wondered if he would order me around on this job. Technically we were equals, but he was popular with Ace and the divers, and rumors said he would be promoted soon. Ace never noticed me. I never went into his office. I had a certain amount of pride. I never liked begging for work. If the company hired me, I assumed there was enough work. Unfortunately, I learned later that Oceaneering always hired more tenders at the start of the season, and many of them never saw the Gulf. These frustrated tenders spent a year in the shop and finally went back to their hometowns. I had a little more patience. I might never become a diver either, but I was willing to work in the shop for two years, or at least until I could afford to buy a car to search for employment elsewhere.

Gary and I finished loading the truck, and I drove eastward. Ace had given Gary directions to a small channel of the Atchafalaya River near Berwick.

I turned off Highway 90 onto a dirt road, drove up a levee and down the other side to the riverbank. A huge workboat, a hundred-footer at least, rested quietly at the water edge. Its spotlights illuminated the back deck and part of the river. The boat was deserted. Tractor tires chained to the sides glistened with condensation. The wheelhouse, high above the deck, was empty.

I got out of the truck and climbed on the boat. No one greeted me. I looked at the stern deck, empty except for a large winch. The winch cable went over the stern into the water. I guessed they had tangled the winch cable in the wheel. The wooden planks on the deck were stained and scarred with cuts and gashes. I looked at the muddy water beyond the stern, swirling and moving quietly, sloshing against the hull. In the distance, a black fog smothered the riverbank and trees.

Gary climbed aboard and surveyed the scene.

"I'll go in first," he said, before I could utter a word. "Hook up the welding machine and drop the torch over the stern," he ordered. He got his dive bag, took off his clothes, and dressed in his wet suit.

I set up the dive station like a good tender, attached a mask to the umbilical, and started the compressor and welding machine. The air was cool and moist. It was February and the river water was cold as ice. I set the radio and knife switch near the stern, and we tested communications. I put five rods in the canvas pouch, turned on the oxygen cylinder, and connected the torch cable to the knife switch. To cut steel under water, we used an oxyarc torch, a simple yet effective tool. A three-hundred amp current combined with a high-pressure stream of oxygen could cut through almost any thickness of steel.

I helped Gary with his weight belt and gloves, and he slipped the Kirby-Morgan mask on his head. I fastened the straps and dropped umbilical over the stern.

"Good luck," I said.

"Hope we can be done in an hour," he said.

Gary jumped in.

I heard his breathing on the radio. I hoped to get a chance to show my skill, even if the depth was only ten feet.

"Shhhhhhhh. . .Damn! This water's cold!"

Gary's gasps and quick breaths hissed from the speaker. "Lot of cable down here," Gary said.

I pressed the talk switch. "How bad is it?"

"Lot of wraps. Cable's on there good and tight."

"Do you think you can cut it?"

"I don't know. . .shhhhhhhh. . ."

"I have the ground clamped to the back of the boat. You ready to burn?"

"Good. . .make it hot!"

I closed the knife switch. "It's hot."

I sat quietly on the stern and listened to his grunts and groans. At least we didn't have to worry about decompression. At a depth of ten feet, a man could stay down all day without decompression.

Gary worked for an hour, then surfaced. He looked grim coming out of the water. He usually had a smile on his face, but the confidence was gone.

He took off his mask and said, "You can do the rest."

I wondered exactly how much he had accomplished.

I changed into my wetsuit and prepared for the challenge. Gary hadn't finished the job. Either he had become cold and wanted to quit, or there was too much cable. I replenished the rod pouch and attached the pouch to my harness. I put on a fresh pair of Playtex rubber gloves and put cotton gloves over them. The rubber gloves prevented electric shock while holding the cutting torch. I put my weight belt on, slipped the mask over my head, and tested the air. It tasted cool and fresh. I looked through the scratched Plexiglas faceplate at the muddy water off the stern. Were there any alligators in the Atchafalaya River? Not in February. They'd be hibernating in their mud holes. Besides, I had something more dangerous to contend with: a cable tightly coiled around a propeller shaft.

I climbed over the rail and dropped into the water. I gasped as the cold seeped into my wetsuit and spread across every inch of my body. It took a minute for my breathing to return to normal. I felt relatively comfortable once my body warmed the layer of water in my suit.

I groped under the hull, relying entirely on my fingers to see in the pitch black darkness. I traced the smooth metal surface of a propeller blade with a length of about six feet. I felt the braided cable wrapped tightly around the propeller shaft. The cable was as thick as my wrist. I tried to form a mental picture of the situation. I traced the coils of cable, touched the bottom of the hull a foot above my head, and wondered how I could position my body in a safe place so when I cut the cable and it uncoiled it would not hit me. I didn't like the idea of having my bones snapped by a rapidly unwinding cable. I found what I thought was a safe place: the center of the propeller blades.

I was situated in the middle of a giant watch spring ready to uncoil at the slightest provocation. The propeller blades could shield me, but I didn't know what would happen once I started cutting.

I groped, found the torch cable hanging nearby, and brought it close to me. I put a burning rod in the end and searched for a decent place to make a cut.

I held the torch in my right hand and grasped the end of the twelve-inch rod with thumb and forefinger of my left hand. I pressed the oxygen trigger and felt the stream coming out of the end. Satisfied the torch was ready, I prepared to cut.

I curled up tighter than a grub in the soil, my knees close to my chest, placed the rod against the cable, pressed the trigger, and said, "Make it hot!"

The metal rumbled at my fingertips as I worked blind. A piece of slag jumped out of the cut and burned a hole in my glove. Pain shot through my left hand, but the water quickly cooled the molten steel, and I continued. "Make it cold," I said.

Gary's faint voice came through my ear speakers. "It's cold."

The rod had shrunk to one-inch. I replaced the rod with a fresh one. I traced my fingers delicately along the ragged edges of the cut. "Make it hot." I continued cutting. I could feel the strands popping when I severed them. How would the cable unravel when I cut through it? Would it grab me and take me to the bottom?

I cut through the last strand. Ka-thunk!Ka-thunk!Ka-thunk! I heard the cable hit the bottom of the hull as it unwound.

I huddled quietly at the center of the propeller shaft behind the blades and waited for the doorknocker from hell to crush my skull. I waited tense seconds. I didn't hear anything more, so I grabbed the cable. The wraps seemed looser. I pushed the cut cable away from me, and it fell to the bottom.

"Cable feels loose now," I said. "One more cut should do it."

"Good."

I cut one more wrap and pushed the torch away. I wrestled with the cable, until the final wrap slipped out of my hands and went to the bottom. "The shaft is clear," I said.

"Good job," Gary said.

I surfaced. The familiar images of the world reappeared. I was happy to return to the surface and focus on the boat hull. I climbed on deck and took off my mask. I smiled at Gary.

"I'm glad we didn't have to spend all night here," he said.

"What time is it?"

"Midnight."

I took off the glove on my left hand and examined the blister on my forefinger.

"You all right?" Gary asked.

"It's nothing."

I changed into dry clothes. I felt elated. Though filled with unusual danger, bottom time always put me in good spirits.

We loaded the truck and drove back to the shop. I walked home and fell asleep before dawn.

Frolich Mud Divers

How different life is at sea, from life on land. The strange world spent on boats and barges among drilling rigs and production platforms that punctuate endless square miles of silver, blue, and green is unknown to most people. Time is measured not by a clock, but by the wind, sun, and waves. Sometimes we spend half a day waiting for rough weather to pass. We may be called to accomplish a simple task, such as turn the wheel of a valve, but the job may take a week.

At sea we are primitive creatures, like sterile worker ants concerned with nothing but serving the Queen of Creation. We work tirelessly from dawn to dusk day after day, with no regard for comfort. For some unknown reason we find satisfaction in plunging to the bottom of the sea, a cold and colorless place. We enjoy being humbled by the power of the sea, the stinging winds, the ever-changing waves, the storms, lightning displays, and torrents of rain. We endure the endless waiting for calm seas to arrive. We endure a scorching sun, slippery deck, and stinging saltwater. In this fluid existence, our senses become overloaded, and we lose ourselves in work. Breathtaking vistas fill our eyes. The hiss of gas into a chamber, the rumble of compressors, and the constant splash of waves bombard our ears. Cold water soaks our skin, and wind nips our faces. Foreign smells invade our nostrils, including seaweed drying in the sun, the foul smell of fish rotting on deck, the unpleasant odor of oil slicks on the water, the stench of pipes covered with shellfish and urchins, the pungent odor of brine in the decompression chamber. The rush of cool, tasteless oxygen into our lungs is refreshing.

When we arrive at the dock and step on land, we can relax, for the work is far away. We become lazy and search for a comfortable bed that doesn't rock. We enjoy the pleasant company of women or drown our worries in alcohol. We continue a life interrupted, or consider life on land as an intermission, before the next job comes, and we begin the cycle again.

We check our bank accounts, which have grown full during our absence, but we don't know what to spend the money on, except beer. We sleep for three days and enjoy the quiet away from rumbling machinery. We will have sex and smell the bayou in our backyards, nap in the afternoon, watch the strange box called television, look through a pile of mail, mow the lawn, tune the car not used for a month, and go for a joyride.

For a man with wife and children, this time must be happy, but I have no family. I consider life on land wasted time, unproductive time, time spent waiting for the next job.

I polish my boots, organize my toolbox, tend to my wounds, and read *Heavy Metal* magazine while waiting for the phone to ring.

✱ ✱ ✱

After Andy returned to college and Pat moved to New York, I acquired a new roommate. Dave was also a tender for Oceaneering, but he had worked for another diving company in New Orleans. He was tall with curly, brown hair and blue eyes. He had scars on his face that suggested he had plastic surgery, but it wasn't enough to repair the damage. Perhaps he had been in an automobile accident or been hit by a cable offshore.

One day we were talking about corruption in Louisiana politics, and Dave told me he was suing the state. I asked him why, and he told me the story of his accident and how federal money had been siphoned off and used for purposes other that what it was intended for.

Dave had been working for Frolich Brothers Divers in Chalmette, and at three o'clock in the morning, he had driven to Buck Frolich's house to load the truck and go offshore on a job. Buck was the owner, and he kept the company trucks at his house. Dave got into a terrible argument with one of the other tenders, and they had almost fought. With his adrenaline pumping, Dave had loaded a truck with compressor and umbilicals and started the trip to Venice, where the boat would meet him and take him offshore. He approached the Mississippi River Bridge going toward the West Bank. A drunk driver in a Cadillac convertible came the other way, going a hundred miles an hour. The Cadillac jumped the median and smashed into the front of Dave's pickup truck.

Dave was in the hospital for weeks. He suffered a concussion, fractured ribs, broken knee, punctured lung, and broken leg. He was in a coma for days, but he distinctly remembered some things while he was in a coma. He saw the paintings outside his room. He felt as if he left his body and floated out of the room. I didn't quite believe him, but he was not the kind of person to make jokes. When he woke from the coma, the first thing he said was, "How are my stocks doing? Where's my AMX?"

The doctor said, "I don't understand it. You should be dead." I don't know why a doctor would say something so callous, but Dave had cheated death. I think it was the adrenaline flowing in his body from the argument that kept him alive. Dave said he learned later that the state of Louisiana had received federal money to erect concrete dividers on the bridge, separating opposing lanes, but the dividers had never been installed.

Dave was durable, all right. He had been in a near-fatal collision, and he was still trying to be a diver. I hope he realizes his dream.

After he recuperated, he seemed more accident prone. One day, while working at the Oceaneering warehouse, he stuck a screwdriver in his thigh.

Dave told me about Frolich Brothers Divers, and the company was looking for tenders, so I decided to leave Bayou Vista and try my luck with Frolich. I had saved enough to buy a car, a diesel Volkswagen Rabbit, so I left the trailer and drove to New Orleans. Anything had to be better than the miserable life on the bayou, where I had made perhaps three dives.

I still had much to be thankful for, however. I had my health, and I was alive. Gary, who I had gone on the wheel job with, had injured himself, slipped and hurt his back on a barge deck. I heard he drove a milk truck in Morgan City. Mark Norris, one of the divers on the Atlantic Richfield job came in one day from a job and found his girlfriend in bed with another man. He shot her, then shot himself. I believe in chance to an extent, but we also make our own future.

✳ ✳ ✳

When the Mississippi River meets New Orleans, it makes a sharp turn at Algiers Point and arcs around the city. That's why New Orleans is called the Crescent City. When French explorer Robert Cavelier, de sieur de La Salle, traversed the river in 1682, he found high ground at what is now Jackson Square in the French Quarter. Disregarding the Indians who still lived there, he planted a cross and claimed the land for King Louis XIV. Though surrounded by swamp, subject to constant flooding, and infested with mosquitoes, this gateway to America's interior was recognized as a strategically important location.

Land is scarce in New Orleans. The only room for expansion is north of Lake Pontchatrain and to the east. A vast system of levees and pumping stations protect the city, because it is twenty feet below sea level.

I lived in an efficiency apartment in Metairie when I wasn't working offshore. Metairie had been a cow pasture in the 1950s. Now it was a growing suburb of New Orleans. Nutrias, or giant swamp rats, lived in the drainage canal that ran parallel to Esplanade Avenue a few blocks from my apartment. Egrets hunted for fish and insects in the shallow water, and a mile north, Lake Pontchatrain stretched as far as I could see. The Causeway

Bridge spanned the lake, some twenty-three miles, and connected the rich farmland and wealthy suburban communities of the Northshore to the city of New Orleans.

New Orleans was a city that never rushed. Things changed slowly. The grim remainders of slavery still lingered. Black people lived in subsidized housing; tourists occasionally got shot in the French Quarter; and all the Roman Catholics sent their children to private schools, while the public schools ranked lowest in the nation. I liked the food, though. I ate red beans and rice and shrimp po-boys.

I didn't spend much time in my apartment. The sea was in my veins, and my real home was on a boat or jack-up rig in the Gulf of Mexico.

Buck, the founder of Frolich Divers, had established a niche for himself, a small block of real estate at the mouth of the Mississippi River where Shell Oil Company operated an oil and gas field. Shell provided living quarters, a dining hall, and movie theater. The deepest water was sixty feet. Many of the small platforms scattered about the field lay in marshes where there was more mud than water. Frolich employed only four divers. Buck liked to sit on his front porch in his shorts at three o'clock in the morning and brief us on the job. I'd load the pickup truck and drive across the Mississippi River Bridge, then head south to Venice. We'd load *Miss Julie*, a fast aluminum-hulled crew boat, and take an hour boat ride to Block 23, East Bay. Fishermen in their little boats and canoes would be out early in the morning around the rigs. We'd pack lunches, work in the bay until sunset repairing lines, then come in and eat dinner.

Old Louie, a black man, was one of the skippers of *Miss Julie*. He had seven kids, and he was in his sixties, but still drove us around on the boat. "Yessir, I got it last night . . ." He pushed through the fog at top speed, engines whining. He didn't wink. He never used the radar, but it was on. Louie liked to eat raw oysters that Charlie brought up. The oysters grew on the platform legs.

Charlie was the senior diver at Frolich. He'd been there for twenty years, I'd heard, and was going to retire any day. He had forearms thick as my thighs. A man of few words, he wore a Mickey Mouse T-shirt and shorts in the summer. He jumped in with no harness and no knife, only an old Desco mask. One time I heard him on the radio banging away at something on the platform leg. Bang! Bang! Bang!

"What's he doing?" I asked C. J., the standby diver.

"Cutting rope with his crescent wrench. He's beating it to death."

Charlie never washed his wetsuit. Whenever we came in from a job, he left it in the back of the pickup truck until we went offshore again. I'll never forget the ripe smell of fish and fermenting seawater in the back of the truck.

B, the other boat skipper, was a short Cajun from Venice with dark skin and black hair. Rumors said he never had a name, and he liked to keep things simple, so he called himself B. Charlie said that B was a fantastic worker. B had been a diver, once, but he had a frightful experience one summer. He had been live-boating with a young, inexperienced tender, and the tender let too much umbilical drift toward the stern of the boat. Before the boat skipper could react, B's umbilical got caught in the propeller. The umbilical yanked him off bottom, and the propeller blades almost chopped B's head in pieces. The skipper shut down the engines immediately, and B found himself dangling two feet from the blades. It was a miracle he didn't get bent.

★ ★ ★

Mud divers spent their lives fixing leaks on various diameter pipelines. We used a device called a split sleeve. We clamped it around the damaged section of pipe. Rubber gaskets on either end usually sealed the leak, once the sleeve was bolted tight. Pipelines invariably leaked in the oil field, for many reasons. Hurricanes damaged the platforms, corrosion ate pipe, and boat anchors sometimes buckled pipes by accident. Wave action on the surface of the water was especially rough on pipe. We also replaced risers. Risers were the section of pipe that connected a pipeline on the sea floor to the processing facilities on top of a platform.

Besides Charlie, Frolich Brothers employed three divers. I liked to work with Bob, the quiet and reasonable member of the team. He rarely raised his voice. Larry, a tall, skinny kid from New York, and C. J., from New Orleans, completed the team. C. J. lost his temper easily. He wore a Savoie helmet. Joe Savoie, a Louisiana diver, took the design from an Italian racing helmet and invented the first helmet with a rubber neck dam seal, allowing divers to work in any position. The lightweight helmet became popular throughout the world.

I came to Frolich in May, the start of the busy summer season. I spent most of July and August offshore. On Friday, July 6, Larry and I used an airlift to uncover a leaking gas line in shallow water. The line was buried under six feet of mud. We took the boat home in the afternoon, but while driving back home, we got a call to report to the Mississippi Grain Elevator Corporation near Belle Chasse, on the West Bank.

Bob met us, and we inspected a huge 53,000 ton ship loading grain headed for Russia. A portion of the dock had collapsed. We checked the ship and found no damage. Hundreds of rats scurried everywhere. The whole place was covered with a fine layer of yellow grain dust. I returned home after dawn.

On Sunday, July 8, Larry and I took the boat to East Bay to change a couple of risers in six feet of water. The sun burned me, and I returned to the dock with a red face.

On Monday, we arrived at the scene of a massive oil leak. We began to install a clamp on the eight-inch line, but received word that a hurricane was coming, so we returned to quarters and took the boat home.

We returned to East Bay four days later to repair whatever had been damaged by the hurricane. The mild hurricane had broken a few gas lines, and risers needed to be replaced. Seas were too rough to work in the morning. We stayed in our quarters.

In the afternoon, we inspected a leak on a three-inch line cut in half. The line was buried under eighteen feet of mud. A Shell representative said he bled off all the lines, but this one was still gushing tremendously, making it impossible to work on. The oil workers didn't know how to turn off the flow of oil to that line. It was a line no one knew about. There were leaks everywhere. Risers hung by a few bolts. Oil slicks turned the water shiny and brownish red.

I noted in my log that the job reminded me of stop-and-go driving. Hurry up and load the boat. Go out to a leak. Wait a half hour for the Shell people to show up. Wait some more while they put gas to the line. Look for the leak. Set up to dive. Check the line. No leak. Wait until they put more gas on the line. Check it again. Well, I guess the leak stopped. Somebody sees a few drops of oil in the water and calls divers immediately. Load the boat. Unload the boat and put the gear on another boat.

On Friday, July 20, we took the crew boat to Block 42 to check a leak. One lonely oil well, white with gull droppings, grew out of the sea. When we arrived, about thirty gulls scattered from their perches. The leak was about 2,000 feet from the well. In the afternoon, we bounced across the waves into deeper water to check a leak that turned out to be deep in the mud, so we couldn't work on it. We enjoyed the evening sky while B went fishing and caught some white trout.

The following day I took the boat home, because a storm was coming.

Most of our time was spent searching for or uncovering leaking lines.

I didn't like the idea of diving in a lake of oil. C. J. once fixed a line in a six-foot-deep hole that was mostly oil. He came out dripping with the brown, foul-smelling liquid that clung to his skin and made him itch. He spent two hours showering and cleaning his gear. He used a special degreaser cream.

In early August, Larry and I ventured into the swamps to fix a leak with a split sleeve. We waited half a day before mechanics repaired the swamp buggy, so we could tow our gear through the grasses. An oil slick covered the water at the site of the leak. We walked through swamp grass, sank up to our necks in mud and stagnant water, and watched for alligators. I never thought I might wrestle an alligator as a commercial diver.

I stood on a swamp buggy while Larry trudged through the mud and installed a split sleeve around a three-inch gas line in a ditch surrounded by tall grass. I stood high on the buggy and surveyed the perimeter for alligators. Larry wore a wetsuit, but didn't need a mask. Welcome to the world of mud diving, where you can get sunburned and eaten by mosquitoes or alligators. Could it get any worse than this?

✳ ✳ ✳

Out in the swamps at the dirty mouth of the Mississippi, working to stop an oil leak polluting the environment and blackening plants, I heard a conversation between a foreman and his workers:

"What would you say to a man who would send a child actor into the land of the wind-chill factor?"

"Here comes the elephant boy dressed in his corduroys, heading south to Illinois."

"That pump don't need no priming, unless it's got a two-by-four stuck inside, or it's Tuesday."

"And what would you say of the intelligence factor of a gorilla raised by its human captor?"

"As much as a human winner raised in the box of Skinner."

Blue Water, Black Death

In April, 1980, Taylor Diving offered me a job, and naturally I took it. I was the happiest man alive. I said goodbye to mud diving, and I moved to the West Bank of New Orleans. I didn't look forward to the same dreary work again, sweeping floors, painting chambers, collecting trash, but I felt the anticipation of all the tenders. They knew something big was brewing. Soon, everyone would be offshore. Taylor was one of the largest diving companies in the world, supporting all the offshore activities of Brown and Root, a billion-dollar construction company. The oil boom was going strong. Welders and mechanics and other workers filled the yards along Engineer Road, even on Sundays. I slept on the floor in my apartment. I didn't buy any furniture, because I knew I would be going offshore soon for a long time.

Taylor stored half a dozen saturation diving systems in its warehouse. The sophisticated deep-diving systems supported the installation of oil platforms and other work in depths exceeding 1,000 feet. A saturation diver was the apogee of the trade. He spent months at a time living in a chamber under pressure and traveled to the sea floor in a diving bell. The term "saturation diving" refers to a scientific theory formulated by Captain George Bond, U.S. Navy. In his experiments conducted at the Submarine Medical Center in New London, Connecticut, Bond asserted that after a given time of exposure to inert gas under pressure, the body will become saturated and absorb no more. Consequently, a diver could remain under pressure for days, weeks, and even months, and the decompression time would remain the same. Bond showed that after twenty-four hours, the body became saturated.

At last I had found a company I could be proud to work for. If I worked hard, I might become a diver in a few years. I might even be a saturation diver. I dreamed of stepping out of a diving bell at a depth of five hundred feet. What would I see there? Would I encounter a giant grouper? Would I face something more terrifying?

✶ ✶ ✶

After a few months of work in the warehouse, I received my first offshore assignment, a position as tender aboard the *M-356*, a Brown and

Root barge. I packed my suitcase and drove to the dock in Venice. I took a sixteen-hour crew boat ride into the Gulf of Mexico, where the water was dark blue. It had been so long since I had seen blue water, I was mesmerized.

My new home was a four-hundred-yard-long flat-bottom vessel equipped with a saturation diving system and dredge. The dredge was a machine the size of a bulldozer that blasted trenches on the sea floor and buried pipelines.

I slept on the top bunk in a small air-conditioned cabin and worked on deck from noon until midnight. I took care of the six divers living in the saturation system, and I also launched and recovered the diving bell. I washed wet suits, sent food to the divers, repaired masks, refueled compressors, and did all the other odd jobs tenders do. Five tenders worked the day shift, and five tenders worked the midnight to noon shift.

✷ ✷ ✷

Life at sea was intolerable to certain souls. Some of the tenders became moody and restless after a month and went home. Who would want to spend countless days under a hot sun staring at an endless ocean, a treeless plain stretching to the horizon, punctuated only by oil platforms that stand in mute silence like guardians of a lost world? I saw no cars, houses, trees for months. I enjoyed no luxuries, except good food. I wore the same jeans and work shirt every day. I lost contact with land, except for an occasional newspaper that showed the stock market quotes.

My companions were fish and sea gulls. The fish, unaccustomed to man, went about their business as they had for hundreds of millions of years. Flying fish sailed by. Sharks circled the barge. One day, a ten-footer circled the barge six times, and Lonnie, a tender, tried to harpoon it. He missed, and the shark disappeared.

Life at sea required great patience and perseverance. Many could not stay for more than thirty days. Separation from family and friends; the lack of mail delivery (in remote places like Bahrain, mail sometimes doesn't arrive for six months); the days of inactivity when storms and rough seas force everyone below deck to play poker and Risk, or sleep, or read books; the constant roll of the barge; the same endless vista day after day after day, waves rolling in, pounding the barge, you can hear them at night sloshing against the superstructure, rattling the boat bumpers and chains; the confinement of a floating vessel, hundreds of miles from land; all these things burdened the mind. For the body, the offshore life was healthy, though austere, with no sex, alcohol, or diversions. Food, however was plentiful and wholesome. Every muscle in the body grew stronger in the constant struggle against wind and waves.

A simple man could enjoy that simple life. Roll out of his berth in the morning, eat a hearty breakfast in the galley, climb on deck to a brilliant sun and a stiff breeze, and work his muscles all day. He didn't have to fight traffic jams, cook meals, or wash his own clothes. There were no weekends. After a twelve-hour workday, there was time to read a book or write letters.

I recorded stock prices into a notebook during the monotonous times, when the bell was on the bottom and the divers worked. I filled the time by washing divers' suits, bringing plates of food for the divers in the chamber, repairing masks, replacing Sodasorb canisters for the carbon-dioxide scrubbers, and refueling compressors. Every thirty minutes the divers wanted a snack or a pitcher of coffee sent to them in the chamber through the medical lock. The medical lock was a small tunnel used to transfer food, masks, suits, and other supplies to the divers inside the chamber.

The most exciting times were launching and recovering the diving bell, especially during rough seas. When a storm came and ripped the sky open and waves crashed against the barge and the barge rolled heavily to either side, bringing the bell out of the water was a task for daredevils. I stood at the winch controls, two tenders grabbed the guide ropes on the bell with long bamboo poles, and the supervisor shouted orders above the noise of the wind and winch motor. The bell swung madly from side to side, the tenders slid on the slippery deck and tried to bring the bell under control, as I guided it into the hooks on the A-frame. Eventually, the bell was brought to rest on top of the saturation system and mated with the chamber. Only when there was a good seal, with no possibility of gas escaping from the chamber, could the divers open the hatch and return to their dry environment.

I never met the divers until they came out of the saturation chamber. For one month, I had heard only the soft gurgling of their voices on the radio when they worked on the bottom. When they crawled out of the chamber, they were sleepy and immediately disappeared below deck. To us tenders, the divers were legends.

There was Fred, fifty years young and still diving. In an industry where the age of thirty-five meant retirement, Fred defied the odds. He liked to set his watch to Greenwich Mean, because he had been to so many places around the world that he didn't want to set his watch so many times. There was Len, who had been in saturation for three hundred days already. He and Grant never complained. They were the mellow ones. Grant dozed in the chamber every day and didn't utter a word when I decompressed him for four hours after gas dives to 290 feet later that summer. Bruce and Roy, young warriors, showed no signs of age. Bruce came from Alabama, and Roy lived in New Orleans.

✷ ✷ ✷

One night, I was awakened by someone shaking me roughly by the shoulder.

"You're needed on the bow," the tender said.

"Huh?" I rubbed my face.

"They need you to make a dive." The tender left the cabin.

All sorts of wild images coursed through my mind.

I dressed and stumbled on deck. It was the middle of the night. Harsh lights stung my eyes. I found a wet suit in the supply van and slipped into it. I put a harness around my shoulders and trotted to the bow.

"I need you to burn off the riser clamp bolts at the sixty-foot level," the supervisor said.

I stared down at the churning water, menacing and black, with streaks of silver from the reflections of the barge lights. I was not fully awake. The barge was anchored a few yards from a platform. I had an idea what I needed to do, but I had never done it before.

A riser was a section of pipe that connected a pipeline on the sea floor with the processing facilities on top of a platform. The riser was secured to the platform with hinged clamps attached to the platform leg.

I slipped my face into the mask and strapped a weight belt around my waist. I sucked on the regulator. Satisfied I could breathe, I crawled over the rail and plunged into the water.

The shock of the cold water woke me. The weightlessness and lack of vision sharpened my senses. I swam to the dark form looming before me. I grabbed the barnacle-encrusted platform leg and descended.

The speaker in my mask crackled. "Where are you going?"

"Huh?"

"You went past the clamp at sixty feet!"

"I did?"

"Go back up."

"I must have missed it." I ascended and found the steel-jawed clamp extending out from the platform leg. "Send down the burning rig."

I had used the oxyarc torch once in school. It wasn't hard; press the electrode against the steel, press the trigger, and vaporize the metal.

I hung on the edge of the clamp and sucked in a cold breath of borrowed air. I could see a couple feet in any direction. No words can describe the intensity of an underwater experience, but imagine hanging sideways on a huge steel structure, breathing air from a regulator, fumbling in the dark, being careful not to scrape against barnacles, mind not functioning one hundred percent, ear speakers crackling with the supervisor's voice. Ten minutes ago I was sound asleep, now I'm under water hanging on a skyscraper burning off bolts.

I found the torch, pressed the electrode against the bolt, and pressed the oxygen trigger. "Make it hot!"

I felt the hot rumble as steel was vaporized by a three-hundred-amp current and a stream of oxygen.

I don't know how long I was down there, but I burned off three bolts, and the tender pulled me to the ladder by my lifeline. When I reached the top of the ladder and popped off the mask, the supervisor stared at me.

"You went to ninety feet. What's the matter with you?"

I smiled.

"Get in the chamber."

I rushed to the decompression chamber stationed amidships. I stripped off my wetsuit and crawled in the chamber nude. I breathed oxygen for twenty minutes at a pressure equivalent to forty feet. Bottom time ended, and I relaxed.

* * *

The next dive was not as much fun. I almost killed myself.

A tender woke me rudely at night again. I dressed and climbed the metal stairs and found harsh barge lights, strange faces of the night shift, a dark sky, and churning black water. I walked to the dive locker and put on some dry jeans and a wet suit top. The neoprene suit felt tight in the shoulders and wrists. The knowledge that I would be in black water with little or no visibility stunned me out of my dream world. I put on rubber booties, looped the lanyard of my knife around the rope belt, and put it in my back right pocket. I walked to the dive station where Harold, the dive supervisor was talking with a tender.

"What are we doing?" I asked.

"Dropping cargo nets of sandbags on a crossing," Harold said. "I want you to follow the down line to the crossing. Then follow the travel line to the crane line and dump a load on the far side. Think you can do it?"

I nodded and looked over the bow where the lights from the barge reflected off the crane line going into the water twenty yards out. Everything was happening too quickly. "Where did you say the travel line went?"

"It goes to the hook on the crane line. The cargo net is hanging just off bottom."

"What's the depth?"

"Ninety-five feet."

"Let's go," said the barge foreman impatiently.

I put on the harness and pulled the nylon strap tight. I slung the ten-pound weight belt around my waist and pressed the buckle shut. I pulled the mask over my head, tested the regulator with a few quick breaths, opened the free-flow valve slightly, and a tender attached the straps around the hood.

"How do you read me?" I said.

"Good." Harold spoke into the phone speaker by the dive station.

I slipped my hands into dry cotton gloves. I turned around and faced the sea, which was rough with three-foot swells rolling in. I jumped in and found the down line.

The water was warm near the surface then became colder on the way down. I went hand over hand along the rope. Darkness enveloped me. I depended on fingers and toes to guide me.

I swallowed. Air hissed quietly into the dry space of the mask and tasted clean. I touched soft mud and gasped as colder water seeped into my wetsuit through wrists and ankles. I groped, found a shackle on the end of a rope, and my toes felt the rough curved surface of a concrete-coated pipe, half submerged in the mud. I found another rope traveling horizontally. I pulled myself along it.

"Are you on bottom?" Harold's voice crackled faintly.

"What? Yeah. . .on the bottom." I moved through the darkness for perhaps twenty feet, then bumped into a large mass. My fingers traced thick ropes and bulging burlap sacks, hard and piled haphazardly. The mass was too large to reach above or around. "I'm at the cargo net," I said.

"Roger. Do you feel the sandbags on the bottom?"

"What? Come back?"

"Do you feel the sandbags on the bottom?" Harold's voice came through a paused breath, barely understandable. My toes scraped rough concrete surrounded by swollen lumps.

"Wait. . .yeah. . .I feel some. . ." The adrenaline was pumping. The unseen giant swung slowly toward me, pushed me, and I took a step back.

"You ready to dump the cargo net?"

"No. Stand by." I had no sense of direction in the black soup. I couldn't concentrate. I tried to stay calm. The cargo net, big as an elephant, swung away.

"Dump the load on the far side," crackled the voice.

I took a breath and didn't know why I couldn't make a decision. Narcosis had clouded my brain. My foot was on the pipe. I tried to make a mental picture of the situation. I didn't know which way to swing the cargo net. I took a guess.

"Swing the big rig to the operator's left." I tried to sound calm to make them believe everything was under control.

"Roger. Swinging left."

I kept a hand on the cargo net. It moved away, and I followed. Don't let go of it. Don't lose it! Okay. Left meant away. It crossed over the pipe. "All stop!"

"All stop on the big rig."

I groped in the soft mud and felt no sandbags. "Dump it anywhere?"

"Are you on the far side?"

"I don't know. I think so."

"Just dump it."

"What do I do?"

"Lower the net, then take one rope off the hook. Go back to the down line and stay out of the way when we pick the net up."

"Roger. . .okay. . .come down on the big rig."

"Coming down."

The unseen cargo net descended like a huge boulder.

"All stop."

"We're all stop on the big rig."

I crawled up the cargo net, traced the heavy ropes to the crane block, and took one rope off the hook. I groped for the travel line. I couldn't find it. I became confused. Stay calm, I told myself. Slow down. It's no good to get excited down here. I traced the smooth steel of a crane block, past tangled rope. I found another rope and followed it back toward the descent line. My umbilical jerked me to a stop. The umbilical was fouled on something. I went back. Where did the umbilical go? I followed it down. I bumped into burlap sacks. Oh no—

"Are you back at the down line?"

"No. . ." I didn't know what to tell him. I was confused. I became anxious. I stopped, concentrated on my breathing, and tried to relax. I still breathed the precious air.

"How's it going down there?"

"Wait a minute—"

"Are you all right?"

"Yeah. . .hose is fouled. . ."

"Come back?"

"Hose is fouled. . .you have to lift the cargo net. . .the umbilical is under it. . .wait. . ." I climbed to the top of the cargo net, found the rope, and put it on the hook. "Okay. . .come up on the big rig."

"Coming up." The boulder rose slowly.

After a few feet I said, "All stop."

"All stop. Can you clear your umbilical?"

"Working on it. . ."

I crawled to the bottom. I groped in the darkness for the umbilical. I breathed harder. My mind was heavy.

"You have to leave bottom soon. Can you clear your umbilical?"

"Maybe. . .wait. . ." I traced the umbilical behind the cargo net and tugged on it. It came loose.

"It should be clear, now. Pick up the diver's slack." The umbilical tightened. The mask wanted to come off my head. "All stop! All stop!" I grabbed the umbilical and yanked it down.

"What's wrong?"

"You're pulling the mask off my head."

"Are you all right? You have to leave bottom now."

"Wait—" I lost touch of the cargo net in the confusion. It was gone. I clawed the empty water.

An urgent voice demanded, "Can you leave bottom?"

"I don't know where the down line is."

"Grab your umbilical. We'll pull you up. Ready?"

I held the umbilical tightly with my left hand. "I'm ready." I ascended, extending my right hand in the darkness so my head would not hit the swinging crane block. My head broke the surface, and a sharp beacon shone in my eyes. I swam to the ladder, climbed on deck, and removed the mask.

"What happened down there?" Harold asked.

"Looks like your quick-release came undone," a tender said.

"I felt the mask coming off my head and—" I caught my breath.

"Three fifteens," Harold said.

I dropped the weight belt on deck and rushed to the chamber. I removed my clothes, crawled through to the inner lock, and leaned against the door. Air hissed in. I yawned, swallowed, and held my nose to clear the ears on the way down, wiped my face on a towel, lay on the bunk, and strapped an oxygen bib to my face. The gas felt cool and dry. I looked up at the porthole and heard the muffled voices of men outside.

It was quiet in that steel prison, except for the hiss of oxygen every time I took a breath. I had plenty of time to contemplate that horrible dive. I tried to relax, but my hands trembled. My right ear throbbed. All the times I had been on the outside looking in, wanting to be inside, and now I was staring at the curved walls of the chamber in shock. The illusion was gone. I had almost been hit by a locomotive. A couple of scuba dives, and I thought I could be a professional. For a moment I saw my career ending. Another dead end. A once-happy innocent kid who wandered into a bad neighborhood and got knocked senseless by a gang of thugs. Maybe the narcosis had confused me. Narc'd out in complete darkness with a swinging cargo net. Scuba was nothing compared to this. It was a nightmare. What if the cargo net had crimped the umbilical? I wouldn't have had any air. They might have found me somewhere on the bottom, or I might have panicked and ditched the mask and tried a free ascent and ended up under the barge. I had to keep track of the umbilical. The damn umbilical got caught, that's all, but I better wake up from this dream, or I'll be dead.

I breathed oxygen for fifteen minutes, took a five-minute air break, then two more oxygen sessions, and the tender opened the valve and brought me up. The air cooled with the release of pressure, and a mist formed. When the hatch popped open, I wrapped the towel around my waist, walked to the dive locker, showered, and put on some dry clothes.

I was depressed for two days after that dive, but I was determined to learn from the experience, and I hoped I would get another chance.

✳ ✳ ✳

My first season with Taylor Diving ended. At least I had made a few dives and spent a considerable amount of time at sea. I knew I could succeed at diving. I only needed more bottom time. All the classroom training in the world was useless. Experience was the greatest teacher.

I worked in the warehouse during the winter. I installed valves and tubing on decompression chambers. The dreary months rolled by. Spring came. I started to lose hope. Many of the tenders that worked for Taylor had been tending for five years and still waited for that elusive promotion to diver. Joe, who had worked with me on the *M-356*, had developed a bad attitude. He said he wouldn't dive as a tender, unless he was paid diver's wages. The supervisors never put him in the water. He quit after his sixth year and began a new career in real estate.

✶ ✶ ✶

In March, everything changed. The shop foreman told me I was going to Mexico. Would my dream come true? Would this be the chance I had longed for?

I put everything I owned in storage, abandoned my apartment, and signed a contract for eighteen months in Campeche Bay aboard the *L.B. Meaders*, a pipelaying barge.

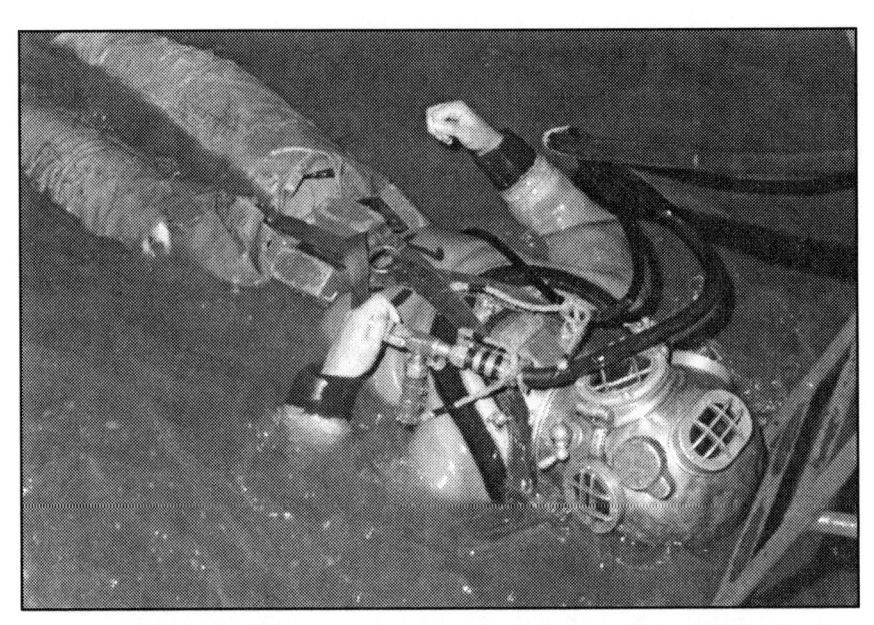

Practicing floating with Mark V dive gear in the muddy water tank at school.

Mr. Byrd, instructor at school and veteran commercial diver.

A diver in Mark V deep sea gear.

Amberjack caught in the Gulf of Mexico.

Author prepares to make a dive in muddy water tank with Kirby-Morgan mask.

A mixed gas dive operation in the Gulf of Mexico. Note banks of helium.

A tug preparing to set anchors. Note anchor buoy.

The gas mixing manifold.

Flare stacks burning natural gas in Mexican oilfield.

A large platform with two oil derricks.

A complex of platforms in Campeche Bay.

A saturation diving system on a barge. Bell sits on top of deck decompression chamber where divers live under pressure. Environment control unit and hot water boiler are in foreground.

Ixtoc burns out of control in Campeche Bay, 1979.

Ixtoc fires rage on top of the water. Many divers lost their lives trying to contain the blaze.

Craig confers with Larry on the stern of the L.B. Meaders, Campeche Bay, Mexico.

Dickie playing with his Nikonos at the stern dive station.

Mark proudly displays his catch, a big grouper he speared at point blank range.

Lee relaxing on the stern of the L.B. Meaders.

Lee with a cobia he speared.

Craig, Joe, and the author by a stern anchor. Joe lost two fingers to the rollers in the pipe ramp.

Mike and Larry confer before a dive. Author holds the Kirby-Morgan mask.

A nice sunset on a tranquil sea.

The huge flare stacks are impressive at night. They light up the sky, creating an artificial day. Frigate birds circle the top of the flames.

A diver comes out of the water after a night dive. Flare stacks light up the stern and produce a deafening roar.

II. MEXICO

Merida, Yucatan

I arrived in Merida on a Taca flight in March. I checked into the Hacienda, an old place near the airport. Palm trees surrounded an attractive pool. I noticed everybody was short, bronze-skinned, and black-haired, and I didn't know much Spanish. I came with my fellow tenders, Steve and Chuck. Chuck had the nickname Pork Chop. Steve had been tending at Taylor for five years. If anyone deserved to be promoted, he did.

In the evening the hot, dry air lifted a little. We walked into town to La Casita on Calle 56. The restaurant looked like a mission. We found a table in the back next to some hanging plants. The place was full of tourists. They chattered about Chac Mool, Kukulcan, and Chichen Itza. I didn't care about Mayan ruins. I felt uncomfortable among all the people. I was anxious and full of energy, ready to embark on my new adventure.

Steve stared at the woman at the table next to ours, and she was embarrassed at having somebody watch her eat, so finally she said, "What brings you to the Yucatan? Are you visiting the ruins?" She was middle-aged, and her friend wore glasses.

"No, Ma'am," Steve said in his hoarse southern drawl. "We're gonna lay pipe all over Campeche Bay."

She looked down at her plate, as if disappointed we weren't respectable archaeologists.

A waiter gave us menus and we ordered beer, fish, and refried beans.

"Do I look like some college professor?" Steve stroked his mustache.

"How does Mexico compare to the Gulf?" I asked Steve.

"Things move a little slower."

"I heard some guys are homesteading down here."

"Yeah. Dickie's been on the *Meaders* for two and a half years."

"How does he do it?" I asked.

"I don't know, but he's easygoing," Steve said. "You'll like him."

Steve motioned to a passing waiter. "*Cerveza, por favor!*"

"I should have ordered *langosta*," Pork Chop said. "This red snapper has no taste."

We finished our meal. The walk back to the Hacienda cleared my head.

✱ ✱ ✱

We left Merida in the morning after a breakfast of rolls and coffee. A Volkswagen minibus took us to the airport, where we boarded a DC-3. The bumpy flight lasted an hour, and I gazed at the stewardess when the clouds obscured the scenery. She wore a long dark skirt and a light blue blouse neatly pressed. All the girls in Mexico were neat and tidy.

We landed in Ciudad del Carmen, a sleepy seaside town. Our company representative took us to a transit house in a residential neighborhood. After a few hours we were taken to a local government office to get our work permits and have our pictures taken. We sat on small wooden chairs in a cramped room with three desks. The door to the street was open, and people strolled by in the hot sun. It was quiet except for an occasional ring of a bicycle bell. The clerk sat in front of a manual typewriter and slowly pecked out one letter at a time with great care. After two hours we were finally ready to board a crew boat and head into the oilfield.

Pemex, the giant Mexican oil monopoly, owned the field situated in the warm waters of Campeche Bay, where the depth ranged from forty to 220 feet. Pemex was the fifth largest oil company in the world. Protected from competition by the government, Pemex enjoyed an enviable position, but it was heavily indebted, undercapitalized, corrupt, and it lacked the infrastructure to produce enough oil for the Mexican people. Mexico had only six refineries. Oil moved to Houston, Texas, where it was refined, then imported back to Mexico.

The Mexican oilfield was the fourth largest in the western hemisphere. The Canterell field held thirty-five billion barrels of oil. The major platform complexes in the Canterell field included Nohoch, Akal, Chac, and Kutz. Many of the platforms were named after Mayan kings. Akal Mo Nhab III, a Palenque king, ruled a civilization whose descendants still speak half a dozen dialects and practice an ancient culture, despite efforts to subjugate them. Chac Mool, messenger of the gods, was a familiar figure seen at many temple grounds in the Yucatan.

My New Home

The crew boat glided smoothly on a calm sea, noisy engines racing at full throttle. I sat on the back deck looking at the moon. Sea gulls floated quietly in small groups on the open water. The lights of Ciudad del Carmen faded as the boat headed into Campeche Bay. We arrived at the *L.B. Meaders* late at night. Many lights on deck cast an eerie glow over the vessel, illuminating a derrick crane on the stern, a control tower and its antennas, a smaller deck crane with its boom down, and stacks of pipe on the bow. Tractor tires hung from chains along the side of the barge, which was about the length of a football field. The crew boat tied off on the port stern, and Mexicans helped us lift our bags onto the deck ten feet above our heads. I crawled up the rusty boat bumper ladder onto the weather-beaten wooden deck scarred with burn marks and gashes. I looked out over the sea, and there was nothing but darkness. The moist air clung to my shirt. I took a deep breath and smelled seaweed, barnacles, and oysters that had dried and decayed along the side of the barge above the waterline. I thought I smelled burning metal and the pungent trail of an electric arc, and nearby, warm air came out of a duct from below.

A strong gust of wind blew over the deck, swept it clean, and I smelled only the fresh, pure sea air.

Steve, Pork Chop, and I stood under the halogen lights. Soon, a man wearing only sandals and blue jean shorts greeted us. He had a wild curly mop of hair and a droopy Zapata mustache. His brown eyes, though partly concealed by worn and wrinkled skin, were bright and cheerful. The right pocket of his tattered shorts held a pocket knife attached to a lanyard. His nose was a little sunburned. "Howdy," he said.

"Yo, Dickie," Steve said.

This was Richard Campbell, who had lived on the *L.B. Meaders* for as long as anyone could remember. He seemed friendly and modest. He spoke in a quiet tone and chuckled from time to time. He seemed immune to the effects of life at sea.

We exchanged greetings, and Dickie led us to our quarters below deck.

My cabin was a cramped space with four lockers, two bunk beds, and a small table. I would be sharing the cabin with Mike, another diver, and two barge personnel. Though small, the cabin was air-conditioned and clean. Stewards changed the sheets regularly. Etiquette dictated that tenders took the top bunk, while divers took the lower bunk.

When I saw Dickie's cabin, I was astonished. Someone had paneled and varnished the walls and lockers. The edges of the walls, the mirror, and both bunk beds were decorated with one-inch rope trim, and both bottom bunks had wooden drawers. A television sat on a shelf above the lockers. The cover on the fluorescent lights was blue.

"Where did you get the wood?" I asked Dickie.

"Shipping crates." Dickie chuckled. "Craig really gets into woodworking."

"This looks like the captain's quarters on a sailing ship back in the seventeenth century."

Craig, the other barge diver, would join us in a few days. He was returning from his home in North Carolina.

Dickie showed me the galley, across the hall. A wall divided the room in half lengthwise. Each half had four tables with long benches. At the far end stood the grill, soft drink machine, stainless steel cooler, ice cream machine, and snack tray.

"The Americans eat on this side of the room, and the Mexicans eat on the other," Dickie said. I thought I knew the unwritten rules of the offshore life: no fighting and no liquor, but this was a new rule, and I wasn't about to question it.

"This cooler is always stocked with fresh fruit, cold cuts, drinks, and desserts. Help yourself any time. Over here is where the line starts. Meals are served every six hours around the clock."

"When do we go to work?"

"Relax. We're standing by. The Pemex inspectors are due in about a week."

I was not accustomed to the slow pace of Campeche. In the Gulf of Mexico, barge superintendents drove their crews hard, not wanting to waste precious minutes. Sometimes they were even reckless, working until the last second, before an approaching storm forced evacuation of the area. A barge was an expensive floating factory that operated around the clock, charging close to 100,000 dollars a day. The Mexicans, on the other hand, had money to burn. They took their time. *Tranquilo, hombre.* Relax, enjoy the day. The work will get done eventually; if not today, then tomorrow. I was going to like it here.

✷ ✷ ✷

When I came on deck in the morning, it was sunny, but a fierce wind blew and whitecaps leaped above the rails. The barge rolled in a slow rhythm. Steve told me we would wait for rough weather to pass before going anywhere. He took me on a tour of the barge. I didn't see many people working. I met Billy, the day shift mechanic who walked with a limp, because he had fallen through a hatch. We also met the warehouse moles from England who worked three levels down, deep in the belly of the vessel, and they had a Deborah Harry poster on the wall. It was like a dungeon down there. I heard the machines humming, and it smelled like dust and grease, and the lighting was barely adequate.

On board, we had riggers from Oaxaca and Veracruz, welders from Texas, foremen from Spain and Portugal, pontoon technicians and supply clerks from England, cooks, stewards, radio operators, mechanics, electricians, and timekeepers. The barge was a self-contained floating hotel with generators, laundry facilities, movie theater, health clinic, and a desalinization plant for fresh water. The only thing it didn't have was a means of propulsion. Tug boats towed it into position and set eight anchors, four off the bow and four off the stern. The barge was able to move in a limited way by pulling on its eight anchor cables like a giant water spider. When it wanted to move forward, it slackened the stern cables and pulled on the bow cables. It could also move from side to side, because two anchors on either end were positioned laterally from the barge.

I met Jim, the barge captain. Mexicans called him the Potato Man. He had a bulging stomach and thin legs. He kept the barge well supplied with food. A boat came every month with refrigerated trailers stocked with strawberries, frozen steaks, and hams.

✳ ✳ ✳

We spent five days anchored in shallow water, waiting for Pemex. Welcome to the floating world, a tiny vessel surrounded by an endless blue sea, under a scorching sun. How different was my world from the landlubbers! I had no bills to pay. Everything I owned was in storage, paid six months in advance. I needed only modest clothes, blue jeans and flip-flops. Food was plentiful. I had no cares, only the potential threat of dangers lurking on the sea floor.

The barge was comfortable. On the bow, neatly stacked pipe joints waited for assembly. Welders' huts ran the length of the starboard side. There a pipeline would slowly grow, joint by joint, slip into the pontoon off the stern, and slope to the sea floor. A 2,000-ton derrick crane dominated the stern. A decompression chamber was welded to the deck on the port side. On a half deck, amidships, were two air compressors, which delivered clean air to the divers when they worked on the bottom.

The first days passed in idyllic bliss. The high point of an afternoon was the arrival of the daily crew boat. We swam off the stern in the warm water, watched videos in Dickie's cabin, and scrubbed the deck plates of the decompression chamber.

Craig Cooper, a barge diver, burned a hole in the dive locker door one day and installed a circular window. He also paneled the door and varnished it. Everyone had to learn how to pass the time, or go crazy. Craig was built like a wrestler. He spoke slowly and never rushed. I felt privileged to be working with a living legend. He had been diving for ten years throughout the world, including the North Sea, Borneo, South America, and the Persian Gulf. When he squinted at me with his icy blue eyes, I saw the hardness of his soul.

Dickie spent considerable time in the weight room, improving his upper body strength. Physical strength was an asset to a commercial diver, as was humility and the ability to work in complete darkness. I don't know what drove Dickie. He owned a spacious house in New Orleans, but he seemed content to live in cramped quarters year after year on a barge. Perhaps he had a dream to retire and someday marry and raise a family, but he never told me his dreams. He was a private person who kept his own agenda.

Mike Sands, the third diver, came aboard. A former Navy SEAL, he lived in Montana. He usually worked only three months a year. The rest of the time he spent hunting and fishing with his son along Flathead Lake. He quickly found a place to do his daily running, the circular platform around the derrick crane. It was a metal grid about thirty feet above the main deck.

I thought running was a good way to stay in shape for the grueling days ahead, so I imitated Mike and ran fifty laps each day.

Mike also liked to paint. One day he painted colorful acrylic lizards in the shower stall of the dive locker. He also painted a new logo on the decompression chamber. He replaced the words "Taylor Diving and Salvage" with "Turkey Driving and Sausage."

Mike always brought a suitcase full of T-shirts he had stenciled, and he quickly sold all of them to barge personnel. One time Mexican customs confiscated all his shirts. It was against the law to conduct business without a permit. A hundred T-shirts looked suspicious. Mike was a maverick and eccentric who complained about barge life and how he couldn't stand life at sea for more than three months. He'd miss his wife and son badly and make any excuse to go home. He was popular with the barge crew, however. He had a playful nature, but underneath, I could see he was still a trained killer, a man of incredible self-confidence and strength.

Pipelaying

Soon we would be laying a thirty-six-inch diameter pipeline, if the weather remained calm. We were subject to the whims of the sea, and her attitude changed every other day.

Pipelaying is a comfortable operation from a diver's point of view, because he must only make a brief inspection dive every six hours, while the welders work in two shifts around the clock.

A pipeline slowly takes shape, as forty-foot sections of pipe are welded together on the starboard side. X-ray machines judge the quality of the welds. If the welds pass inspection, a whistle blows, everyone leaves the welding huts, and the barge moves forward. The pipeline moves to the stern on rollers. Toward the stern, an aluminum band is wrapped around the welded area, and a chemical hardening foam is applied to the gap between the band and exposed metal of the pipe to protect the welded area from corrosion. Tensioning shoes, hard rubber supports at regular intervals, prevent any lateral movement of the pipeline. The pipeline moves down a ramp, leaves the barge, and slides onto a pontoon.

A pontoon is a buoyancy device that allows the pipeline to slope gently toward the sea floor. The pontoon is about two hundred feet long, consisting of three hinged sections. Each section has compartments that can be pressurized with air to produce the desired amount of buoyancy. The pipeline rides down the center of the pontoon on rollers.

When seas become rough, welders attach a plug on the end of the pipeline, and the pipeline is lowered to the sea floor. When the weather calms, the barge moves into position, a diver connects a cable to the end of the pipeline, and the barge pulls the end of the pipeline up into the pontoon, up the ramp, and into the welders' huts, where new sections can be added again.

The welding area is a potentially dangerous place, especially when the pipeline moves to the stern. Everyone must stand clear when the whistle blows. Hands or arms can get crushed if caught between the pipeline and tensioning shoes.

★ ★ ★

The tugs picked up anchors one night and towed the barge to the platform complex named after a Mayan king, Akal. I can always tell when it's time to go to work, when I'm awakened by the sound of anchor cables being pulled off their drums at high speed. When I'm in my bunk, I hear the high-pitched rumble coming through the walls. Setting anchors takes about two hours.

I quickly ate a breakfast of eggs and bacon and climbed on deck. The barge wasn't rolling too badly. I had acquired my sea legs the previous year, so I didn't have to worry about seasickness anymore.

I walked to the stern and watched a tug set an anchor. The crane picked up an anchor buoy, raised it high above the deck, and turned toward the tug, off to the port side. The buoy looked like a Christmas tree ornament, one hemisphere painted red, the other white. It was about eight feet in diameter. It made a loud clunk when the crane set it on the tug. The deck hands disconnected the cable. The tug raced toward the horizon, with the anchor cable ripping through the sheaves. The tug went about a thousand yards and dropped the anchor.

Directly astern, perhaps a mile away, six yellow platforms joined with walkways grew out of a blue sea like a little fishing village on pilings. In the center, two towers rose twice the height of the platforms, and bright yellow flames shot high into the sky. The top of the flames turned orange, and black smoke appeared out of them. The platform on the left had a walkway leading to a tower bent at an angle, and a shorter column of flame, perhaps fifty feet high, came out of it.

To my right, I saw another group of platforms about five miles away. Distances were deceptive looking across water. I saw four flaming towers, and the smoke rose in distinct columns until all the columns mingled together in the sky and the smoke drifted off to the left with the wind. Pemex was burning its natural gas, a byproduct of an oil well. I thought it was a waste.

To my left, four drilling rigs, various distances apart, grew out of the sea on tripod legs, like lonely sentinels at the end of the world.

Steve jumped in with scuba gear and inspected the hitch at the starboard stern. The hitch was a particularly dangerous area where the pontoon connected to the barge. The ramp behind the hitch leading up to the welding area was open to the sea, and water surged in with tremendous force on every barge roll.

Joe, a veteran tender at Taylor, had lost two fingers one season. He had been washed into the ramp by the surge and knocked against a set of rollers. The rollers had pivoted and crushed his right hand.

***

The pontoon arrived later by tugboat, and the Mexicans secured it to the starboard side with two hawsers. The brown sea monster was covered with barnacles, shellfish, and clumps of coral. Not one inch of metal remained exposed.

Steve and I donned scuba gear and flooded the forward compartments of the pontoon. I enjoyed being in the water, out of the hot sun. I helped Steve attach a crane line to the front of the pontoon, then we climbed out of the water.

The crane picked up the pontoon, while the tug steered the back end. Soon the pontoon came to the stern, the technician in the pontoon shack opened the fingers on the hitch, and the crane set the pontoon into the hitch. The barge shook with a loud clunk! when the pontoon landed and the hydraulic fingers closed.

Steve and I jumped in again and connected the hydraulic control hoses to the pontoon.

We were almost ready to lay pipe.

***

We waited two days for calm seas, then went to work in the afternoon. Dickie connected a cable on the bottom, and the barge picked the pipeline off the sea floor. Mike jumped in, hung on the end of the pontoon, two hundred feet from the stern, and guided the pipeline into the pontoon. The barge slowly backed up, and I watched for an hour as the pipeline moved up the pontoon into the welders' huts. When Mike climbed out of the water, the sun had set. In the distance, the flares of the platforms cast brilliant halos, and the platforms were silhouetted under a reddish haze.

I secured the dive station, shut down the compressors, and went below deck at 8:30.

At four o'clock in the morning somebody turned the light on in my cabin and said, "You're needed at the stern." Mike instantly jumped out of bed.

"Get up," he said to me.

"What's going on?" I asked, still groggy.

"Just get up there."

I dressed and climbed on deck to a churning sea under a purple sky. Dickie told me a storm was coming.

Steve and I set up the dive station while the barge pulled ahead and lowered the pipeline to the sea floor by a cable. Craig jumped in and disconnected the cable. Dickie was on the radio and Mike was standby diver. Seas were already running three feet when dawn broke. It didn't take much wind to start throwing that water around.

Craig spent about fifteen minutes on the bottom, talking calmly, like he was working on a jigsaw puzzle, then Dickie told Pork Chop to pick up his slack. Pork Chop decompressed him, and Steve and I jumped in with scuba, pressurized the front two tanks on the pontoon, disconnected the hydraulic hoses, and a tug pulled it away. Six-foot seas arrived later in the morning. We waited.

Craig came in my cabin and said, "Looks like the storm changed direction. Pontoon's coming back. Get up on deck."

We were on deck all day and night. We installed the pontoon again, Mike connected the pull cable, Dickie guided the pipeline in, and we retired to our bunks around 1:00. I was exhausted.

Pontoon Check

We spent a day laying pipe. The divers made inspection dives at 6:00, noon, 6:00 in the evening, and midnight. Scuba was typically used during the day, but on the midnight check, we used the Kirby mask and umbilical. The diver swam along the pontoon and checked that the pipeline was riding securely on the pontoon rollers and that there was no damage to the concrete coating of the pipeline. Sometimes chunks of concrete may be knocked loose when the pipeline bounces on the rollers, and this may expose the metal surface of the pipe, which is undesirable. Seawater is corrosive to metal. The diver swam to the end of the pontoon, made note of the depth, and followed the pipeline to the sea floor, to check the slope of the pipeline and how it settled on the bottom.

✱ ✱ ✱

Pork Chop and Craig made the first pontoon check at 6:00 in the morning. The deep blue water, more restless in the early morning, as if awakening from a peaceful slumber, the wind, blowing cool across the deck, and the sun, not yet fierce in the cloudless sky, greeted me when I stepped on deck. A school of porpoise leaped into the air far away. The creatures did not approach the barge.

At noon, Steve and I put on wetsuit tops and blue jeans and prepared for our inspection dive. Jeans provided adequate protection from jellyfish particles in the water and barnacles on the pontoon. Two nights ago, I had learned a lesson about diving without protective clothing. Asked to clear a buoy flag that had become tangled around an anchor cable, I had jumped in quickly wearing only a swimsuit. I dived under the pontoon, and the barnacles cut a deep gash in my left calf.

With my wound bandaged with gauze and duct tape, I stood at the stern, ready for the rough transition from ordinary time to bottom time. I held my mask tightly with one hand and the regulator with the other. With a heavy steel tank on my back, I plunged ten feet from the barge deck to the water. The shock of impact knocked me out of my dream state. The sea tossed me around. I kicked vigorously to propel myself under the surface turbulence.

I swam to the pontoon and grabbed the guide wire. I wiggled my jaw and blew my nose until my ears cleared. The water was cool, a refreshing escape from the scorching sun. Breathing air from my regulator, I looked through the dirty window of my mask at the particles floating by. I adjusted my mask, cleared the regulator, pulled the loose fin strap over my bootie, and turned my attention to the pontoon.

Steve and I inspected the hitch area. Steve cleared a small piece of concrete out of one of the locking fingers. I found a blenny that had made a home between two steel plates on the hitch. I nudged it with my finger. The tiny fish, barely two inches long, attacked my glove in defense of its territory.

I watched the blenny for a few minutes. Why had it picked a humble perch at the stern of a floating fortress to make a home? Steel walls protected it on three sides. The pontoon, richly stocked with barnacles and shellfish, provided food. Perhaps the niche where it rested, though surrounded by turbulence, was peaceful and calm. Predators would find the turbulence around the hitch dangerous. The blenny sometimes walked on its pectoral fins, like a seal. The solitary creature looked almost comical, with bulging eyes on top of its head, a tapering body, and continuous dorsal fin. I moved my hand closer again. The blenny nipped at my index finger. I retreated.

Steve and I swam past the hydraulic hoses on the panel above the bottom tank and followed the pontoon down and away from the barge. The rollers were spaced about thirty feet apart in a V-shape and the pipeline rested on them. As we passed the hinge connecting the first and second sections of the pontoon, it groaned quietly. Everything appeared to be in good shape except for a small crack in the second section where air bubbles escaped.

We swam to the third section, reached the end, and my depth gauge read fifty-two feet. The pipeline, its forty-foot sections of gray concrete punctuated by silver bands marking the welded areas, came out of the end rollers and sloped gently toward the bottom and disappeared in the mist. A remora, its body undulating, hugged the top of the pipe and followed the slope to the bottom. Remoras usually attach to other fish such as sharks, whales, and turtles with their sucker-like organ on top of their head. They eat scraps of food left behind by their hosts. Perhaps the pipeline appeared to be a giant fish the remora could attach to.

Above, bright surface light exposed the turbulence, where voices chattered, machines hummed, and waves clashed with the barge. Below, the great emptiness loomed..

We swam over the pontoon and returned toward the barge on the other side and continued our inspection, then we swam under the pontoon to the dive ladder.

We surfaced, removed our tanks, and Dickie greeted us. We showered, changed, and filled the scuba tanks using a small compressor outside the dive locker.

We had little to do in the afternoon except take a nap or sunbathe. I still had too much restless energy, so I organized the dive locker. I crammed the wetsuit booties and Kirby hoods in the cubbyholes along the back wall; hung the crescent wrenches and flashlights on their lanyards behind the door along with the crowbars and sledgehammers; pushed the box of manila rope under the work bench; placed the knife switch in the corner next to the broken radio; sorted the hose fittings; hung the buoyancy vests on the rack with the wet suits and harnesses; stuffed the backpacks along the back wall; rearranged the little things like fishing hooks, O-rings, silicon grease, carbon dioxide cartridges, batteries, chamber handles, valves, and Teflon tape in the boxes on the shelves in the center of the locker; and I didn't know what to do with the chemical lights. I stuffed the heavy box of burning rods under the bench next to the spare depth gauge. Eight scuba bottles rested vertically on the side wall along with plenty of fins and masks and old jeans. The dive locker would not have been complete without the Playboy playmate above the shower stall. Wearing nothing but a fishnet, she was our fantasy.

Midnight Dive

The only reason to wear a watch was to time a diver's decompression in the chamber; otherwise, time was meaningless on a barge. We were ruled by the rhythm of the sea, the ebb and flow of the waves against the barge, the rise and fall of the sun, and the number of pipe joints we had deposited on the sea floor. I did not know whether the day was Monday or Friday, and I didn't care. There was no weekend at sea. I had a vague notion that it was the month of April, but soon, the idea of months and seasons would also fade. It was always summer. Only two kinds of time existed, bottom time and surface time. Bottom time was short, intense, and unforgettable. Surface time dragged on and on.

The barge spent five days laying pipe. One day, Mike and I made the evening pontoon check using scuba gear. Mike went to the bottom wearing a bailout bottle, a small tank containing only a fraction of the air of a standard scuba tank. I followed him and reached the bottom at 130 feet, where the water was cold. The pipeline settled into a gray mud that stretched forever. No words could describe the awesome emptiness of the sea floor, where everything familiar had faded away.

I straddled the pipe and tightened the strap of the backpack that held my scuba tank. My denim jeans protected me from the rough concrete. My fins and rubber booties touched soft mud.

Mike raced past me, ascending to the surface. I thought something might be wrong. I followed quickly.

By the time I reached the end of the pontoon, Mike had disappeared. I swam to the ladder and surfaced.

I found him in the dive locker. "What happened to you?"

"I ran out of air. I was sucking on fumes all the way up."

I guess Navy SEALS liked to challenge themselves.

✳ ✳ ✳

The time came for me to make a midnight pontoon check. I had made only a few night dives, and I was apprehensive.

At 11:30 I climbed on deck. As I was collecting my jeans, wetsuit top, and booties under the port air duct, the second shift of barge workers appeared sleepy-eyed, with Styrofoam coffee cups in one hand and cigarettes in the other. They worked from midnight to noon, so they had to adjust their biological clocks somehow. I walked into the dive locker and dressed. I put on a nylon harness with metal rings. I strapped a ten-pound weight belt to my waist and walked to the dive station. Steve connected the masks to the umbilical. Mike stood in front of the dive station and made notes in the log.

I looked at the black choppy water reflecting the barge lights. I took a big breath. The harness and wetsuit top felt tight in the chest. The barge lights shone on half of the first section of the pontoon, but the last two sections were under water.

I slipped the mask hood over my head, and Steve attached the straps and clipped the umbilical into the harness. I put on fins and cotton gloves while Steve threw umbilical in the water.

"How do you read me?" I said.

"Fine." Mike's voice came through the ear speakers.

I was reduced to tunnel vision, looking through a scratched Plexiglas faceplate. I jumped in.

Everything conventional disappeared: a firm deck, warm moist air, bright lights, engines purring, men talking, the smell of coffee. Now, a surge, shadows bouncing, cool wetness, the dark form of the barge hull, a crackling voice. Head wrapped in a rubber cocoon, I'm almost light as air with no scuba tank on my back.

I gasped for breath, kicked hard to the pontoon, a dark barnacle-encrusted giant cradling a pipeline on V-shaped rollers between the tanks. My umbilical trailed behind, snakelike, silver wraps of duct tape visible. I grabbed the guide wire and pulled myself toward the end of the pontoon. Faint light, bending at crazy angles, reflecting particles, danced with the surge. Air hissed into the mask. It did not burn my eyes in the dry space, tasted clean, but was mixed with a little condensate. I felt comfortable inside a Kirby. I had the option of turning on my free-flow valve, giving me unlimited air.

"Pipe's riding smoothly down the center," I said.

"Good." Mike's faint voice crackled next to my ears.

Comfortable, able to concentrate, with warm water inside the wetsuit, I looked back, checked the drift of the umbilical, which was fine, opened the free-flow valve full blast for a second to blow some of the water out, reached back and pulled the fin on coming loose on the right foot, tightened the weight belt, and swallowed to clear the ears as the depth gradually increased. In a few minutes I reached the third section. It was quiet.

"Have some concrete missing near the end of the pontoon. Pipe's bouncing on the stern roller."

"You're at the end?"

"Roger."

"Give me a pneumo on top of the pipe."

"Roger. Take it."

Hanging alone in a silent cave, weightless, two hundred feet from the barge and far below the surface, where the pipeline left the pontoon and sloped unassisted into the darkness toward the sea floor, left hand holding a bracket, right hand holding the end of the narrow gray pneumo hose against the concrete, I waited for bubbles. Some light lingered. The pontoon and pipe gave off an eerie luminescence, and I had two feet of visibility. The small remora appeared again, hovering above the concrete. It stayed just beyond the end of the pontoon. The persistent fish still looked for something to attach to.

Air trickled out the pneumo hose.

"Got bubbles."

The pipeline moved. I knew the welders had completed more joints, and the barge was pulling ahead. Concrete particles scraped loose, floated away, and the pipe groaned as it slid on the rollers.

"Come on back." The distant voice reminded me of another world..

I returned along the guide wire and fought a current all the way. When I reached the first section, the barge hull came into focus. It seemed to defy gravity, suspended above nothing but darkness. I climbed the ladder, and soon I breathed familiar air again.

"That's a no 'D' dive. Your depth was sixty-two feet. Close up shop. I'm going below." Mike disappeared.

I didn't have to spend any time in the chamber decompressing. Breathing the warm, moist air again, standing firm, glad to be back, I looked into the darkness at the faint glow of the flares on the horizon, at the black water that seemed less ominous, and my excitement subsided. I didn't notice that the stern was deserted. Steve had probably gone to shut down the compressors.

I showered, changed into dry clothes, rinsed the gear with fresh water, hung the clothes under an air duct, and went below. My apprehension faded. Bottom time at night held fewer terrors.

Almost a Fight

Blessed with five days of good weather, the barge made steady progress. The barge could lay about a half mile of pipe in a day, so the Akal structures slowly receded as we moved forward. The tugs periodically repositioned the anchors, allowing the barge to continue moving by tightening its bow anchor cables and slacking the stern cables.

I snorted bloody mucous when I surfaced from daily pontoon checks, because of sinus problems. Ear infections also tormented us. The treatment was to avoid water. Steve stayed out of the water for a few days, and I missed a few pontoon checks. I developed a habit of rinsing my ears with hydrogen peroxide after every dive. I didn't mind the painful earaches, pain in the sinuses, or barnacle cuts, because I loved being in the water. Every dive was an escape from the hot sun and monotonous routine of barge life.

Tension between Dickie and Mike erupted into a quarrel. Dickie and Craig were the official barge divers, which gave them a privileged status. They were considered permanent residents of the barge. Mike was something of an outsider, and he resented the situation, because he felt he was a better diver than Dickie. Mike had about ten years of experience, while Dickie had only six.

One hot afternoon, Dickie was sitting on a port stern bitt, acquiring a tan. Mike approached and shoved him.

Dickie leaped off his seat and cocked an arm. "Back off!" Dickie growled.

Mike retreated. "Did you see that? He almost punched me." Mike feigned innocence to the bystanders.

Steve, Craig, and I stood nearby watching the scene.

"There's an anchor down there," Dickie protested.

Mike saw he had no sympathy from us, so he stalked away, muttering. "He picks a fight with me, and he'll be sorry. You can bet who the winner of that fight will be . . ."

Mike disappeared through a hatch.

"He's a nutty guy," Steve said.

"Yeah," Craig said. "I saw him come out of a bar naked once and jump on the hood of a moving pickup truck. Scared the hell out of the driver."

✳ ✳ ✳

Mike didn't challenge Dickie anymore, because fighting was forbidden on the barge, and a violation meant an instant ticket home. Mike worked only three months a year, so he couldn't jeopardize his position. Mike often criticized Dickie, however, and questioned his diving ability. Mike wanted to be barge diver, so he intended to belittle Dickie at every opportunity.

I didn't have any trouble with Mike, except for one time when I forgot to put a fresh towel in the chamber and received a tongue lashing.

Although Mike was a rebel who never ceased complaining about how miserably the company treated its divers, I admired him. Mike's ability was enviable. He was as quick and agile as a porpoise under water, and we called him Flipper. He often told me about his SEAL training. One time his team set charges under water at Subic Bay, Philippines. A boat came by at high speed and plucked the divers out of the water before the charges exploded a few minutes later. Mike said he had to lock his arm into a rubber strap at the stern of the boat as it passed. He thought he dislocated his shoulder when he was thrown into the boat.

I didn't notice any rivalry between Craig and Dickie. Both were steadfast and reliable. Dickie had been on the barge for two and a half years. I admired his perseverance. He was humble, and I heard him chuckle frequently on the radio when he was under water.

Steve, Pork Chop, and I wanted to be divers, which meant a doubling of our pay and a heightened status from servant to master, but I knew it might be many years before I saw a promotion. Steve had been tending for five years, and his attitude grew worse as the months passed. I don't know how he managed to stay in the business for so many years. One day he even told me he hated salt water. His wife was pregnant with their first child, and I know he missed the domestic life. I was a bachelor with nothing to tie me to the landlubber life. I could stay at sea for years, if necessary.

✳ ✳ ✳

The barge set the unfinished pipeline on the sea floor and towed to a new location. The derrick crane set an oil separator package on the top of a platform. We did no work for six days. We made scuba dives around the platform, speared fish, and collected spiny oysters. A typical day featured movies, scuba dives, running laps around the crane deck, sunning on top of the pontoon control shack, and watching the Mexicans work.

Juan and Santiago, the foremen from Spain and Portugal, kept the

Mexican riggers busy. Most of the Mexicans were teenagers, making more money than they have ever made in their lives. They made about 22,000 pesos a month, which translated to 600 U.S. dollars. They came on the barge thin and scrawny, and in a few months, became healthy and strong. Some of the boys couldn't have been more than fourteen or fifteen years old. They chipped paint, assembled wire slings, operated air tuggers, assisted the welders, unloaded refrigerated food containers, and performed countless other tasks. Some of the older men wore dress slacks and dress shirts, which quickly became stained with oil and grease. They had unique habits. They stowed fruit such as apples in cubbyholes around the barge and always included a bowl of soup with every meal. They were also thieves, and some of them brought guns on board. A scuba mask was taken one night, while hanging under an exhaust duct to dry. We kept the dive locker locked.

✶ ✶ ✶

Pork Chop developed a rash on his arms and face by the end of April. Steve thought it might be an allergy to something he ate. I had no theories, but the sea can produce strange maladies. On the *M-356* the year before, I came out of the water one day and developed a rash that covered my entire arm. I think the water had been infested with jellyfish particles. The rash didn't incapacitate me, but it itched like hell. After a few days, the rash disappeared.

Pork Chop would have to return to the States, if he did not feel better soon.

Spiny Dive

While the derrick crane set a structure on top of a platform, the divers played.

We jumped off the stern and headed to the structure a dozen yards away. We wore scuba gear and carried paint scrapers, hammers, spear guns, and nylon mesh bags for carrying whatever we collected.

I settled on a horizontal cross brace at a depth of 110 feet, while Craig and Dickie looked for grouper at greater depth. I chipped off a large spiny oyster with my paint scraper and hammer and dropped it into my bag. The water was clear and warm, except at the bottom, which was shrouded in mist. The bottom was at a depth of 130 to 140 feet.

I kicked with my fins, glided along horizontally, and passed a clump of antler coral growing on the structure. My mind was refreshed, the heat and noise gone in the home of the gill-breathers. I looked up. The tremendous barge had been reduced to a matchbox, the pontoon an insect ovipositor. The legs of the structure, rivaling the largest pine trees, rose to meet the surface light. I ascended along a platform leg encrusted with growth and straddled a cross brace at sixty feet. My blue jeans protected me from the rough surface. I tapped at the base of a spiny oyster and dislodged it. Mike and Steve tapped with their paint scrapers below me. The origin of the sound was difficult to detect under water.

An abundance of sea life covered the entire structure. Oysters, mussels, sea urchins, barnacles, coral, sea fans, tube worms, hermit crabs, and other strange invertebrates made homes on the artificial reef.

In the area surrounded by the latticework of tubular steel legs and cross pieces, hundreds of fish congregated. They liked the protected area, which gave them a point of reference. Barracuda hunted; triggerfish dined on barnacles; and dolphin fish, red snapper, pompano, and amberjack glided along in the clear water. They were not disturbed by our presence. An amberjack swam by me. A hook was in its mouth trailing weights and a polypropylene line. A triggerfish approached and tried to chew my gloves. I pushed it away with my paint scraper. Two barracuda, mouths open, dagger teeth displayed, gave me an angry look some distance away. Mike ascended and chased a six-footer, but the barracuda shot away to the other side of the structure. I filled my bag with oysters and glanced at my pressure gauge, which read 400 pounds. Far above, flooded by bright surface light, the ladder on the stern bounced with the surge, and the anchor cables stretched as far as I could see. I cared little for what might transpire on the barge. My quiet world with its spectacular view would remain a mystery to the barge personnel.

Dickie and Steve ascended and climbed the ladder. Craig followed, with a barracuda trailing ten feet behind. The barracuda wanted the fish in Craig's bag. Craig removed his fins and quickly ascended the ladder. I left the structure, kicked through the open water, and aimed for the ladder. The barracuda did not seem to be interested in my bag full of spiny oysters, but it was a curious fish, and it hovered a few yards from the ladder. I kicked toward it with my fins, and the barracuda darted away. I climbed on deck.

Mike surfaced a few minutes later, and I said, "Those barracuda were aggressive today."

"Yeah. It must be dinnertime."

"What did you get?" I asked Craig.

"Couple snapper."

"Let's go tomorrow," Steve said.

"We'll be too far away from the structure. Wait till we reach the other end of the line. We can do some more scuba diving there."

The divers showered, changed, and went below, leaving Steve and I to recharge the tanks and rinse all the gear with fresh water. We dropped the spiny oysters in plastic buckets full of bleach. After a few days the sea growth would dissolve and we'd be able to see their true colors.

I found spiny oysters with a wide variety of colors. Most were white with orange at the hinge. A few were red, brown, yellow, or purple. Some had spines more than two inches long; some were joined together like Siamese twins; some had coral growing on them. I didn't eat the fleshy meat inside. I collected them for their beauty. They had little value. Some could be cut and made into jewelry. Some could be used as ashtrays, or decorations on a coffee table. I didn't know what I would do with mine, but it was exciting to hunt for jewels of the deep. I wanted to find an oyster with the longest spines, the most brilliant colors, or an unusual specimen, such as three fused together.

How did oysters grow long spines? R. Tucker Abbott, famed author of beautiful illustrated books on seashells, found the answer. When the animal wants to enlarge its home, shell secreting cells in the mantle deposit a layer of calcium carbonate on the edge of the shell. Periodically, the spiny oyster sticks a finger of mantle and shell secreting cells up into the water and starts to make new shell around the fleshy protuberance. As it deposits carbonate, the fleshy part withdraws into the shell, leaving a long, beautiful spine.

Dos Bocas

Pork Chop took a crew boat to see a doctor in Ciudad del Carmen, but his rash didn't improve. The doctor told him to eat only fruit and vegetables, but his condition grew worse and his eyes became puffy, so he returned to the States. His replacement was named Mark, another veteran tender still waiting to be promoted. He had worked in the North Sea, a fearsome place, with treacherous weather and brutal cold. Campeche Bay, with its warm water and calm seas, must have been like a dream to him.

Craig took a short vacation, and his relief man was a forty-five-year-old from Arizona. Lee had worked for fifteen years in practically every offshore oilfield in the world. He was what they referred to in the industry as "hard core." In a business where thirty-five was considered old, Lee was a rare old-timer. He had graying hair and a pale face, and he had difficulty hearing. Many years of diving in the cold waters of the North Sea had drained the circulation from his extremities, and that was probably why Craig affectionately called him Grampa Munster. The deafness in his left ear was probably caused by years of exposure to the high-pitched scream of dredge machines. Lee carried a Styrofoam cup wherever he went, because he constantly chewed tobacco. He was always spitting into his cup, even when he wasn't chewing.

✳ ✳ ✳

We spent twelve days laying a twenty-four-inch diameter pipeline from the Akal-J platforms across a calm greenish-blue sea, and Mike and I made the dawn pontoon checks. Akal-J was the largest platform complex in the Akal field. Akal-J looked like a floating city, with blue lights and four tall flare stacks that burned brightly in the night. We moved away from the vicinity of the structure after the first day, so we didn't have any oil slicks or burning flares, which turned the stern deck into an oven.

I enjoyed the mornings. A cool wind always blew, and the Mexican sun wasn't hot yet. Jumping in the water always refreshed me.

I had gained strength from many scuba dives, and my confidence grew. I was slowly adapting to the underwater environment. Perhaps some of Mike's unassailable self-confidence had inspired me, too.

After completing 400 yards, we were interrupted. Pemex wanted us to inspect the structure on the other end, so we set the unfinished line on the bottom and buoyed off the end.

The barge picked up anchors and towed to the structure, and we made a scuba dive before sunset to inspect the platform legs. Lee came up with a five-foot barracuda. He said he wanted to take the skull home after he scraped it clean. He seemed slow on deck, but he was a twenty-year-old in the water.

✶ ✶ ✶

Steve and I loaded the *Eagle Ray* crewboat with a decompression chamber, two compressors, masks, umbilicals, and radios one morning. Dickie, Lee, and Manuel, a Pemex inspector, hopped aboard, and we bounced across the waves.

"Where are we going?" I asked Dickie.

"They got an SBM that's leaking oil," he said.

An SBM, or single-buoy mooring system, allowed supertankers to fill their hulls with oil without having to enter shallow water. A pipeline ran along the sea floor to the SBM, where a flexible hose descended from the buoy and connected to the pipeline. Supertankers parked next to the buoy, without fear of running aground.

We bounced along for a couple hours and rested in the galley. When we approached the SBM we saw the oil slick following the current, and the shiny water smelled bad all around the buoy. The SBM looked like a big orange can with rubber boat bumpers strapped around it. The buoy was about twenty feet tall and forty feet in diameter and it moved slowly up and down with the swells. Below the surface of the water, six barnacle-encrusted chains held the SBM in place. The chains stretched to the sea bottom. The *Eagle Ray* pulled alongside a Mexican ship anchored nearby. I saw no activity on board the ship.

Dickie jumped in the water, made the inspection, and came out covered in brown oil. The oil coated the umbilical, which made it slippery. I had a hard time pulling Dickie up. As I decompressed him, Lee lit his pipe and walked around on deck pretending to be a supervisor. I thought his actions were stupid with oil fumes everywhere, but I guess he needed to impress the men on the ship, who looked down at us curiously.

The sun on the cloudless day baked the wooden deck, the hand rails, the chamber, the diving hoses, oxygen bottles, and compressors so they were almost too hot to touch. I watched the chamber depth gauge through a tiny slit of my right eye.

Manuel came up to the chamber and put his hand on my shoulder. "*Amigo*, I want to speak to the *buzo*."

"Sure. Just press this switch when you want to talk and let it go to listen."

He put his face close to the speaker and his forehead wrinkled up like he was uncomfortable talking to a box. "What did you find?"

"A damaged hose and a leak in one of the flanges. Do you have a blueprint of the SBM?"

"I can try to find one. Can you repair it now?"

"No. The whole flange has to come off."

"Let me call Dos Bocas and see if they have drawings there." The inspector went below and I gave the chamber a good vent. The temperature in the chamber must have been 120 degrees. I didn't envy the diver.

After twenty minutes, Dickie came out wearing a white towel. "Damn oil itches like crazy. Did you wash my suit?"

"Steve took care of it."

"Good. Where's Lee?"

"Probably in the galley."

"Secure the gear and shut down the compressors. There's nothing more to do here."

Steve and I spent half an hour trying to wash the oil off the umbilical hose. While we sat on the back deck, we heard the captain of the *Eagle Ray* start her engines. First came the whine of the air starter, then the steady rumble of a diesel engine idling. The second engine kicked in. We quickly untied the hawsers, and the boat roared away over a smooth blue sea.

"Finally a breeze." Steve said.

"Want something to drink?"

"Get me some iced tea, with lots of ice."

I came back with two large glasses. We cleaned the Kirbys. We could hardly talk with the engines going full throttle.

"Did they tell you where we're going?" shouted Steve.

"Dos Bocas," I shouted back.

In the late afternoon we arrived at an inlet lined with palm trees. The surf broke on a white, sandy beach. Behind the palm trees the land had been cleared and big storage tanks stood where trees used to be. The Mexicans were building an oil processing plant and a pumping station. It might have been a Sunday, because I didn't see any activity. We passed a few small boats tied to a wooden dock. We tied off the *Eagle Ray* on the other side of the channel and walked along sandy soil deeply scarred with tire tracks toward a long single-story building perhaps two miles away. We passed tall mounds of dirt along the construction site and soon our boat and the inlet disappeared. We felt strange and lighthearted on land, far away from our barge. The four of us and Manuel went into a building that had a fan but no air conditioning. Manuel left us for about fifteen minutes, then came back with a set of blueprints and an engineer. While Lee and Richard tried to explain what had to be done to the SBM, Steve and I sat and listened to the conversation, which was mostly in English, but sometimes Lee tried to clarify a point in Spanish.

After a while Steve and I went outside and sat in the shade of a tree.

When Lee came out of the building he said, "Dickie and I are going into Paraiso for some beer. Manuel will take you back to the boat."

"How you gonna get there?" Steve asked.

"The engineer's got a truck."

It was dark, and we heard the katydids and crickets chirping. We felt better once the hot sun was off our backs. We followed Manuel down a dirt road, and soon we were deep in the construction site, surrounded by sand piles and half-finished structures of the oil processing plant.

"Manuel, this doesn't look like the right way." I said. "We never passed these buildings before."

"Keep walking. The ocean is this way. Can't you hear it?"

"I think we're lost, Manuel," Steve said.

"Don't worry, we'll find it."

We continued to follow Manuel, who walked at a slow pace like a man on a stroll in the park. We saw a group of men sitting around a fire in the distance. They were drinking from bottles. We approached slowly, and they saw us.

"*Alto hombre!*" A man wearing a straw hat shouted at us. When he stood I saw he held a gun.

Manuel spoke to them quickly in Spanish, and the man sat down by his campfire.

"What did you say?" I asked.

"Who were they?" Steve asked.

"Construction workers," Manuel said. "They live here. I told him we were looking for our boat, and he said the inlet was just over that ridge. He told us to be more careful next time. He almost shot us. He thought we were *banditos*."

"You better take care of us, Manuel," Steve said. "I don't know Spanish, and I sure as hell don't want to get shot by some drunk in the middle of nowhere."

The construction workers looked at us suspiciously but let us pass. When we crossed over a tall sand dune, we saw the *Eagle Ray* on the other side of the inlet.

"How do we get across?" Steve asked.

"There's a guy sitting on the dock down there. Let's ask him."

Manuel did the talking again. Steve and I followed and waited. The man on the dock called out to somebody on the other side of the inlet, and soon the purr of a little outboard motor broke the silence. In ten minutes we boarded the *Eagle Ray*. Manuel went to his cabin to file his report. The rest of us stayed on deck.

"What happened to you guys?" Lee asked. "We've been waiting over an hour."

"Manuel gave us a tour of the whole plant." Steve said. "What kind of beer did you get?"

"Old Bohemian. That's all they had."

"Look at this. Half the case is gone already." Steve grabbed a bottle.

We sat on the port side of the boat, drank beer, and listened to the sound of the waves pounding the beach behind the palm trees. The lights on the boat reflected off the black water in the channel. In the distance we saw a campfire in front of a hut.

"How many beers did you have, Lee?" I asked.

"Who's counting? Give me another. That's all I need. A bottle of beer and a woman."

"You have to go to Carmen for that," Dickie chuckled.

"Think I could sneak in one night on the crew boat?"

"I don't care what you do, but if anyone from Taylor sees you in town, they'll send you back to the States."

"There are some pretty *senoritas* at the Safari Club that are almost worth the trouble. There's a girl there named Yesenia. I'll never forget her. I think she was from Veracruz. Probably gone now."

"What the hell are we waiting for, anyway?" Steve asked.

"Goddamn boat captain. He's probably in town drunk," Lee said.

"All we do out here is hurry up and wait. Hurry up and wait. I been working for five years. When are they going to break me out?"

"I don't know. The boom years are over. They can pick anybody they want, now."

"If I don't break out soon I'll quit. I can make more money as a crane operator in Alaska."

"Mike Pailet tended for six years before he broke out."

"It's not right."

"You guys have it rough," Lee said. "When I came to work at Taylor in '66 I tended six months on a dredge barge, then they broke me out."

We got drunk on Old Bohemian, sitting on the port side of the *Eagle Ray*, and Lee told us the story of a hardheaded diver who never took anybody's advice.

"I knew a German diver, once," Lee began. "His name was Helmut. Carried around a big ego. It's funny; in this business, they're the first to get killed or crippled." Lee turned his head and vomited on the deck.

Steve laughed. "Watch where you're aiming that thing."

"So what about Helmut?" I asked.

Lee wiped his face on his sleeve. He turned to me and continued talking as if nothing had happened.

"You could never tell him what to do. He put on a lot of fat one winter, and when the season started he was in bad shape. It took two tenders to put his weight belt on. I told him the belt was too tight, but he didn't listen to me. When he surfaced from a 240 foot dive he complained of back pains. We ran him on a Table Six, and that didn't help. After another Table Six he went in for good. After that he couldn't move his legs and couldn't make love. He sued the dive company. I think they gave him two hundred thousand. He had a good wife, though. A beautiful woman. She went to work at TG&Y."

The tight weight belt cut the circulation in Helmut's waist, interfering with the elimination of inert gas dissolved in his tissues. When he surfaced, bubbles probably formed and pinched critical nerves. Stories such as these always humbled me.

"Where's that boat captain?" Dickie asked. "We have to get back to the barge. Lee, you feeling all right?"

"I feel great. Leave me alone."

"I'm getting bitten by mosquitoes," Steve complained. "I'm going inside."

We put the second case of beer in the air-conditioned galley, and I tried to find a comfortable resting position for the long ride back to the barge. The captain eventually appeared out of nowhere. We left Dos Bocas for the open sea. I was tired from the heat and couldn't sleep because of the roar of the diesel engines as the boat raced along the black water under a starry sky.

Dickie played with a deck of cards. I wondered how he always kept the same even temper. He never complained about the living conditions, the work, or the fickle sea. He even chuckled when he worked under water, and the only time I saw him angry was when Mike shoved him. He could spend a long time at sea and not seem affected by it. Why was he staying out so long? He couldn't be in debt.

We arrived late at night, and Dickie gave Juan a big bear hug when he stepped on board.

The Portuguese laughed when he saw all of us stagger to the dive locker with our eyes glazed.

"Do you have any beer for me?" he asked.

"Just one case."

"Where is it?"

"In the chamber. I'll bring it down to you after I get something to eat."

"You boys had yourself a real party, didn't you?"

"Yeah. Four of us and a bunch of mosquitoes."

"Get some rest. We're standing by."

"On what?"

"A French ship is making a lift on the structure."

Lee Gets Injured

We did some pipelaying in early May. Mike had taken a ten-day vacation, so I tended Lee. He and I also made pontoon checks together. After a pontoon check, I brought him a cup of coffee, and we played darts in the lounge above the dive locker.

One night, we set the pipeline on the bottom. Lee made the dive to disconnect the pull cable from the end of the pipeline.

Disconnecting a cable can be difficult, especially if seas are rough, because the three-inch-thick cable strains with the surge and can snap like a whip.

I tended Lee from the ladder, while Dickie was at the dive station radio. He gave us a hint of upcoming work. "You guy's better get your rest. All hell's gonna break loose after this line."

"What are we doing?" I asked.

"Risers, clamps, Z-bends. Everything. We're gonna be working around the clock for weeks."

It sounded exciting. I looked out over the water and felt the wind on my face. Somewhere out there rough seas were coming our way. On the horizon, a drilling rig with a beacon stood alone in the darkness.

Two Mexicans leaned against the railing and looked at the shiny umbilical going into the water. "You want some *mota*?" one of the Mexicans asked me.

"How much?" I asked. *Mota* was their term for marijuana.

"Forty dollars a kilo in Oaxaca."

"I'll let you know."

"How much does a color television cost in your country?" the other one asked me.

"I guess you can get a cheap one for three hundred," I said.

I thought it strange that Mexico and the United States could be so close geographically, yet so distant culturally. What I take for granted, they dream about. Last night, the Mexicans made a campfire on deck and fried red snapper they caught. With their reddish-brown skin and raised cheekbones, they probably had Aztec or Mayan blood, and they were making good money, but I never knew what was on their minds. They were descendants of warriors chipping paint, while their Spanish bosses raked in billions from the oil. They probably hated Americans. They could be good friends, though. I had given George, a rigger, an old pen knife, and he always offered to carry my suitcase on the crew boat and invited me to his house to eat goat and meet his four wives. Though the influence of the Spanish dominates Mexico, the customs of older cultures still prevails.

I felt Lee moving on the end of the umbilical, 155 feet below.

"Pick up his slack," Dickie said. "He's coming up."

I pulled the umbilical slowly, and soon Lee stood on deck. I removed his mask. He didn't say a word.

I followed Lee to the chamber. He stripped and crawled inside.

I pressurized the chamber to forty feet and made myself comfortable on a bitt by the controls.

The dive had been short, and Lee breathed oxygen for ten minutes, then I released the pressure to the chamber. He didn't say a word after coming out of the chamber. I rinsed his clothes with fresh water. Lee disappeared into the dive locker.

Later, the crew boat arrived, and Craig come aboard.

Lee got on the boat, and when I asked Dickie about it, he said, "He felt dizzy after that last dive. He thinks he might have ruptured an eardrum, so he's going to see a doctor in del Carmen."

"He didn't tell me anything," I said.

"Keep an eye on him."

"He looked all right."

"Ask him how he feels next time he comes up."

That's how they are, I thought. Those hard-core divers don't feel any pain until later. They could come out of the water missing a finger and not know it. That's how tough they were. He had walked to the chamber in his usual slow, easy stride.

✳ ✳ ✳

The next morning, seas had calmed, so Craig connected the pull cable. Dickie guided the line into the welding huts, and the barge started laying pipe.

Two days later, we set the pipe on the bottom again on a dark windy night, and the barge picked up anchors. Was this a change of plan or an interruption due to weather? I didn't know. No one told me. We were always being interrupted.

Swells pounded the barge the next day, and the barge rolled heavily while under tow. We were at the mercy of the weather and the Pemex officials. I didn't know which was worse.

Lee returned. He told me his eardrum had been bruised, not perforated. He wanted to stay out of the water for a while. That meant I would be making two pontoon checks a day. I didn't mind.

A Barge Overturns

We were standing by in some strange place where the depth was 155 feet and the water was dark blue. We had been laying pipe for three days, then the barge dropped the line to the bottom. Lee made a dive at midnight and attached a buoy. I couldn't see any platforms, only one empty sea, restless and unpredictable. Steve boarded yesterday, but Mike hadn't returned yet.

A few hours after dinner, I was relaxing in my bunk, when Lee walked in and said, "We got a little job on the *332*. Let's go."

"What do I need to bring?"

"Just some wet suits. The crew boat should be here in about twenty minutes."

My stomach churned. That was the jolt I had to get accustomed to. In a cozy bunk, absorbed in a book or sleeping, I'd be on a rolling deck the next moment, fighting noisy machinery, wind, and stinging saltwater. Booby traps lurked everywhere. Crane lines swung above my head, cables under tension blocked pathways, slippery coils of rope lay on deck, and twisted sheet metal with jagged edges liked to skin my knuckles.

Would I be getting in the water? I practiced clearing my ears a few times.

I went to the dive locker, packed a nylon bag, and met Lee on the port side. We boarded the crew boat and found seats in the air-conditioned galley. It was a bumpy ride, and I couldn't sleep.

We arrived at midnight, where diving was in progress off the stern. A tug had hit a supply barge, puncturing its side. The supply barge had flipped, sending dozens of pipe joints to the bottom. The barge divers needed more bodies to salvage the joints.

As I stood on the deck of the barge illuminated by an inferno 200 yards away, I was awed by the scene. A huge three-level platform, flanked by two flare stacks, grew out of the sea on sixteen legs. Golden flames a hundred feet high stood like giant candles holding out the darkness, and the flat water reflected silver and gold. We shouted to be heard above the burning roar. Behind the large platform stood a smaller one, and behind it stood an unfinished platform with eight legs coming high out of the water. White and blue lights around the large platform cast eerie halos where the light of the flares did not reach, and the steel structures with their reddish glow rose above our heads in the dark sky. The sea was calm. We met a diver at the stern station. He explained the situation.

"Welcome aboard," he said to Lee. "What's the *Meaders* doing?"

"Standing by to lay some pipe at Akal." Lee glanced down at the black water.

"Appreciate the help." The diver stroked his beard. His bloodshot eyes told of many sleepless nights. "They want to salvage all ninety-nine joints in two days."

"Think you can do it?"

"We're getting three to six joints per dive. Bottom time is a hundred and eight minutes. The depth is seventy-four feet. We should be finished day after next, if we can find the joints. They're scattered all over the bottom."

"How are you picking them up?" Lee asked.

"We had a special clamp made. Look, here's one— it slides on the end like this. We have milk jugs tied off above the clamps, so you can fill them with air from your pneumo to give them buoyancy. They're heavy bastards."

On deck lay the crudely cut piece of steel, about one square foot in size. It was an inch-thick plate with a slot cut into it. We crouched around the clamp and studied it.

"Are you diving tenders?" Lee asked.

"Everybody. Two divers are almost burned out. The Mexicans are tending the hose and the tenders are running the chamber. Two fifteens and one ten in the chamber. I'll put you and your tender in the rotation in about three hours, so get something to eat, if you want."

"Okay." Lee stood.

The diver looked seriously at Lee. "Those pipes are on top of each other, so some of them might shift. I don't want anybody getting trapped under one. Make sure the diver goes back to the down line before signaling the crane to pick the joint up, because we had a clamp slide off one, and the pipe nearly smashed one guy's foot."

"Some of those pipes must be full of mud," Lee said.

"Right. Real heavy. Don't get under one. Slings are good, but the sudden strain when they come out of the water—"

"I know what you mean."

The crane picked one of the joints out of the water and set it on a barge on the port side. Water poured out of the forty-foot-long pipe held by two slings, and some splashed on deck.

Lee and I found the galley below deck where it was quiet, but the rumble of compressors and the roar of burning natural gas still echoed in my ears.

We ate drumsticks and mashed potatoes that tasted delicious.

I returned to the deck and relieved a tender at the chamber who also looked like he had endured many sleepless nights. Lee disappeared, probably to find a bunk for a short nap before his dive, which would be near dawn.

I operated the chamber for four hours. I tracked the time with a cracked and wet wristwatch that somehow still worked. The divers breathed oxygen for fifteen minutes at forty feet, switched to air for five, returned to oxygen for another fifteen minutes, took another air break, and completed one ten-minute oxygen breathing session before I brought the chamber to the surface. They left their steel prison, ate something, and slept before their next dive.

When the sun stood above the horizon and the painful natural light replaced the comfortable anonymity of the darkness, the platforms lost their fantastic qualities. They became familiar steel shapes, and I was glad I would be diving in daylight in the strange place.

Lee jumped in shortly after dawn and salvaged four joints.

My turn came, and the cool water felt better than the burning deck. I was glad for the opportunity to make a dive. I needed all the experience I could get.

I landed on the bottom, where visibility was only a foot, but if I looked up I saw light filtering down to a depth of perhaps twenty feet. Some light was always reassuring.

I groped around in the mud and searched for a pipe joint. I moved awkwardly through the thick water in a semi-upright position. I held a line connected to the crane line somewhere out there. I made an arc around it, and soon my foot kicked rough concrete. I took a breath of warm air. Not knowing where I was, I made a guess and told the radio man to swing the crane to port. The rope loosened. I pulled it tight. The crane sling came to me, and I walked with it to the end of the pipe. I ordered the radio man to lower the crane line. Soon the metal clamp hung next to the thirty-six-inch diameter pipe. I couldn't lift the clamp. It needed buoyancy. I fumbled with the milk jugs. I stuck my pneumofathometer hose in one and held it upside down.

"Give me air to the pneumo," I said.

"Roger. Coming to you."

I filled two plastic milk jugs, and the clamp became lighter. I carefully pushed the slot of the clamp on the pipe. The clamp was still heavy enough to mash a finger. I repeated the process for the other end, worked slowly, methodically, and breathed normally. My breathing was under control—I'm always conscious of my breathing—then groped back to the down line.

Reaching a safe position, I said, "Come up on the crane."

In the murky water, I waited patiently. Soon a long, dark form appeared, silhouetted by surface light.

The pipe cleared the water and disappeared.

I looked up at the surface light and saw life. I was not alone. In the distance, a sea turtle glided by through the water. Moments like that made bottom time special, when I could forget my loneliness and appreciate a fellow creature of the deep whose life must be an endless journey through thousands of miles of empty space.

The dark oval shape with flippers grew smaller and vanished.

"Pipe's on the barge. Go out and find another one," came the garbled voice through my ear speakers.

Crawling along the bottom toward the place where the last pipe rested, I hunted again and eventually found a familiar concrete shape half buried in mud. I worked steadily, stayed calm in the darkness, kept a hold on the tag line, salvaged this one, and another, and then the ear speakers crackled and said, "Leave bottom."

"Roger. Leaving bottom." Hand over hand, I made the slow ascent along the manila line from the unknown back to the world of people, a solid deck, fresh air, and normal pressure.

I quickly ditched the gear, walked to the chamber, stripped off the wet clothes, and crawled in the hatch nude. The tender took me down to forty feet. I found a towel and wiped my face and wrapped the towel around my waist. I reclined on the bunk, strapped the oxygen bib to my face, and slowly inhaled the cool, tasteless gas. The chamber felt like an oven, not dry heat but humid heat, and I perspired. Soon it became unbearable, but I had to remain for one hour. The saltwater itched. In fifteen minutes the first vent brought some fresh air into the chamber. I contemplated the dive and rested. I felt proud to accomplish something. Maybe I could work in dark water. All I needed was more dives. The stifling heat in the chamber and the smell of stale saltwater under the deck plates didn't matter after a good dive. I had worked hard to salvage three joints in about two hours, but Lee got four. Despite his age, he still performed miracles under water.

I thought about the sea turtle. I saw the black form again, the flippers working smoothly, and I wondered what species it had been. The only other time I had seen a sea turtle outside of captivity was in a beach in Florida where a big leatherback had washed up. It had a heavy growth of coral and barnacles on its shell and blood was seeping out of its mouth. I remembered the sad eyes and wondered why it had washed up. There was no evidence that it had been attacked. I had tried to turn it over, but the smell was terrible, so I had pushed it back into the surf and left it.

After the decompression I showered, dressed, and operated the chamber. The job continued through the day and into the night. After midnight I went below and slept. At dawn, I operated the chamber again. Late in the afternoon we had salvaged all the joints, and took the crew boat back to the *L.B. Meaders*. We arrived after dark.

L-bends at Nohoch

Mexico, enchanting land of many cultures, great beaches, ancient ruins, pyramids, and active volcanoes, had become my home. The wonders of the Yucatan beckoned. Time travelers can snorkel along the underground river at Nohoch Nah Chich, which means giant bird cage in Mayan. Nohoch Nah Chich is located in the Quintana Roo region of the Yucatan. It is a large underwater cave that features human remains and fire pits from the last ice age. For those willing to brave the heat, the ruins of Chichen Itza rise out of the jungle only a few hundred miles inland from Campeche Bay.

Years later, my wife and I visited Chichen Itza. I climbed the ninety-one steps of the Kukulcan pyramid and admired the view from above the treetops. I walked across the ball court and tried to imagine the game the Mayans played with a small rubber ball kicked through a stone hoop high above the ground. Some people say the captain of the losing team was beheaded. Others say the captain of the winning team was beheaded because decapitation offered a shorter way to heaven. The game represented the battle between life and death in the Third Creation.

I hiked through the jungle to the natural sinkhole, or cenote, where people were sacrificed. I toured the observatory, a sophisticated stargazing structure, aligned so the Mayans could see Venus. I stepped among the cool corridors of the nunnery, the living quarters of the elite; and the Temple of the Warriors, with hundreds of columns standing in formation.

The Mayans were meticulous sky watchers. Their concept of time was different than Western man. Time had no beginning and no end. It was a series of great cycles lasting roughly 5,125 years. The Mayans devised a calendar more accurate than the Gregorian calendar, and they tracked time millions of years into the past and future. They predict the present cycle will end in the year 2,012, which amazingly corresponds to a cosmic alignment where the plane of the Milky Way galaxy will align with our solar plane.

The Mayan civilization flourished for thousands of years, then mysteriously declined. Wars, hurricanes, or droughts may have contributed to the culture's demise.

✳ ✳ ✳

I floated on an endless sea, dotted by platform complexes and drilling rigs, in the cradle of the Yucatan Peninsula. Much work still needed to be done to complete the infrastructure to the oilfield.

The industrial world needed oil badly. The oilfield was being built hastily, and Mike often said that the next hurricane that came through Campeche Bay would destroy the house of cards. Already, a few years before, Ixtoc had spilled 140 million barrels of oil and burned out of control for 295 days.

✳ ✳ ✳

Dickie left the barge for ten days of vacation, and Mike returned with a duffel bag filled with T-shirts he designed. He sold a hundred T-shirts in about three days.

The barge moved to within fifty yards of the Nohoch platforms. Seas were calm, and the black and silver water danced under the barge and platform lights. As soon as a few anchors had been set, Craig dived to inspect the jacket leg and found a clamp on the bottom where the L-bend could slide into. Mike jumped in and surveyed the bottom.

An L-bend is a long, curved section of pipe that connects a pipeline on the sea floor with another section of pipe that rises vertically along a platform leg, or jacket leg, and connects to the oil processing equipment on the top of the platform. The section of pipe that rises vertically is secured to the platform leg with hinged clamps. We would set the L-bend between the pipeline and platform, and another team of divers would weld the sections of pipe together.

✳ ✳ ✳

I slept for a few hours while the riggers prepared the slings. The sun rose, I walked to the stern, and the L-bend hung from the derrick crane on two thick cables a few feet above the water. The concrete-coated pipe extended beyond the width of the barge, and one end turned and rose vertically perhaps twenty feet, ending at a flange.

The morning quickly turned into a nightmare. The barge was not rolling badly, but when one large swell came through, one end of the L-bend touched the water. Water flowed into the pipe, making it heavier. When the barge rolled again, one of the cables snapped, sending the L-bend to the bottom. The second sling broke because it couldn't support the weight of the whole L-bend.

The situation was not good. A barge that charged 100,000 dollars a day was going to be seriously behind schedule if the L-bend couldn't be raised soon. The superintendent and the assistant superintendent appeared on the stern with frowns. Even the cooks and stewards came up to see what happened. The Mexican riggers stood by the stern rails with nothing to do.

Lee talked with the superintendent for a few minutes, then he said, "They want us to double wrap two chokers on one end."

"They picked a bad time to send a pipe to the bottom," Mike said. "Two of us are burned out already. We can't dive until tonight."

"We'll dive tenders," Lee said.

"Burned out" meant that Craig and Mike had too much residual nitrogen in their tissues from previous dives. They couldn't dive for twelve hours.

Lee made the first dive and successfully connected one sling; then all the divers were burned out.

As I was decompressing Lee in the chamber, Mike approached. I saw the killer instinct in his eyes, cold and serious, and the green had been bleached out. He said, "You're next."

I grew apprehensive.

Lee finished his decompression, and I dressed in a wetsuit top and jeans.

"What's down there, Lee?" I asked.

He looked at me for a moment through tiny slits, and I wondered if he had heard me, because I stood to his left, his deaf side, but then he said, "Rig it any way you can. The tube turn is coming out of the mud. You should be able to rig it just behind mine."

I put my harness on, attached my knife, put on rubber booties, wrapped a strip of duct tape around the jeans at my ankles, grabbed a pair of fins and a dry pair of cotton gloves, put on a ten-pound weight belt, snugged it up, and walked out to the stern. Mike stood by the dive station next to Chink. Steve had dragged the dive hose over and looped twenty feet over the side. The crane line disappeared in the water fifty feet off the port stern.

I put the Kirby-Morgan band mask on my head and said, "How about a little air over here."

"You need air? What do you need air for?"

Mike opened a valve, and the reassuring hiss of gas came into the mask as I cracked the free-flow valve. Steve cinched up the straps around my head, and I put the gloves on. I climbed over the rail and put the fins on. Holding the rail, looking down at the water ten feet below, breathing the dry compressor air, wearing cotton gloves, feeling the wet suit tight in the

105

shoulders and wrists, wiggling my toes in the booties, feeling heavy with the weight belt, I was ready.

"How do you read me?"

"Pretty good. Remember you have to make two wraps."

"Roger."

I was always apprehensive before a dive. Where I would go no one could follow. I had to be self-confident and self-reliant. I had no idea what surprises the bottom held. My fear knew about the potential dangers, the marine life, the currents, the steel traps. I went humbly, but surprisingly, once I jumped in and glided through the weightless medium, the apprehension vanished, time ceased to exist, the moment eclipsed past and future, and I reveled in the strange, new world.

What was I supposed to do? Wrap a three-inch-thick steel cable twice around a pipe and shackle it into itself. That's all. In school they called it "wrestling the alligator." I was going to 132 feet, a depth where narcosis would probably sap my mind of clarity. The pipe was three feet in diameter. Lee did the same thing with the first cable and made it look easy. How much did the L-bend weigh? Probably 200 tons, and only Lee knew how it landed on the bottom, but he didn't tell me. Mike was on the phone, ready to give me a hard time. Steve would be my tender. I appreciated Mike for giving me a chance to perform. Mike would keep track of the bottom time, and he'd tell me when to come up. He'd take a pneumofathometer reading as soon as I reached bottom, so he'd know my exact depth. All I had to do is worry about the job, wrapping a heavy steel cable around a pipe that might be half buried in mud. The Mexicans stood around looking at my gear. I wondered what they thought. Everything outside the faceplate was in focus. The platform stood clearly in the sun. Barely a ripple rolled across the sea, and the crane line hung motionless.

I jumped in, swam to the crane line, dived head first, grabbed the cable, and descended feet first. My ears cleared easier that way. I looked down, couldn't see anything yet, only a gray, bottomless chasm. I took a reassuring breath and descended hand over hand into the unknown. The crane line stayed in focus before my eyes. Soon sunlight diminished and only my breathing and the occasional crackle of Mike's voice in the speakers interrupted the silence. No fish disturbed the empty space.

I passed through a thermocline at perhaps 100 feet. The water became colder. A pipe appeared, like a column to some ancient temple rising at an angle out of the mist.

My feet touched soft mud. At a depth of 132 feet, colors had vanished, and the water was murky. Visibility was about ten feet. The massive steel pipe grew out of the mud, and the crane block hung above it.

Nitrogen narcosis already affected my mind. I found it difficult to concentrate. Making a decision took minutes. I was disoriented. It took a great deal of willpower to act. Without the pressure of limited bottom time and Mike's goading on the phone, I could have blissfully stared at the pipe forever.

Air hissed into the mask. I was alone in the quiet deep, next to a train wreck. No fish swam by. What was I doing here? I had a job to do. "On the bottom," I said.

"Remember, two wraps," Mike reminded me.

I swam to the cable hanging beside the pipe. It was too heavy. Take the shackle off. Take the shackle off. "First thing I'll do is take the shackle off the sling."

"Don't lose it." Mike's voice crackled, faint and distant.

I crouched, unscrewed the nut, and took the pin out. I breathed normally, but there was a strange numbness in my face, and my mind didn't work. I heard reverberation in the background. I held the fifty-pound shackle and replaced the pin. It took a great deal of effort to concentrate on the simple task. I climbed on the pipe and put the shackle in a safe place near the other sling.

"How's it going down there?"

"Okay. Wait—" I grabbed the cable with both hands and pushed it over the top of the pipe. I crawled under the pipe, found the cable, and pulled it through. I raised a cloud of debris. I stood, pushed the cable, and it flopped over the pipe again. It was heavy. The cable could mash my fingers if I got them caught between cable and pipe. My breathing became labored. I didn't want to work too hard, because under water was not the place to be out of breath.

"How's it going?"

I held my breath and strained to hear the words. "I have it over the top . . . just have to pull it through the bottom and shackle it up."

"You've been farting around down there for thirty minutes. Hurry it up."

Where did the time go, I wondered. "This thing's coming up out of the mud at a forty-five degree angle . . ."

"Just make a double wrap, understand?"

"A few more minutes . . ."

I retrieved the shackle and returned to the bottom, next to the eye of the sling. Reclining in the mud, I planned my next move. What was my next move? "Come down on the big rig." I gazed up at the crane line.

"Roger. Coming down."

The crane block descended quietly.

"All stop."

"We're all stop."

I was glad seas were calm; otherwise, the crane line would have been bouncing up and down, making my job much more difficult.

Working slowly and deliberately, I rested the horseshoe-shaped shackle on the cable, brought the eye of the sling to meet it, and pushed the shackle pin through the eye. I screwed on the nut and rested. "Shackle's together. Let's get this mess out of the mud, so I can see what I've got."

"You have the shackle on there?"

"I think so. What the hell— get up on it."

The block rose slowly, the steel noose tightened, and the shackle snapped against the pipe with a loud thunk.

Two hundred tons of pipe shook.

"All stop!"

"All stop. How's it look?"

"Cable's tight. Shackle looks good. I'm ready to leave bottom."

"Leave bottom."

That's it. It was over. I relaxed. Up the greasy crane line I ascended hand over hand and almost punctured a finger on a burr.

My head cleared, the smoky mist receded, and it felt good to be returning to the surface world. I made a slow, controlled ascent. When I reached fifty feet, Steve pulled me to the barge.

"You have a six-minute water stop. Hang at the bottom of the ladder."

I grabbed the bottom rung, rode the surge, relaxed, and gazed through my faceplate at sunbeams probing the emptiness below. My bottom time had been forty-eight minutes.

I climbed on deck, removed my mask, and tasted fresh air.

"Three fifteens," Mike said.

I wasn't free yet. I had to breath oxygen for three fifteen-minute periods in the chamber pressurized to forty feet. Each oxygen breathing period was followed by a five-minute period breathing air, because too much oxygen irritated the lungs.

I walked to the port side, removed my clothes, crawled to the inner lock, and pressed the heavy steel door shut. Steve opened the intake valve, and air roared into the chamber. My ears cleared.

As I decompressed, I looked up through the porthole and saw the L-bend swinging through the sky. Laying on that aluminum bunk breathing oxygen, I was floating, too. Everybody was happy.

✳ ✳ ✳

In the evening, with the sun touching the sea, I climbed on the half-deck and refueled the compressors. The Mexican riggers secured fresh slings to the L-bend. The daily crew boat arrived and tied off behind the material barge. Dickie came aboard, and Lee left for ten days.

Three hours later, with food in my belly, I came on deck, and the L-bend was hanging in the air on three slings. The compressors rumbled, so I knew we would be diving, soon.

Steve and I tested communications to the masks. The stern was a busy place. Men walked in and out of the shadows, Mexicans crouched behind the air tuggers. Chink stood quietly looking up at the L-bend as he drank a cup of coffee, and some welders leaned against the railing. I don't know what the welders did when we weren't laying pipe. I guess they slept or played cards.

At ten o'clock, Dickie jumped into a black, churning sea. Steve tended him, I fed hose, and Craig worked the radio.

The light we had installed in the dive station worked well. A depth reading could be taken easily, and Craig could see what he was writing in the log.

The L-bend descended below the waves between the structure and the barge, and Dickie guided it to the bottom. He came out after an hour, we removed his gear, and Steve led him to the chamber.

I wiped out the mask with a paper towel and set it in a coil of umbilical hose next to the bailout bottle.

"Did he get it?" I asked Craig.

"Yeah. It's in the clamp. Bolts are tight."

"Who's next?"

"Mark will de-rig, then we'll have to wait. I don't think the next L-bend will be here before dawn. Isn't that right, Chink?"

"It's on the way. That's all I know."

When Dickie came out of the chamber, the night shift men had come on deck, and Mark was in a wetsuit top, ready to go. I strapped the bail-out to his harness, and he slipped into it. A few minutes later, he jumped in, swam to the left sling, and disappeared under water. I tended him by ladder and listened to his breathing. I don't think he needed all his bottom time to disconnect everything. Soon he stood on deck, and I decompressed him.

I shut down the compressors after midnight, and I got some sleep. The next few days passed in a blur. We set three more L-bends by diving around the clock. We dived on a 140 foot table with forty-eight minute bottom times, a five-minute water stop, and three fifteens in the chamber. The sun scorched us during the day, but when night came, the mood changed. Everything grew quieter, not as harsh. The deck cooled. The pace slowed. We had the whole sea to ourselves while the world slept.

I tended Mike from the ladder, listened to his grunts and gasps on the radio, and tried to learn his skills. Mike didn't volunteer information. I had to pry trade secrets from him.

When Mike worked on the bottom, he liked to carry on a conversation with a fellow named Mr. Bill. Mike, the fearless warrior, would teach Mr. Bill the dangers of diving. The squeaky, high-pitched voice of Mr. Bill, the famous Play-Doh character, would come on the radio. "Ohh, Noooo!" Mr. Bill would shout. Sometimes Mr. Bill would be flattened by a riser or a piece of pipe, and Mike would have to continue the job alone.

Forty minutes into the dive, a tugger cable popped, and Craig told me to pull him up.

"Why?" I asked.

"He ripped the clamp off the jacket leg."

I pulled up his slack, and after his water stop, I pulled his full weight across the water toward the ladder. Saltwater dripped on my jeans and flip-flops. Mike probably weighed 180 pounds, but with the weight belt, it seemed like 250.

Mike climbed up the ladder, threw his gloves on deck, and removed the mask.

"You pull those tuggers too hard," Craig said.

"If the clamp's not on tight, it'll pop off."

"Not on my dives."

"Maybe I know how to use a tugger."

"Those were half-inch bolts." Chink took off his blue baseball cap and wiped his forehead with the back of his hand.

"I'll go down and see what's going on," Craig said.

"I guess I was dreaming if I thought one damn job would go smooth."

"What are you going to tell Ignacio?"

"I don't know yet."

"Let's go, Mike," I said. I was worried because he had four minutes to get to forty feet in the chamber after surfacing.

We walked to port, and I pressurized the chamber.

An hour later, Mike came out. I put a fresh towel in the chamber, rinsed his clothes, and came to the stern.

Craig jumped in, and when he reached bottom, he said the clamp hadn't been damaged, just needed new bolts. We sent them down, and he set the clamp.

Mark made a good dive. He pulled the tube turn into the clamp and tightened the bolts. I had a lot of respect for Mark. He approached every dive with seriousness, and Craig gave him the opportunity to make challenging dives. I wondered why the company had not promoted him. When he came out of the water I helped him take off his gear and gave him a nudge toward the chamber.

"Don't push me, son," he said quietly, and I left him alone.

Night came, and we slept a few hours, but then, I heard anchor cables, so I knew the barge was moving. Somebody turned the light on in the cabin and told me to go to the stern. The way Mike came out of the bunk you'd think someone was dropping mortar rounds in on us. When I reached the dive locker Steve was already suited up, ready to make a dive. Everybody else was standing around droopy-eyed.

Dickie said, "We got a salvage job. A tug dropped an anchor and fouled the cable in its wheel."

"Is that the tug on the port side?" I asked.

"Yeah. You have to move the dive station over there and run a new supply hose off the half deck. You know how to operate a forklift?"

"No."

"Mark will help you."

"How much cable they got in the wheel?" asked Mike.

"I don't know," said Dickie. "Captain Jack threw it into reverse and jammed it pretty bad. You guys need to set up the burning gear."

After an hour we were ready. Steve went to the bottom and surfaced in twenty minutes. I gave him two tens in the chamber. I rinsed Steve's clothes, sat on the bitt, and looked down at the crippled tug with its back deck low to the water. When Steve came out, Mike dived and cut the cable out of the wheel with the oxy-arc torch. I tended him for a long time, but he was near the surface, so he didn't need any chamber time. We finished at dawn and moved the dive station back to the stern. Later in the morning we started the last L-bend, and the bright sun was painful to my eyes. I was tired.

Dickie set the L-bend on bottom. Chink told us to forget about the clamp. The barge had been ordered to another location. He told us to wrap a sling around the tube turn and jacket leg.

Craig dived, connected the sling, took measurements, and buoyed off the pipeline.

Exhausted, I slept in the afternoon as the barge towed away. My biological clock was being reset.

✷ ✷ ✷

I had one night to recover my strength and lost sleep. It was a quiet interlude, but I sensed it wouldn't last. I heard the anchor cables going out before dawn and knew we were on location. I had an uneasy feeling, not knowing what to expect.

Somebody stuck his head in the room and said, "You're needed at the stern."

Mike jumped out of bed. "My wife can't understand how I can be awake in a second," he said.

"It's probably the SEAL team training," I said. I dressed, shaved, gulped down breakfast, and climbed on deck.

I found Mark getting ready to go in the water. Craig was briefing him. Steve stood with them in a mechanic's suit and flip-flops, and his hair looked wild. We were anchored near a six-legged platform, but I didn't know the name of it. Mark had a pair of gloves, and the masks were on line. I assumed the compressors were running.

"All right," Craig said. "Go down and measure the circumference of the jacket leg and tell me if you find any clamps. You got some rope?"

"Yes, Sir." Mark looked at the horizon. "Here comes the sun. It's gonna be another hot one."

"Is the chamber ready?" I asked.

"Ya'll better check it," Mark said.

I walked to port, looked inside, found a couple fresh towels, and returned. The churning water lost some of its mystery when the sky brightened and we could see to the horizon. I helped Mark with his gear, and he jumped in. I tended him, and Steve uncoiled hose from the dive tree. Mike stood against the stern rail and frowned at the structure.

"What are we doing?" I asked Craig.

"Setting a Z-bend and some clamps, then we got another one someplace else."

A Z-bend was an L-bend with an extra curve in it.

Mark's breathing came through the phone, and soon he reached bottom. "There's a clamp with the door open."

"Let's get a pneumo at the top of the stand-off." Craig took the depth reading and wrote something in the log.

I stood by the ladder. The restless water lunged at the structure. The early morning bombarded my senses. The information came in, but my brain didn't process it. The powerful blue water played tricks on my eyes, the unsteady deck wanted to throw me off balance, and the umbilical danced like a snake. I felt the diver on the end. His voice crackled from the speaker. I tried to understand what he said between breaths, and I imagined being in the cool water, away from the burning sun. I picked up the diver. Saltwater dripped on my clothes and feet. My hands felt raw from gripping the wet umbilical tightly. The diver surfaced, and everybody scrambled to remove his gear. I undid his quick-release, helped him pull off the mask, caught the weight belt, and held the bailout bottle as he removed his harness and threw his gloves on deck. He hurried to the chamber, stripped, and crawled inside. I took the chamber to forty feet before the bubbles formed in the diver's body.

We waited for the Z-bend to arrive on a material barge. Mike took a nap on top of the pontoon shack. I rested in my cabin.

That night, as I was about to get comfortable with a book, Craig came in and said, "We're setting it tonight."

"Looks like another sleepless night."

"I'd say we'll be diving in three hours."

I climbed on deck later. The Mexicans had started rigging the Z-bend with six slings on the material barge tied off to our port side. Seas were choppy and the wind blew from starboard. I felt tired, but once work started and adrenaline flowed, momentum carried me. Steve had already connected two masks to the umbilicals. Mike and Craig stood by the dive station. Steve always seemed to be one step ahead of me. I was always the last to know what was going on. Whenever I came on deck Steve had the compressors running and the masks on line, and he looked at me as if to say "What do we need you for?"

Dickie came out of the dive locker dressed in a long-sleeved denim shirt with fancy metal rivets around the pockets. The left sleeve was laced with slag burns. He wore ragged jeans and patched booties and carried a flashlight. The lanyard to his Queen Steel knife in his back pocket was looped around a ring on his harness. "Do they have the Z-bend rigged yet?" he asked Mike.

"It should be swinging around any minute. Do you want me to buy you a new set of jeans when I go in?"

"No. These are my good luck jeans."

The blue and white lights of the derrick crane illuminated the massive structure that towered into the night sky. It felt exciting to be on a rolling barge working in some wild place with huge machinery. Soon one of us would go down into the restless sea and do something that required courage and strength. Few people in the world had any idea of the risks involved or the skill needed to do it and come out alive.

The crane motor purred, and the giant pipe swung around until it hung motionless off the stern, balanced perfectly on six slings thirty feet above the churning, shimmering water. The Z-bend spanned the width of the barge. Men looked like insects beneath it. I didn't know how Dickie was going to set it, but he had set many before, and although no job like this could ever be called routine, he had enough experience to approach it calmly.

"They want the back end a hundred and fifty feet from that leg—" Mike said, pointing to the structure.

Dickie looked at the Z-bend, the tugger cables connected at either end and the slings with their big shackles. "I wonder how much visibility there is." He took a roll of duct tape and taped the flashlight to the top of the Kirby hood.

"That's the dumbest thing I ever saw," Mike said.

Dickie ignored him.

More men came to the stern. Chink and Juan appeared, followed by some Mexicans who crouched behind the air tuggers. A few welders and a cook in a white shirt and checkered pants stood by the rails and watched.

"Look's like we're ready to go," Chink said. "Where do you want it?"

"Drop it to fifty feet, then I'll ride it down," Dickie said.

Chink spoke into his walkie-talkie, Juan gave commands in Spanish to slack the tuggers, and soon the pipe disappeared below the water.

Dickie jumped in and performed his magic. Only another diver could appreciate the challenges a man faced under water. A forty-eight-minute dive didn't seem like a long time, but to a diver, it was a day's work. Nothing felt more exhilarating than coming out of the water after a successful dive.

Dickie's gasps and heavy breathing came from the speaker. He talked constantly and made the arduous work seem easy. Sometimes he chuckled, and sometimes he gave a command to move a tugger cable as he maneuvered the massive pipe to its resting place on the sea bottom. I didn't know if the flashlight helped him see.

When Mike said, "Pick up his slack. He's leaving bottom," I knew Dickie was finished.

Mike dived to remove the slings around the Z-bend. He unshackled two, Craig disconnected two, Mark removed the last two and the tuggers, and we shut down the compressors.

I didn't know what was coming, or how long our rest would be. I just followed orders. The sun was high in the sky. My eyelids felt heavy. I slept for a few hours.

✷ ✷ ✷

A clamp is two cylinders joined by a short metal tube. Half of each cylinder is a hinged door that can be opened fully. The larger cylinder wraps around a platform leg, or jacket leg, and the smaller cylinder is where the vertical part of an L-bend or Z-bend slips into. A diver uses air winches to move clamps into position and close the doors, because they are so large. Setting a clamp can be a tricky operation, especially during rough seas, when the clamp can bounce around.

Steve set the clamp at ninety feet, and Dickie set the clamp at thirty feet.

I jumped in at dusk to secure the bolts on the clamp at ten feet. It was a simple but exhausting job, comparable to tightening a bolt while being tossed around in a washing machine. I held on for dear life to a barnacle-encrusted flange with my stomach up in my neck as a powerful surge came through, then the bottom dropped out and I hung in the air as the water receded. I wrestled with a bolt until the next wave hit. I used muscles I never thought I had, and if it wasn't for the jeans, my legs would have been shredded. I don't know how long I was in the water, but when I came out my arms and stomach muscles were sore and my legs felt cramped. Dickie told me later I had worked 124 minutes. I showered, changed, and helped Steve and Mark secure the dive station.

Mr. Bill and the Riser

Setting a riser in rough seas is like riding a Brahma bull at the rodeo. I had never set a riser, but I knew it was a mean beast. Dickie broke his thumb trying to set one.

A riser is a straight section of pipe with a flange on one end that connects to an L-bend on the bottom. A riser is secured to a platform with clamps on the jacket legs. The pipe comes out of the water and rises to the platform deck. The trick to setting a riser is aligning the flange on the L-bend with the flange on the riser and, at the exact moment, dropping a steel pin, or drift pin, through both holes. Two drift pins have to be stabbed to stabilize the riser, so bolts can be inserted. The diver has the unenviable job of riding the vertically hanging pipe and stabbing the drift pins. The drift pins are too heavy for a man to lift, so they are tied with ropes above the flange holes. When the time is right, the diver cuts the rope and hopes the drift pin falls through both holes. The procedure sounds easy, but it's not.

In the afternoon we set up the dive station. The sea was in an ominous mood. The derrick crane lifted the monster pipe off the center deck until it hung vertically. It was the biggest piece of plumbing I'd ever seen, a drainpipe to a god's bathtub. It was about two hundred feet long, three feet in diameter, and had a concrete coating. As the boom swung around slowly over the water toward the platform I saw the drift pins tied above the flange at the bottom. They each probably weighed more than a hundred pounds and were tapered on one end. Mike had told me they would be used to line up the riser flange with the Z-bend flange on the bottom and keep them relatively stationary so we could insert bolts. The flange was about five feet in diameter with thirty bolt holes. Two air tuggers on a platform walkway ten feet above the water and two tuggers on the stern deck would provide horizontal stability.

Mike came to the stern wearing a long-sleeved velour shirt. He didn't need a wet suit in the warm water. He slipped into his harness and cast a worried look at the riser hanging almost motionless near the platform leg. Setting a riser in rough seas frightened me. Mike may have been crazy, but he was not stupid. With his vast experience, he could judge whether or not the job was worth taking the risk.

"It's gonna be a bitch with those swells coming through," he told Dickie at the dive station. A six-foot wall of water came along at an oblique angle and continued off to port. The structure stood firm, but the barge rolled with it.

"Let's shut it down, then," Dickie said.

"What do you say, Chink?"

"Let's give them a good report."

"Get that O-ring ready. I'm gonna set the drift pins and put two bolts in." Mike snapped a weight belt around his waist.

"The hell you are," Dickie chuckled.

"He can do it. I've seen him," Steve said.

"We'll give it a try," Chink said. He spoke into his walkie-talkie, and the riser flange disappeared into the dark water.

"Ignacio better not show his face up here," Mike said. Mike didn't care for the Pemex inspectors, who were constantly changing their minds. He slipped the mask over his head and jumped into the water. I tended his umbilical by the ladder a few feet from the dive station.

A crazy Navy SEAL was going to 140 feet to wrestle with a mad bull.

"Come down on barge tugger number one," Mike said.

The foreman gave a hand signal to the Mexican crouched behind the tugger.

Cable disappeared into the depths. I couldn't see what Mike was doing, but I could feel the tension. I kept a tight line. Everybody listened to his talking and breathing.

"Swing the big rig a few feet to the operator's left," Mike said.

Chink stood next to Dickie and relayed the instructions to the crane operator with his walkie-talkie. "Come up on the barge tugger."

The Mexican pushed the lever. The air winch tightened the cable as far as it could. With a final put-put-pock, it stopped.

Mike's gasps punctuated his speech. "Come down a few feet on the big rig . . . all stop! . . . Whoa! . . . this is like riding a wild horse! . . . trying to stab a drift pin now . . . get in there . . ."

Dickie listened attentively. Mike knew what he was doing. I pictured him trying to drop the drift pin through the bolt hole during a calm interval between ground swells. I didn't know how he was going to do it. I thought he needed both hands to hold and aim the pin and needed both his legs wrapped around the bucking pipe to give him stability, so how could he cut the rope on the pin?

A swell came through and lifted the barge. The tugger cable strained terribly. The steel plate the tugger was welded to groaned. The tugger popped free, hit the stern railing with a loud clunk, and the Mexican rigger flipped over and lay flat on his face a few feet away, laughing.

"Watch out, Mike!" Dickie shouted.

"What's wrong?"

"Tugger broke free. It almost went over the side."

"I see . . . pick up the diver's slack . . . one drift pin is in! . . . Arghhh! . . . Riser's pivoting around now every time a swell comes through . . . If I don't get this other pin in fast, the first one is going to get bent . . ."

"Don't get hurt."

"Whoa! Just took a ride that time . . . Trying to stab the second drift pin . . . It's in . . . Stay in there, baby . . . don't pop out . . . Get a bolt down here!"

"Bolt's coming down."

Steve shackled one of the bolts to the quarter-inch manila down line and dropped it over the side. The riser moved back and forth near the platform. A wall of water came through and almost touched the bottom walkway of the structure.

"I have the bolt . . . dropping it in . . . Send another bolt . . . This flange is still moving around a lot . . . How's the weather up there?"

"Getting worse. It's starting to rain. Your bottom time's almost up."

A welder came to the stern and threw up his hands in disgust. "What do you expect me to do?" he shouted. "If you try to use that tugger right away, it'll pop again."

"Weld it down," Chink shouted.

Mike breathed heavily. He grunted.

"Let me get the bolt in . . . Guess who just showed up . . . It's Mr. Bill . . ."

"It's scary down here, Mr. Mike." A high-pitched voice came from the dive speaker.

"Don't be afraid, Mr. Bill. You want to help me set this bolt? Get down there and tell me when the bottom flange lines up with the top so I can drop the bolt through."

"I don't know, Mr. Mike."

"Trust me."

"It's so dark I can't see anything."

"Turn your flashlight on so the boys and girls can see what we're doing."

"Good idea. Look at the size of that thing!"

"It's called a riser. You see this gap between the two flanges? We never want to put our fingers in there, because the flange can come down and cut them clean off."

"I'll re-remember that. What's that over there?"

"That's a structure. It's like a big house sitting on top of the water..."

Dickie pressed the talk switch. "You have a few minutes left."

"Roger on that. Mr. Bill's helping me set this bolt."

"Ohhh, nooooo!"

"Mr. Bill?... Mr. Bill?... I guess I'll have to do it myself."

We listened to Mike's labored breathing for a few minutes, then his voice returned.

"Second bolt's in. I'm leaving bottom."

When Mike reached the deck, I undid his quick-release. He took his mask off and dropped it. He jerked the buckle on his weight belt, breaking the one wrap of duct tape around it, and the belt fell on deck.

"What a ride!" he shouted.

"Three fifteens," Richard said.

It was raining heavily. I decompressed Mike, then Craig jumped in and tried to drop a few bolts, but the sea punished us for trying to continue. The barge rolled heavily and a tugger cable broke, so the riser swung wildly on the surface. Dickie said the bolts were being mashed to pieces on the bottom. Craig came up without accomplishing much, so he recommended we stop work.

Mark dived and removed the bolts and drift pins so we could try again in the morning. The barge pulled a few hundred feet away from the platform, and we shut down the compressors near midnight.

In the morning rough seas pounded the barge, so I went to the divers' room after breakfast and found the crew mellow in their bunks.

"When do you suppose we'll head back?" I asked.

"Don't know," Craig answered. "Swells might come down tonight."

We watched a movie, then I returned to my room and took a nap.

The wind slacked off after dark. The barge moved toward the structure under a full moon. We resumed diving.

We were nocturnal creatures again, working in the shadows, surrounded by an ocean of darkness, but it was cooler and the water took on a secretive mood. When Mike left the surface and disappeared, he entered another dimension. Only his tugging on the lifeline and voice on the phone told us he was out there. We stabbed the drift pins and dropped bolts into the flange all night.

Daylight came, and we had almost all the bolts and the O-ring in. Steve dived and removed the drift pins. He also inserted the last bolts. A morning breeze invigorated me. I enjoyed the sun. Whitecaps marched across a dark blue sea. After decompressing Steve, I returned to the stern and found two machines that looked like jack hammers, but they had sockets on the end.

We spent all day and night tightening thirty flange bolts with an hydraulic impact wrench and torque machine. We affectionately called the machines Big Bertha and Mighty Mite.

I made a dive at night on a 140 foot schedule with a forty-eight-minute bottom time.

I wondered if it would be black on the bottom. My stomach felt light, but I was getting in the water, which was like sugar to an ant. Dickie briefed me on what part of the flange to work on.

"Remember," he said. "Don't impact too much on a bolt. We need an even gap; otherwise, the flange will leak."

My apprehension was always greater diving at night, but, surprisingly, when I reached bottom I had ten feet of visibility. The light came from the moon and from the bioluminescence of plankton, coral, and other marine life. In the subdued light, a black wall of darkness threatened to close in. Shapes became larger and grotesque. The ghostly image of the structure loomed in the distance as big as a city block, and the riser rose toward the surface like a giant down spout.

I overcame my fear by concentrating on the task. Alone with my thoughts and the occasional voice from the ear speakers in my mask, I worked slowly, methodically. Breathing was all that mattered. Perched on the flange, I wrestled with the impact wrench, stuck on a nut. The impact wrench was about my height. The wrench loosened, and I told the surface crew to raise it. The tugger cable tightened, the machine rose, I moved it to the next nut, and told them to drop it. The wrench slid on the nut only after I attacked it like a man possessed. I tried to remember not to over-exert myself. I focused only on the flange. I didn't want my thoughts to stray, because they might invent more things to be fearful of. I remained conscious of the position of my umbilical. The umbilical gave me air, and the path home if I became blind.

I placed the backup wrench on the bottom nut, then pressed the trigger. The socket pounded away at the nut with a painful rat-tat-tat-tat-tat, and the vibrations coursed through my bones like an electric current. The nut slowly turned as the machine worked with a thousand pounds of torque.

I impacted on six bolts and surfaced after what seemed a long time. I crawled in the chamber and rested, too tired to think. I felt totally sapped, like I'd worked a whole day, but the oxygen gave me the energy to continue.

Dickie tightened the last bolts and checked the gap around the flange. By midnight, we started swinging the clamps around to meet the riser. All night it remained clear, but in the morning it rained hard. We tightened the clamp at ninety feet.

In the afternoon the skies cleared. While Craig tightened bolts on the clamp at thirty feet, someone at the top of the platform threw half a watermelon down. It hit next to the dive station a foot from Chink. Bits of watermelon juice sprayed his pants, so he told the crane operator to give the living quarters at the top of the platform a nudge with the boom to shake them up.

We finished the riser job at dinnertime. It seemed like a great burden had been removed. We had all the time in the world. Mike wanted to make a scuba dive, so I joined him. We explored the structure. We found spiny oysters on the jacket legs and filled our mesh bags. Later, Dickie and Craig went down after dark. I had slept little the past three days, but I needed to be in the water.

Dickie Breaks His Thumb

The barge moved to the other side of the platform during a heavy rain. When I took a walk on deck in the morning, ten-foot ground swells glided in, hitting the starboard side. The wind felt cool, and the sky was overcast. Only a few men stood on the rain-soaked deck. They drank hot coffee and cocoa. Above the control tower an American and a Mexican flag showed a few missing seams and tattered edges. A steward appeared out of a hatch near the stern. He threw two plastic bags of garbage over the side. The stern deck looked like it had been swept clean of all loose debris, rope, and cables. Along the circular wall that formed the base of the derrick crane stood, in varying rusty condition, dozens of yellow fifty-five-gallon drums, a giant cast iron barbecue grill, a ten-foot-long anchor, a metal table for splicing slings, and two coils of sheet metal. Everything had been tied securely with cable. A strange moth lay dead under one of the halogen lamps. I took it to the dive locker and pinned it to a piece of cardboard.

Mike came in and said, "Let's go for a scuba dive. You have the tanks charged?"

"Yeah."

"Craig and Mark are coming, too. Let's see what this structure has."

They showed up a few minutes later, and Craig said, "We're pulling out of here in a few hours. Let's get some fish." He grabbed his spear gun in the cubbyhole on the back wall.

We jumped in and quickly descended to twenty feet to avoid the wave action on the surface. The platform had twelve legs. It was like a huge fortress rising up from the deep. All the legs were covered in marine growth and disappeared in a fog that covered the bottom. Hundreds of fish swam lazily within the perimeter of the structure.

We descended to 120 feet where I wrapped my feet around a cross brace and knocked off dozens of spiny oysters into my nylon bag with a hammer and scraper. Craig and Mark explored the lower levels, disappearing and reappearing out of the mist. I noticed that most of the spinys were on the insides of the legs at 100 to 120 feet. Mike was around somewhere, but I didn't know what he was doing. I glanced at the pressure gauge. It read 400 pounds. I felt anxious, because I wanted to return to the barge. Mike appeared below me. He seemed busy collecting spinys. I ascended to sixty feet, straddled a horizontal, and waited. The water was murky, and in the vast columns of the fortress I felt insignificant. I focused on the hollow hiss of air on every breath. It was a comfortable solitude, heavy spiny bag hanging from my rope belt, barnacles and shellfish pressing against my jeans, and I looked up at the quiet storm attacking the barge.

Mike's bubbles floated past me, then he ascended. I followed, hugging the jacket leg, then swam freely in open water toward the bottom of the boat bumper ladder. Monstrous waves hit the starboard side of the barge. Mike grabbed the bottom rung of the ladder with one hand. He held a bag of spiny oysters in the other. I was thirty feet below him. He tried to remove his fins. A particularly strong wave slammed into the barge. Mike dropped his fins and bag of oysters. He scrambled up the ladder out of sight. His gear drifted down. I was more anxious, with only 100 pounds of air left, and I didn't know if I'd get back on the barge. I decided to try another ladder further toward the bow. I grabbed the bottom rung. I removed one fin, and a wave came in that almost tossed toss me on deck. I hung on with one hand. The surge flipped me upside down. The barge rolled, the wave receded, and I seized the moment. I ripped off the other fin and climbed to the top of the boat bumper with my prized cargo intact.

On deck, Mike greeted me. "Are you all right?" he asked.

"Yeah. A wave flipped me, but I held on."

"Soon as my fins came off, I felt like I was going to the bottom."

"Too bad about your spinys."

"Where's Craig and Mark?"

"I think they swam to the stern ladder. It's not so bad there."

"Wish I had thought of that."

"I'll tell Craig to order a couple sets of fins and masks."

We walked back to the dive locker, where Craig chided us for surfacing on the starboard side.

✱ ✱ ✱

The barge towed to another structure. I slept an entire night, the first sound sleep in weeks. I awoke late in the morning and spent most of the day cleaning my spiny oysters. I dipped them in bleach, scraped off the sea growth, and sprayed them with silicon, to make them shine. One specimen had a particularly attractive orange and red color with miniature spines. I didn't know what I would do with the spinys. I dreamed of selling them to gift shops in New Orleans.

Late that afternoon, the barge anchored near the Nohoch A platform, and we set another Z-bend. Steve checked for clamps and opened the door on the bottom clamp. I gave him two fifteens in the chamber. Dickie set the Z-bend on the bottom, and Mike removed the slings. He reported that the bottom clamp was welded to the jacket leg, so we would have to cut it off, to slide it down and insert the vertical part of the Z-bend into it. The sun was going down, and I didn't look forward to another sleepless night. We were diving on a 140-foot schedule with a bottom time of thirty-eight minutes.

Craig dived and cut off part of the clamp arm with the oxy-arc torch. Mark finished the cutting, then we waited while the welders fabricated another clamp. Five hours later, it was ready. I tended Steve, who tried to set the clamp, but it was the wrong size. I made the dive to remove the clamp.

I wrestled with a hinged monster twelve feet in diameter for twenty-six minutes at a depth of 136 feet. When the clamp slid off the platform leg, it raised a cloud of barnacle and shellfish debris. I came out of the water physically and emotionally drained. I rested in the chamber, wiped off the saltwater, and the oxygen revitalized me.

The welders adjusted the size of clamp, and Mark set it. Dickie dived to set the Z-bend in the clamp. The bolts on the clamp were bent, so Dickie couldn't close the door to the clamp.

Dickie surfaced.

"Why didn't you check the damn bolts?" Mike snapped.

Everyone's nerves were raw. Seas were getting rough, and we hadn't accomplished anything. Chink wanted to get the Z-bend in the clamp before midnight.

Dickie came out of the chamber, dressed, and took a stance by the dive station. "You gonna make a dive?" he asked Mike, who stood by the stern railing and glared at the water.

"You expect me to clean up your mess down there?" Mike shook his head.

Dickie looked at Chink.

The barge foreman sighed. "Get in the goddamn water, or I'll run ya' off."

Mike trotted to the dive locker. He returned with his favorite velour shirt and jeans. Cursing to himself, Mike leaped in the water and made a spectacular dive. In fifteen minutes, he set the clamp at the right height, put spacer bars in the door, and tightened the bolts, so the clamp was tight around the jacket leg. Then he pulled the Z-bend into clamp with the help of air tuggers.

When Mike finished his decompression, Craig dived, closed the clamp door around the Z-bend, and tightened bolts. One hour after midnight we were almost finished. Johnny, the night shift foreman, relieved Chink.

Steve jumped in and disconnected the slings, but when he surfaced, he said, "The crane line caught somewhere and snapped the clamp off the jacket leg."

Johnny stayed calm and took a sip of coffee. "I don't need that kind of news to start my day."

Johnny, Dickie, Craig, and Steve formed a huddle. Dickie stroked his mustache. "What's down there?" he asked Steve.

"The Z-bend's sitting on bottom with a broken clamp."

Johnny frowned. "We have to go off location, now."

"What do we tell Ignacio?" Craig asked.

"I don't know. Let's say the bottom settled and broke off the clamp. Send somebody down and run a choker around the jacket leg and tube turn so at least the Z-bend won't drift away."

"That sounds reasonable," Craig said.

Mark dived, and after his decompression, we shut down the compressors and slept while the barge pulled up anchors. Nothing seemed to go right on that job. I was glad to get some sleep. We had been working about forty-eight hours.

✶ ✶ ✶

The barge set anchors near Abkatum, an old four-legged structure weatherbeaten and rusty. It had a red escape pod on the top deck used to evacuate personnel in case of hurricanes. The sea was dark green and calm. We were going to set two risers. Craig called for additional divers and a supervisor from a nearby barge, because it was going to be another marathon of nonstop diving. The bolts lay on the stern deck, and each one was so large, it would have to be lowered with an air tugger. I knew we would be impacting bolts for at least a week. I looked forward to more bottom time, and I didn't care if it meant no sleep. I hoped the weather stayed fair and seas remained calm. The sea could destroy our work in a few hours, if the wind picked up and rocked the barge.

Divers from another barge started the first riser, and I slept for a few hours, expecting to work during the night.

I tended four divers the first night. We dived on a 120-foot schedule with sixty-eight-minute bottom times. The divers had a four-minute water stop at thirty feet. Chamber time was two fifteen-minute periods and two ten-minute periods breathing oxygen. We tightened bolts with the hydraulic impact wrench all night and the next day. Close to noon, the supervisor told me to go below and get some sleep.

Awakened in the evening, I ate a meal and climbed on deck. I tended two divers and decompressed them.

My turn to dive came, and my heart raced, especially because the dive would be at night. I'm more paranoid when I haven't had enough sleep. Fear, paranoia, and uncertainty accompanied every diver, but when I jumped in the water, the feelings vanished and I lived in the moment.

Perched on the ledge of a giant flange at a depth of 120 feet, I breathed cool, tasteless air. Some light filtered down revealing the monster structure nearby, but beyond, darkness swirled in chilly silence. My umbilical, the tugger cable, and hydraulic hoses to the torque machine snaked up toward the barge. I passed the time watching the Select-a-torque machine work in agonizing slow motion. For each piston stroke, the nut made a quarter turn, then the piston retracted. One cycle took about three to four minutes. The backup wrench on the other nut jammed frequently and I had to hammer it loose before instructing the tugger crew on the surface to raise the torque wrench. I measured the gap on the flange. It was three finger widths on the backside and two on the front. I was alone, with nothing but my thoughts and breaths. Where were the fish? I didn't see any within my five-foot radius of visibility.

My sixty-eight minutes came to an end, and I returned to the friendlier world of the surface.

After my chamber time, I slept a few hours, then relieved Steve sometime before dawn. I didn't know what day it was, or what time it was. I didn't talk to the growling supervisor. When the sun came up, I had never seen the water so intensely blue. When I picked up the diver, it was Mike, and he seemed tireless as ever. As usual, he found something to complain about.

"You ought to get a new torque machine, Don," he said when the mask came off his head.

"What's the matter with it?" the supervisor asked.

"It's not working right."

"Sure it is."

"Stay here all week, then."

"What do you care? They're happy with the gap."

"The flange will leak."

"Give him three fifteens," the supervisor said, ignoring Mike.

Mike and I walked to the chamber.

"What's the matter with the machine?" I asked.

"Piston arm broke twice last night."

I took Mike down to forty feet and stared at the needle on the gauge.

Lee come out of a hatch. He must have boarded on the previous night's crew boat.

Lee came over. "Who's in there?"

"Mike. How was your trip?"

"Not bad."

He looked well rested. "Who went in?"

"Craig and Mark."

Lee walked to the stern and talked with the supervisor. I gave the chamber a good vent. It started raining. After Mike's chamber time I changed clothes, found a raincoat, and went to the stern.

Ignacio, the Pemex inspector, seemed satisfied with the gap on the flange, so we pulled the torque machine out of the water. Next, we tightened the riser clamp bolts. I tended Lee who took care of the clamp at sixty feet. Steve finished the thirty-foot clamp, and I slept a few hours while the barge moved to the adjacent leg, where we started on a Z-bend and another riser. It rained hard the rest of the day and the sea churned, but the work continued into the night. At any moment we had a diver decompressing in the chamber, a diver on the bottom, and a standby diver sitting next to the supervisor. Day and night blurred. We slept when we had a chance and ate during a lull, but there was nothing like going to 120 feet to charge a tired soul. No matter how exhausted we were, we wanted to feel the ocean against our bodies. We craved it. We were sea lions at home in the depths, and the barge and bunks were only sand and rocks to briefly rest on before returning to the crashing waves.

I was getting more experience, growing stronger, becoming more confident in the water. A trip to the unknown was always intimidating, where I would be alone, having to rely totally on my own abilities, but magically, once I entered the water, fear and anxiety dissolved and I was like a child again, absorbed in the moment.

We set the Z-bend on the bottom after dark. A ferocious squall hit while I tended Lee. The rain filled the sea to overflowing, and the barge rocked. Lee came out of the water, and I decompressed him in the downpour wearing a hooded raincoat. Lee lay on his comfortable bunk inside his steel cocoon, which effectively sealed out any wind, noise, or rain. I was amazed that my watch still functioned after all the salty spray it had received.

The barge superintendent decided that the weather prevented us from setting the riser, so the crane made a lift and we pulled away from the platform to wait for the eventual calm.

We rested for half a day. The sun came out and the sea settled down. We waited for orders from Pemex. An inspection diver came on board and photographed the bottom of the barge to record the condition of the paint. He wore extra long flimsy fins. We weren't impressed. Steve dived with him.

The barge moved on location in the evening. We started diving again. The riser hung in the water near the structure, and Dickie jumped in, with Mike at the dive station. Dickie talked a lot whenever he was in the water, explaining everything he did, which is the proper way, so topside knows what is happening, but Mike still disparaged his efforts. We heard Dickie breathing hard. The ground swells came through steadily. The riser must have been shifting violently, and Dickie didn't make much progress.

"Guy's barge diver and he doesn't even know how to set a riser," Mike grumbled.

Mike always found an opportunity to criticize Dickie, but I didn't see how Mike could be a barge diver, if he wanted to stay offshore only three months a year.

Dickie surfaced after putting one bolt in, and we helped him take off his gear by the ladder.

"You're bleeding," Steve said. "Hey, Mike, his hand's bleeding."

"Two fifteens and two tens." Mike didn't show any pity.

Dickie held his right arm like it was in a cast. He said nothing.

Steve helped him walk to port. I dried out the mask and came to the chamber to see how Dickie was.

"He's in pain," Steve said. "He needs to go in and see a doctor."

"What happened to him?"

"Drift pin dropped on his hand."

I cringed at the thought of having a hundred-pound steel rod drop on my hand.

✳ ✳ ✳

Dickie took the crew boat in to del Carmen when he stepped out of the chamber.

I tended Mike that evening. He set the riser and inserted two bolts and the aluminum O-ring. We dived continuously through the night. In the morning, all bolts had been inserted. We used the hydraulic tools again. Mighty Mite broke after two dives. Big Bertha was more reliable.

In the evening I jumped into a calm sea. The water was clear on descent along the pipe toward the flange, and I had good visibility. I reached a depth of 112 feet. The impact wrench was suspended by a cable and sitting on a nut. I spent sixty-eight bone-numbing minutes with Big Bertha in the dim light. The vibrations of the impact wrench coursed through my body and turned my muscles into gelatin.

When I ascended, I witnessed something that made the dive worthwhile. I forgot my tiredness, forgot the job, forgot myself. A school of fish filled my viewport. A hundred-foot-long silvery shape with a thousand eyes moved gracefully through the transparent water, diagonally upwards, not fleeing out of fear but giving me enough room, folding to accommodate my presence. The fish were almost close enough to touch, but at forty feet, the school turned and disappeared into open water, leaving me with my bubbles. I looked up and followed my umbilical to the surface. It looked like a snake dancing in the turbulence, and when I reached thirty feet, the supervisor told me to stop. I hung from the jacket leg for four minutes, then surfaced.

I stripped and crawled in the chamber. Wrapped in steel, sheltered from the elements, I let the oxygen work its magic.

Rough seas sprayed the starboard side in the morning under a clear, brilliant sky. We finished impacting on the second riser, and Pemex wanted us to impact on the first riser again. Lee dived to loosen the clamps, and Mike started with the Select-a-torque.

When Mike came out of the water, Chink wanted to know the gap on the riser flange, but Mike said, "Leave me alone. You people bug me too much."

I decompressed him, and we stopped diving while welders attached a section of pipe on top of the platform where the riser would tie into.

We started diving on the first riser later that day. We loosened the bolts on the front side of the flange to close the gap on the back, which was two and a quarter inches. We tightened bolts all night and narrowed the gap to one and a half inches.

I tended Mike past midnight, and when he surfaced he said, "That's all you're gonna get. It's tight."

Pemex wanted us to continue closing the gap, so we dived through the night. I tended Lee. Steve kept me company.

"Anybody heard about Dickie?" I asked.

"Yeah. He broke his thumb in three places. Lee said he got blood poisoning, too."

"Damn." I fished Lee. I felt him moving on the end of the umbilical. Steve leaned against the stern rail. "He's going back to the States."

"For how long?" I asked.

"Don't know."

"With him gone, maybe they'll break you out."

Steve shook his head. "Not this time. They passed me up again."

"What do you mean?"

"Those pricks in New Orleans are sending somebody down."

I sympathized with him, but there was nothing I could do. "At least you're making a lot of dives," I said.

"Yeah. Working twice as hard for half the pay. I'm getting tired of it. I can do anything under water they can."

I shifted my weight by the ladder and pulled up some slack. "You know what I think?"

"What's that?"

"Nobody else would do all this surface work but a tender itching to get in the water."

"You got that right."

By evening the following day all the divers and tenders had tried to tighten the gap on the flange. When Mike finished his dive, he threw his mask on deck. "That's all you're going to get. Where's that taco-eating inspector? One and a half inches. That's all!"

"Don't get sore at me," Chink said. "I'm just doing what they tell me."

"Yeah, right."

"You want me to get him up here?"

"It doesn't matter. I'm going in soon."

We made two more dives. I went to sleep around midnight.

Beer Run

I woke at noon and found us under tow. In the galley, the captain and the superintendent drank coffee and couldn't decide where we were going. In the middle of the night, the barge had turned around, so by late afternoon, I saw the same structures that we had been anchored near for the riser job. I returned to my bunk. Mike was packing his things and Lee was reading a book.

"Where are you going?" I asked Mike.

"I'm taking Dickie's bunk before the relief diver gets here."

Mike seemed happy to occupy the bunk of a barge diver. Dickie, with a broken thumb and blood poisoning, would be gone for at least two months. Steve sulked and spent much time alone in the dive locker when he learned he would not be promoted. He disassembled masks and rearranged the work bench countless times. He rarely raised his voice or grumbled like Mike, but his eyes grew weary, he didn't shave regularly, and his face acquired a permanent frown. He didn't move with as much energy. Mark, who had come on board cheerful, stopped smiling. I knew if Steve and Mark didn't get promoted, I didn't stand much chance, either.

I looked at my calendar. The month of June had been hell. All those risers and L-bends had turned us into manic-depressives. Days of nonstop diving charged us with incredible energy, then we crashed and slept for twenty-four hours while the barge towed to another location, or rough seas interrupted our work. I hoped we would do some pipelaying soon and recuperate. I was weary from many sleepless nights.

I still had a great thirst for bottom time. Although I envied the divers when I stood on deck and got drenched by rain or scorched by the sun; although I hated the long, boring hours of tending and operating the chamber; I still carried out my tasks efficiently. I always put a fresh towel in the chamber, cleaned the masks after every dive, and refueled the compressors without being told. I hoped the divers would have sympathy, and put me in the water more often. For a chance to experience more bottom time, I was prepared to spend many months at sea.

Mike left with his duffel bag. Some time later, a short guy in jeans and a red T-shirt came in the cabin.

"Hey, The Troll is here," Lee said. "How are you doing, Larry?"

"Pretty good," the new guy said.

Larry was an ex-marine who lived in Tyler, Texas. He had a tattoo of a skull on his upper right arm. He was about the height of a troll with powerful arms and a thick neck. Larry belonged to the 1,000-footer club. He had been on a saturation diving job to install the Cognac platform in the Gulf of Mexico near the mouth of the Mississippi River. The water depth there was about 1,000 feet.

✳ ✳ ✳

I had hardly noticed Dickie's departure in the blur of action in June, but soon, it felt as if a family member were missing. Those risers were brutal, yet Mike always seemed to come out unscathed, with a little help from the intrepid Mr. Bill. Navy SEALS were underwater magicians.

I looked at my logbook and was surprised I even kept accurate entries during the past few weeks. I had forgotten what food tasted like, forgotten about everything but the relentless job. About the only habit I still had was shaving. I never forgot to shave. Maybe this feeling was what shell shock was like. Would I really last until the end of the year? I didn't want to get hurt. If they sent me down to set a riser I'd be more careful than Dickie. If seas were too rough, the hell with it. I'd refuse. If I refused, though, they'd send me home. I didn't want that. I had to tell myself I wasn't going to get hurt. I was invincible. Nothing was going to hurt me.

✳ ✳ ✳

We enjoyed a four-day truce from our sea battles. I slept until noon, ate steak without rushing, roamed the deck, swept the dive locker floor, sunbathed on top of the pontoon shack, watched the Mexicans chip paint, and watched videos.

The dark blue water rippled against the barge, and on the horizon a few platforms with flares burning reminded me that we floated on top of a huge oilfield..The scorching sun turned me into a bronze statue. Occasionally, sea birds flew by across a milky blue sky. It was peaceful and relaxing, and we took swims off the stern. Mark and Lee made a scuba dive and came out with one pompano. Lee lost a spear to a barracuda. Mark had returned a few days before, but Craig was still in. I wondered why he was taking so much time off.

For exercise, I climbed on the crane deck and ran laps around the walkway. Some of the grating was loose and I had to duck under a beam every lap, but it was the only place to run, and the view was good.

I looked out at the sea that extended to the horizon in every direction and knew it could be a dangerous place for anyone adrift. The sea could hypnotize and cast a spell over me, if I spent a long time with her. I felt mesmerized already from hearing the slow slopping of the water against the hull on the hot calm days; from feeling the excitement when the wind picked up and hurled whitecaps over the rails; from being in the quiet narcotic depths, weightless; from seeing that vast blue plain, ever restless, moody, big enough to swallow the sun and throw us around with a sigh; from standing on the stern at night, gazing at the mysterious water reflecting the moon and barge lights.

The barge towed to a new location. I watched the sun set off the stern. A three-legged drilling platform caught the wake of the barge, and the sun touched down near the platform, its diameter only a third of the platform's height, its fires subdued. I looked at it without pain. A wavy trail of smoke drifted through the red and yellow light and met the platform. The trail headed toward the sun like a winding road in the sky, and another smaller drilling platform rose out of the sea to starboard. The endless water slopped lazily, calm and silvery, with no oil slicks, no floating bags of garbage, only a few lonely sentinels on an empty horizon.

✷ ✷ ✷

A new day brought more surprises. Steve and I loaded the compressors, umbilicals, and chamber on the tug, *Mr. Harry*. Lee, Larry, and Manuel joined us, and we took a trip that lasted about an hour. The boat tied off next to *Sarita*, a huge Norwegian ship with a derrick crane. She was setting a platform. The ship had begun driving pilings into the hollow legs with a steam hammer. An oil slick around the platform told us something was wrong.

Larry dived and inspected the bottom. When he came out, slimy brown oil covered him and the umbilical. He took off his mask. "Looks like they drove a pile into a pipeline."

"That's a first," Lee said. Lee, Larry, and Manuel formed a circle.

"Better check your surveys of this area. Looks like an old line going in that direction." Manuel went below to radio his report.

Larry pointed to an orange buoy in the distance. "It probably goes over to that SBM."

Larry took a shower to rinse the acidic oil off his body while Steve and I found some rags to wipe the hoses.

The oil slick extended for miles in an ever-widening brown trail.

"Look at all that oil," I said.

"I like how they build an oilfield," Steve said.

"Nobody knows except us."

"They're better off not knowing. Hell, they don't care. What's a little oil spill?"

Afterward, we took a forty-five minute ride to a tanker. We tied up along the port bow, and the men on the ship dropped a rope ladder with thin wooden slats. It must have been fifty feet up to the deck of the ship.

"What are we doing here?" I asked.

"Making a beer run," Lee said. "You and Steve get up there and lower the cases with this rope."

The climb up the flimsy ladder was slow. I didn't want to think about the trip down. Steve and I went into the ship cooler and carried twenty-four cases of Old Bohemian to the side of the deck overlooking *Mr. Harry* and lowered them one by one. Lee stuffed them into the chamber.

It started to rain heavily. The wind on the deck of the ship knocked us around, but we lowered the last case down to *Mr. Harry* without mishap. We were drenched, and I didn't look forward to climbing down a slippery rope ladder. I lay on my stomach, dropped my feet over the side, felt for the first slat, grabbed the rope, and made my way down. I tried not to look at the boat, only forward, watching each hand slowly slide a foot and tighten, moving a step at a time, holding that rope with the grip of a dead man, until finally I jumped onto the heaving deck of the tug. Steve climbed down after I did, and we returned to the *L.B. Meaders*.

The derrick crane lifted the chamber onto the center deck of the barge, and we smuggled the beer into the dive locker. There weren't many men on deck, because of the rain, but I'm sure some saw us. After our cargo was safely stowed away, we returned the compressors and chamber to their proper places, washed the masks, cleaned the dive hoses with soap, and finally dragged our bodies to the galley for a midnight meal.

In one day all the beer disappeared out of the dive locker, destined for small, private refrigerators of privileged men who kept quiet, because liquor on board was forbidden, at least in the Gulf, but in Mexico we stretched the rules. The barge sat quietly, not able to do a thing because of rough seas, and all the men were in their rooms sleeping, reading, or drinking beer.

The divers relaxed in the lounge above the dive locker. Craig had built a couch and chair from wooden crates and put foam padding on top. Posters decorated the walls, so we had a comfortable escape from the drab living quarters below deck. Juan joined us. We had two cases of beer, and Larry had a bottle of Scotch.

Lee pointed to Larry's Scotch. "Where did you get that?"

"Won it from Ted Hicks in a booray game."

"Is he any good?"

"No. Not with booray, but you should see him when we play poker. Last year he won 80,000 dollars on one hand."

"I heard about that."

Larry took a sip of Scotch. "Bobby Taylor's good. He won 25,000 last week."

"Ted's not doing too well lately," Mike said. "He raffled off his 12,000-dollar gold watch. John Peters won it."

Larry looked at me. "You ought to play poker with us sometime."

I shrugged. "I never played it. I don't make that much."

"What are they going to do with that oil leak?" Steve asked.

"I don't know," Lee said. "Maybe that's what all the waiting is about. I can't believe they drove a piling into a live line."

"There's a lot of oil coming out," Larry said.

"They don't care," Mike said. "Look what happened with Ixtoc."

"Yeah. Whole Texas coast was covered with six-foot tar balls." Mark chuckled. "I was on the *L.B. Meaders* when it happened. There was oil all over the place. The surface of the water was on fire. The bell would come up through the burning oil like a chocolate-covered doughnut, and they had fireboats spraying the hoses to keep them from burning."

"Taylor wanted me to go on that job," Mike said. "I told them they were crazy."

Larry sat closer to the table and cupped his glass with both hands. "The Mexicans lost three or four divers. Taylor killed one. That's when they shut it down. I was there when the Taylor diver got killed. His hose was caught in the wreckage, and he couldn't move because the oil was shooting out so fast. You could hear him on the phone saying how his mask was filling up with oil."

"Couldn't they stop the oil?" I asked.

"The conductor pipe had ruptured under the blowout preventer, so they tried a bunch a nutty ideas," Larry said. They tried dropping a few tons of little lead balls down the pipe, but that didn't do any good. It was a mess."

"They sent those Mexican divers one after another, like sacrifices to their sun god," Mark said.

"I don't know where they get some of those Mexican divers," Lee said. "We were sent to a dredge, one time and I went down to inspect the sled. It was riding twenty feet off bottom. The pipe wasn't even in a ditch. The Mexicans had supposedly been making ditch checks, but they never even bothered to go to the bottom. We had to start the whole line over."

Beer bottles littered the table. We were all getting a good buzz.

"It's a shame those boys got killed," Mark said.

"They had to prove how macho they were. When somebody dares a man in Mexico, there's no way he can back down."

The divers reminisced about friends that had been killed. A Taylor diver had been sucked into the mud pumps of a dredge, one summer. All that remained was a mangled torso floating on the surface. The company scattered the dive crew around the world, to make it harder for the lawyers to reach them. Larry said that Taylor killed about one diver a year. Another diver had been killed on an experimental dive in the North Sea. He had made a dive to 2,000 feet in a Norwegian fjord and had passed out. Carbon dioxide poisoning was the suspect, but nobody knew for sure what had caused his death. Larry told us not to work for Comex, the French company. A whole saturation team working for Comex had been killed in the North Sea one year. Six fresh bodies replaced the team, and they were killed, too. Those were accidents no company wanted to reveal.

Lee reached toward Larry. "Give me some of that Scotch."

"Help yourself." Larry gave him the bottle.

"The North Sea. I had enough of that place. Too cold." Mark leaned back in his chair.

"You were there last year, weren't you?" I asked Mark.

"For three months."

"What was it like?" I asked.

"Rough, son. Fifty-foot swells. They came rolling in, and the barge was as high as the top of the structure. We had a storm one time. The barge had to cut its anchor cables and run for shallow water. I saw a welder tie a torch to the end of a broom handle. He didn't want to get too close to cut the cable. When that thing parted, he danced out of the way. Whoom! The anchor cable whipped through the sheaves and into the water faster than a scared moray."

Everyone laughed.

"You have any beers left over there?" Mike asked.

Steve glanced into the cooler. "Yeah."

"Throw me one."

Lee slammed his empty bottle on the table. "Give me a *cerveza*, too. You'd think a tanker could at least have Tecate."

We opened fresh bottles and settled in our chairs.

"What's that say on your shirt, Juan?" Larry asked.

Juan looked like he hadn't shaved for a week. He wore a greasy T-shirt with a Spanish saying across the front.

Juan grinned. "My life is full of sweat and tears. Do you like it?"

"That's good," Larry said.

"My girlfriend in Portugal gave it to me."

"Is she waiting for you?"

"Yes. Maybe I'll marry her, if I ever get off this barge."

"How old are you?"

"Twenty-one."

"You're just a kid."

"I've been in the North Sea, in Bahrain—"

"How old's your girl?"

"Eighteen. Let me tell you something. Every time I go on a date with her she brings her mother. We are still strict in my country, not like in your country where they have all those wild women." He cocked his head back and emptied his bottle.

"Is that the sound of an anchor cable?" Steve asked.

"You're hearing things. Have another *cerveza*." Lee pushed a bottle toward Steve.

Mike looked at Mark. "Put some music on will you?"

Mark rummaged through our meager collection of tapes.

I drank my beer and stared at a poster on the wall. The words on the poster said "Happiness is wanting what you have, not having what you want." I thought the phrase applied well to our austere existence. "You're full of stories, Lee," I said. "I heard you've been diving fifteen years."

Lee nodded.

"That's a long time."

"I had some good years and some lean years. Spent a lot of time in the North Sea on dredge barges. I lived in Costa Rica in the mid-sixties."

"What was it like back then?"

"A glass of beer was a dime and whores were a dollar fifty. There wasn't much to do in those sleepy little towns."

"You had to learn Spanish, didn't you?"

"That was the easy part. Getting up was hard. I'd have a cheese tortilla and coffee and look at the people in the street. There weren't many cars. A lot of people had burros. I could have settled down there. I don't know why I ever left."

"What were you doing there?"

"We were supposed to build a road. Some kind of development scheme financed by an international bank. They had money to spend, and we built a road that went nowhere. It ended in the jungle past a dried stream bed. I don't think anybody used it. It was a good road, though."

"I want to hear a better one than that," Larry said.

"Like what?"

"I don't know."

"Did I tell you the one about the guy in the merchant marine who kept getting clap?"

"I heard that one already."

"All right. Want to know why Costa Rica is different from the rest of Central America?"

"Why?"

"Because the Spaniards found nobody to conquer, and there was no gold. There were Indians, but they didn't surrender like the Aztecs. They burned their crops to starve the Spaniards. Anybody that settled there had to grow their own food, so Costa Rica is mostly middle class today. Not too many rich and not too many poor."

"They don't have an army do they?" I asked.

"No. Thirty percent of the budget is spent on education."

Mark put a new tape in the machine, one that he had brought from home.

"What kind of music is that?" Mike asked.

"Asleep at the Wheel," Mark said.

"Play something else," Mike protested.

Mark frowned. "That's a good tape, man."

"Put that Christopher Cross tape in."

"Whatever."

"That's better." Mike leaned back and stared at a purple sea fan on the wall.

"When's Dickie going to be back? Anybody heard?" Steve asked.

"I don't know." Lee stood, and headed for the door.

"How much longer are we going to be standing by?" I asked.

"Let me go talk to Manuel," Mike said. "I don't care if he's asleep. I want some answers."

Larry looked at Mike. "He doesn't make the decisions. Some bureaucrat in Mexico City does."

I walked out to the stern. Mexicans were reading comic books under the glare of the halogen lamps. I urinated over the side by the dive ladder. Beer always went through my body quickly. Two sea gulls floated on the water and bobbed up and down with the swells. The barge groaned as it turned on its long axis. The purple and white lights on the derrick crane were like stars in a dark sky. Steve came out of the lounge. He joined me by the pontoon shack. We looked at the dark water and listened to the gurgle and splash as it hit the sides of the barge and swirled around and through the pontoon hitch.

✲ ✲ ✲

We waited two days for *Sarita* to move, so we could lay a bypass line around the one they punctured.

The Troll roamed the hallways late at night and urinated in trash cans. I studied the stock market. Mike painted with his watercolors. Lee played darts. Mark acquired Craig's habit of smoking filter-tipped cigars. All the waiting could drive a man crazy.

One evening the barge pulled close to the structure and the pontoon arrived. It had a new stern section, not as rusty as the forward two sections, with less barnacle growth on the tanks below the water. Mike made a dive and secured a cable around the bottom of the platform leg. Lee shackled the end of the pipeline into it to keep the line from shifting away from the structure as we lay pipe. Mark and I flooded the pontoon, attached the control hoses, and tied a buoy to the end of the pipeline when it reached the end of the pontoon and started its descent.

A Buckled Pipeline

The barge finished laying the bypass line, and we spent weeks connecting the end of the line to a single-buoy mooring system at a depth of 140 feet. We had to remove all the bolts from a flange where the old pipeline connected. Four divers and a supervisor came from another barge to help us.

We had removed all but four bolts, but all the divers were burned out. Don, the supervisor, refused to dive tenders, so we had to cease operations.

The barge captain wasn't happy. He asked Steve if we had been paid for the dives on the riser job, and Steve said, "Yeah. We got paid, but the supervisor doesn't want to put tenders in the water."

"I thought you didn't want to dive because they weren't paying you."

"I've made plenty of dives without getting paid for them. Of course I don't like it."

"Sitting around doesn't make us look good."

"Go talk to that supervisor. He doesn't think we can do the job."

"Too late for that. Pemex already called the Oddberg divers."

"Don't blame us. We wanted to dive."

"Looks like we're gonna be on standby for a while."

Steve and I went into the dive locker. He said, "I wonder why he doesn't want us in the water. That's a lot of money we're losing."

"Lee can't say anything?" I asked.

"No. You can't argue with Don. He's ex-Navy and expects us to take orders."

"You and Mark have the experience. They should let you dive."

"I've been putting up with this bullshit too long. I'm getting tired. They don't care about us. Hell, pretty soon I won't care, either."

"Seems like it's just a bunch of politics."

"I'm no good at playing that game."

"Me, either."

The *L.B. Meaders* moved off location, and a ship owned by Oddberg, a Norwegian company, came to remove the last bolts and separate the pipeline. The ship had a saturation system with a moon pool, which let the bell launch from the bottom of the hull. It was a dynamic positioning vessel, well designed for rough seas. Normally it would be working in the North

Sea, but there was so much work in this oilfield that everybody was in Campeche—Norwegian, Mexican, American, French, and British divers.

★ ★ ★

The next few days brought confusion and extra work, because of a lack of communication between shifts. We returned to the work site to pick up the pipeline and weld on a flange. Mike made the first dive, secured a down line, and positioned the barge over the line.

To lift a section of a pipeline off the sea floor, the barge used a number of davits, small cranes, on the starboard side. The *L.B. Meaders* had six davits running the length of the barge. The divers connected five davits, but when the pipeline surfaced, too much pipe extended beyond the fifth davit. That part buckled and fell in the water.

We worked through the night and into the morning. We cut off the damaged section, welded a blind piece on the end, set it on the bottom for a measurement, and picked it up again. I guess the supervisor figured the hard work was finished, so he let tenders dive again.

Before dark, as a fantastic sunset unfolded shooting yellow, pink, turquoise, and blue streaks across the sky, I jumped in and took a pipe profile. I followed the pipe, and the supervisor took a depth reading at each davit, so we could determine if the pipe was coming up evenly. The pipe was at 100 feet. Natural bottom was 140 feet. My bottom time was ten minutes.

The barge welded on a flange, we set the pipe on the bottom, and it lined up perfectly.

For two days we wrestled with the big chains that moored the buoy to the sea floor. I made a dive and connected one chain.

Finally, we were done. Mike, who had grown mean-tempered after three months, packed his bags. "Time to celebrate," he said. "Time to go fishing. If you're still around, maybe I'll see you next year."

"Would you sign my logbook?" I asked. I handed it to him.

"Looks like you got a few dives here."

"Almost fifty."

He initialed each entry. He put his watercolors in the briefcase and stuffed his clothes from the locker into a duffel bag. "You know what? If I can get a job as an artist, maybe I'll retire. I just had a great idea. I could paint sports handbooks. What do you think? A skiing book called The Downhillers, a tennis book called The Racketeers. Then I could do a golf book, a running book, a fishing book. . ."

I smiled.

Mike chattered until early morning and kept me awake. He talked about the time he shot a dog on a hill above Flathead Lake. He thought the dog was rabid. He talked about his wife, who faithfully waited for him in his trailer in Kalispell. He grumbled about the company and boasted about a plot of land he owned in Montana, where he would build a house.

I slept most of the day while the barge picked up anchors. I walked on deck when the crew boat came around dinnertime. Steve joined me on the port side. He looked weary. We watched Mike leave. I didn't know when I would see the tireless warrior again. Faces changed on the barge, but the sea remained the same.

Craig came aboard. He had shaved his beard. His cheeks looked sunburned.

"Who do I tend now?" I asked Steve.

"You're tending Lee." Nobody wanted to tend Lee. I resigned myself to that pipe-smoking, Skoal-spitting, hard-of-hearing veteran and thought he might teach me something.

The 1,000-Foot Club

We were supposed to lay pipe soon, but seas became rough in the afternoon, and the pontoon returned to shallow water. The barge anchored next to a small platform, and the derrick crane made a lift, which gave us a chance to go scuba diving. I collected about twenty spiny oysters at 120 feet. The water was comfortable at that depth. Visibility was excellent, and I saw many fish in the area inside the structure legs, including some big amberjack, pompano, red snapper, grunts, sheepshead, blue tang, and dolphin.

I cleaned the spinys, and at night the barge rolled noisily as seas steadily increased and we lay in our bunks. My new roommate, Larry, seemed to be a reasonable fellow, quiet and unemotional. He had seen the horrors of war in Vietnam, and he had been diving for six years. He had also been on a saturation diving job to 1,000 feet.

Saturation diving was slightly different than simply jumping in the water, surfacing, and decompressing in the chamber for a few hours. A saturation diver lived under pressure for weeks or months in a deck chamber. A diving bell transported him to the work site. When the work was finally finished, the diver spent days decompressing. Only then could he exit the chamber. A saturation diving job required a large investment in surface equipment, including vast amounts of helium gas. As a result of scientific research in the 1950s, the commercial diving industry adopted saturation diving techniques in the 1960s and proved that men could work for almost unlimited amounts of time at extreme depths. Captain Bond of the United States Navy showed that after a given period of exposure to inert gas, a diver would absorb no more. His tissues would be saturated. The consequences of the discovery meant that the decompression time to remove the inert gas from his tissues would be finite.

Larry described how he felt living at a pressure of 1,000 feet, thirty atmospheres, in a steel chamber with five other men. The chamber was pressurized to a depth equivalent to where the divers would be working, so the diving bell became merely an elevator transporting the divers to and from the work location. I taped our conversation, so I was able to reproduce his exact words.

"Can you tell me about the job?"

Larry grabbed a bottle of Scotch and poured a glass. "My wife told me she was pregnant with our second child when I went into Sat," he started. "I told her not to worry. I told her they had made other dives to a thousand feet, but really this was the first, so nobody knew what would happen. We was all hyped up, you know. The first thing we noticed when we reached working pressure was that we couldn't talk to each other. My joints ached, and I had back pains. It felt like my bones was next to each other. One day out of boredom I did ten chin ups off the shower curtain and couldn't breathe after that."

"Why not?" I asked.

"The atmosphere. It was so thick. Rodney dropped a pair of headphone covers and they just floated down back and forth like a leaf. You could brush your teeth and spit and all the toothpaste would spread out and kinda slowly drop into the sink. Nothing fell straight down. It was real easy to over breathe that Kirby. I didn't notice any high pressure nervous syndrome, but my wife said in my letters I'd lose my train of thought. I'd start on one thing then stop in the middle and start something else."

"What was it like in the water?"

"On the bell run I took the travel line over to the grout station. They had set the bottom structure. It looked like a big castle coming out of the mist. Parts of it were painted white. The bell guides. It looked like something out of Edgar Allen Poe. You had your thermoclines and shades of blue. You had visibility at night. I looked up and could just about see the surface."

"You could see the surface?"

"Yeah. I'd be out there and look up, and suddenly it dawned on me. A thousand feet."

"Did you see any fish?"

"After thirty days we had some grouper come in. Eight-footers. Probably weighed 800 pounds. They had a lot of sharks near the surface. People was fishing for 'em."

"Water must have been pretty cold."

"We had the hot water suits, so we couldn't feel it. It didn't seem as cold as the North Sea."

"What about the helium?"

"That felt cold."

"What mixture were you breathing?"

"I don't know exactly. About 99.9 percent helium and .1 percent oxygen."

"Did you have any work, or was it mainly inspecting?"

"We was there mainly in case something went wrong. If they broke a piling, we cut it in sections. The whole job was controlled by computers. They had sixteen mooring buoys going down with chains. They could move the structure an inch in any direction. They had RCVs with video cameras. One RCV picked up a suitcase on the bottom."

Remote controlled vehicles were often used in place of divers to perform limited functions under water. Equipped with hydraulic manipulator arms, they could turn valves, inspect sub-sea structures, or salvage small objects.

"A suitcase?" I asked.

"Probably from a boat."

"Those must have been some big pilings."

"I'd say they was about six hundred feet long. They had a special steam hammer imported from Italy to drive them." Larry sat quietly on his bunk and sipped Scotch.

"What was on the bottom?" I stared in awe at the warrior and envied him.

"Just mud."

"You think the bottom was stable enough?"

"I'm not sure. The mouth of the Mississippi has lots of slide areas. They lost whole structures out there where the shelf drops off."

"I wonder how deep the Gulf gets."

"A lot of places go to three thousand feet. I think the Mississippi Canyon is seven thousand feet."

"Did you feel excited about going so deep?"

"It was no big deal, really. I had been to five hundred feet in the North Sea. They did have to develop some new equipment, though. We had new burning gear. They had a one-thousand-amp welding machine and new winches. Everything had to be designed for the increased pressure."

"How much did they pay you?"

"Day rate." Larry smiled.

"You're kidding."

"I had agreed to make the dive before they told me about the pay, so I got screwed on that. I made another dive in the North Sea a few weeks later and got a three-thousand-dollar bonus."

"Same depth?"

"That dive was to one thousand and forty feet."

"You make it sound like it was routine already."

"We had a lot of problems on that dive. Half the crew thought they was bent. My hands felt like a tuning fork. I had vibration in the fingers. That was high pressure nervous syndrome. When it was over and I came out, my knee joints felt like they was rubbing together. I couldn't climb stairs. When you come out you feel drained. It takes about three days to get back to normal."

"Is it worth it?"

"It don't matter to me. I'd do anything to feed my family."

"There aren't too many people who belong to the thousand-foot club."

"You want to know what's really weird?"

"What?"

"Sometimes I'd be down there, and I'd get out of my bunk to go to the toilet and I'd take two steps and forget where I was going. I'd order a pitcher of coffee and forget about it until it got cold. Some of the guys couldn't remember their names when they came out. After a week they was okay, but it definitely affects short-term memory."

"And nobody knows the long-term effects of breathing helium."

"Yeah. Maybe in a few years one of my legs will be shorter than the other." He laughed.

"Helium's a strange gas."

"Yeah. Your mind's crystal clear." Larry cleared his throat. "The stuff leaked out the chamber, too. They had to add gas all the time."

"That's amazing. What else does helium do to you?"

"You lose your appetite. Everything tastes bland. We used a lot of salt and pepper. It makes you feel cold all the time. You get cold from the inside. Even with blankets on and a sweater I felt cold. I drank coffee, but it didn't help much."

"What about your voices?"

"That was funny. Topside always had a hard time communicating with us, because we sounded like Donald Duck. Trying to order dinner was impossible. They just sent down a menu and we checked off what we wanted. We drove those supervisors crazy. We'd get boozed up and send a whiskey bottle out the medical lock, and they'd be there trying to hide it from the oil company rep. They'd ask us who smuggled the whiskey in, but we just played dumb. They'd talk to us like we was children, give us a long lecture, and when they was finished, we'd say, 'Come back on that.'"

"How long did it take to decompress?"

"They brought us up at four feet an hour. I think it took ten days to come up. When we got up to a hundred and thirty-two feet, we stopped for over an hour."

"It must have felt good when that hatch popped open."

"Yeah."

✷ ✷ ✷

Rough seas continued to pound the barge. Ten-foot waves hit the starboard side, carrying salt spray through the pipe ramp. The barge rode the waves easily, though. In the galley the Mexicans played poker, and the welders played booray. Francisco, the Spanish steward, was playing with the welders. Somebody told me he had lost four thousand dollars the night before.

Shark Talk

We made a spiny dive in the morning, then the pontoon arrived, we installed it, and the barge began laying pipe. I didn't know where we were. We were going to lay 800 joints, then another barge, the *332*, would take over. It was on the other side of the platform acting as the pull barge. It kept a tension on the cable attached to the end of the pipeline, so as we moved forward, the pipe would remain close to the platform. The pontoon had four sections. The end was at least a hundred yards from the stern of the barge.

At noon, a ten-foot shark swam around the barge twice, then disappeared. Somebody threw a few welding rods at it, but it stayed on a leisurely course twenty yards from the barge, below the surface.

I had never seen a shark under water. Many of my dives had been at night in poor visibility, so I wouldn't have seen a shark, anyway. I had no fear of what I could not see.

Near midnight, the crane broke down, delaying pipe transfer from the supply barge, so we did not make any progress all night.

Larry and I stayed in our cabin and talked about sharks with Mark and Harvey. Harvey was the barge medic. He had spent time in Vietnam as an enlisted man.

I asked Larry what kind of shark circled the barge, and he said, "It might have been a bull shark. Hard to tell."

"You couldn't get me in that water," Harvey said. "I don't know how you guys do it day after day with those killing machines down there."

"You don't see too many around the rigs," I said.

"It takes only one bite, and it can take a leg off." Harvey spoke excitedly.

Larry didn't twitch an eyebrow. He sat quietly on the bunk.

"They say most people who are bitten hardly ever see the shark," Mark said.

"They're attracted to blood, aren't they?" Harvey asked.

"Yeah," Larry said.

"They don't bite because they're hungry. They just bite for the hell of it," Mark said.

"Or they'll bite something to test what it is, but by then it's too late," Larry said.

148

"They'll hit it with their nose," Mark said.

"They have the sensory system—"

"Lateral line system," I said. "They can detect vibrations in the water. Slow ones, like a wounded fish makes."

"Same signals as a thrashing swimmer makes," Larry said.

"I was swimming between two islands in deep water, about a hundred and thirty feet. I mean you'd start thinking about that shit. Something rubs against your leg. When I was in the Philippines I saw blue sharks. Streamlined, coming at me. When you have unlimited visibility they're like death coming through the water."

Larry and Harvey poured more drinks. I didn't drink. I munched on an apple.

"I saw a beached great white one time," Harvey said.

"They have the record for the most attacks against man," Mark said.

"It had four rows of teeth, and they were razor sharp."

"I was in Hawaii in Sixty-four," Larry said. "I don't know what happened, maybe temperature changes or current changes, but all the sharks came in. They had schools of sharks in the shallows. Fifteen-footers. Twenty-footers. They closed Waikiki beach. People was baiting them with beef carcasses and shooting them with high-powered rifles. Some Hawaiian kids would free dive, tie ropes around their ankles—"

"They're crazy," Harvey said.

"It happened in Padre Island last year," Larry said.

"I hope it never happens here," Mark said.

"I don't know if it was changes in feeding patterns, or currents, or what."

"I caught a ten-foot hammerhead once at the mouth of the Mississippi," I said.

"Sharks don't usually go in fresh water," Harvey said.

"They've caught them upstream," Larry said. "I used to swim in Sebastian. When I was in diving school I'd dig for clams in Sebastian Inlet, the Indian River side. I'd swim my distance swims out there because it was pretty calm. I found out it was a shark breeding ground." Larry chuckled.

"They get pissed at that shit, too," Mark said.

"I'd dig those cherrystone clams, and we'd have steamed clams, baked stuffed clams, and clam chowder—"

"You guys ever see a shark when you're working?" Harvey asked.

"No," Larry said. "We don't look like a fish with that umbilical trailing behind us."

"They could probably bite clean through that umbilical," Mark said.

"I'd like to see the look on a tender's face after he pulls it up," Larry said.

"And what about you?" Harvey said. "You'd be down there with no air."

"I'd have to haul my ass back to the surface pretty quick."

Mark and I laughed, and Harvey had a look of horror on his face.

Mark Spears a Big Grouper

The pipelaying went smoothly through the end of July and into August. The welders suffered in the heat of the pipe ramp amid the fumes, X-ray machines, and grinding wheels. They sweated under their goggles and leather bibs, and we heard the crackle of welding rods day and night as the pipeline took form and left the stern into the water. Life became easy for the divers. They still got their depth pay, but we had to deal with boredom. My logbook showed I settled into a routine.

July 27 – Laying pipe
   6 am – wake, breakfast
   6:30 – pontoon check
   8:30 – writing
   11:00 – lunch
   11:15 – nap
   5:00 – dinner
   5:30 – pontoon check
   7:00 – movie or reading or stocks
   9:00 – running
   9:45 – reading, mail, stocks
   11:00 – pontoon check
   12:00 – sleep

I visited the blenny on my pontoon checks. The secretive little fish loved its niche by the stern. It seemed curious about my presence, sometimes leaving its protective space to observe my gloved hand. The sea was so full of life. The pontoon was practically a coral reef. The moment something dropped under water, a fish, barnacle, shell, coral, or some other form of life started growing on it or claimed residence near it.

One day Craig woke me past midnight and told me to take a scuba bottle to the bow. The welders lost an X-ray machine in the pipe and a man was going to go in on a trolley and retrieve it. There was plenty of room inside a thirty-six-inch-diameter pipeline, but the man definitely had to be immune to claustrophobia. He was going inside a black tunnel under the sea, and the last four hundred feet was at an angle downward. He would have no communications and nobody knew if there was enough air in the pipe, so they wanted him to strap a scuba tank on his back so he could suck on a regulator, if he felt bad. I thought the task was worse than diving. I was glad they didn't ask one of us to crawl in that pipe.

Eric's eyes bulged when I showed him how to breathe on the regulator and check his pressure gauge. He was totally unfamiliar with the equipment, yet his life might depend on it. The foreman checked the knot at the end of a small sled with wheels, and he gave Eric a flashlight.

"Put the regulator in your mouth like this and breathe normally." I demonstrated.

"You mean like this?" He clumsily put his teeth around the rubber mouthpiece and took a few breaths.

"Right. And this is your pressure gauge. It'll tell you how much air is left in the tank."

"In this tank here?"

"Yeah."

Eric looked to his right. "You better keep a strain on that rope. I don't want to go on no roller coaster ride."

The foreman nodded. "Don't worry. I got two good men here."

I wished him good luck. He strapped the tank to his back, lay on his stomach on the sled, and entered the pipe head first. The men held the rope carefully and fed it while Eric pulled himself along. I went below for a cup of coffee. Thirty minutes later I returned to find the X-ray machine had been retrieved.

"Where's Eric?" I asked one of the men.

"Washing his face."

"Where did he find it?"

"I don't know, but he feels good to be out of that pipe."

I checked the scuba tank and found that Eric had used more than half the air. He must have been breathing hard, I thought. That's one thing about a skilled diver. He always stays calm under pressure. Never breathes that regulator too hard. You can always tell the experienced from the inexperienced. The veteran diver will have 500 pounds left when everybody else is out of air.

I went to the stern and charged the tank with the small compressor outside the dive locker. I noticed about twenty cabbage butterflies hovering around the lights. They must have all broken out of their cocoons at the same time. I returned to my bunk for some sleep before the noon pontoon check.

I came on deck around ten o'clock in the morning. It was warm and sunny. Mark and Craig were in the water on the port side shouting at Steve to throw them a rope.

"What's going on?" I asked Steve.

"Mark speared a grouper."

With the help of some of the Mexicans, we hauled the great fish out of the water. It was the biggest grouper I had ever seen. Mark and Craig dragged the fish to the stern and picked it up with a forklift.

I raced for my camera and took pictures. "Where'd you get that monster?" I asked.

Mark pointed. "Craig and I took a tug over to that structure this morning."

Mark and Craig were rabid divers. They would get in the water at any excuse.

"Mark got him right between the eyes," Craig said. "He was dead right away, otherwise, he would he dragged Mark across Campeche Bay."

Mark laughed.

I looked at the olive-colored Jewfish with its rounded caudal fin, eyes bulging, and the small hole in the head where the spear went in. I felt the slippery body, and it must have been seven feet long and weighed about eight hundred pounds. "How big do they get?" I asked Craig.

"I don't know. They keep growing and growing. I've seen them as big as Volkswagens. Could swallow a man whole."

I took more pictures, and Mark stood proudly by his catch and smiled. We showed the fish to the cooks, who said they were going to cut it, fry some of it, and make soup with the rest. We ate grouper fillets for a week.

No Air!

The barge stood by for three days waiting for a supply barge carrying twenty-four-inch pipe. We occupied our time with scuba diving and card games. Mark speared a two-foot grouper, and Craig surfaced with three red snappers. The superintendent lost money to the welders playing booray and poker every night.

We started laying a seven-mile line, which could take two weeks. I made the dawn pontoon checks with Lee.

When we were still close to a structure, Craig and Mark dived in the morning with their spear guns. Craig surfaced, appearing slightly rattled. "The grouper were aggressive. One almost knocked my mask off."

"The current's really bad," Mark said, panting.

"It's the worst I ever felt in my life," Craig said. "When I reached the ladder I almost got sucked under the barge. Then I ran out of air."

Craig showed only a face slightly tinged with pink; otherwise, he showed no emotion, and he wasn't breathing as heavily as Mark. I looked over the stern, and the surface appeared calm, except for an eddy by the pontoon hitch, but as I looked closer, I saw jellyfish particles and other ingredients of the great soup approaching the barge as if drawn by a magnet. The current was strong.

Craig had explained his crisis with aplomb. After ten years of diving, he must have experienced more terrifying things than running out of air and being sucked under a barge, but I couldn't imagine what they were. Running out of air is at the top of my list of terrifying things, especially if I'm at 130 feet. Close behind are being squeezed into a dishwasher (I tend to get claustrophobic) and riding a roller coaster.

✷ ✷ ✷

That afternoon, I practiced Spanish from a workbook, but the verbs seemed too hard, and I didn't think I would ever speak the language well. Later I watched a movie called *The Great Riviera Bank Robbery* where thieves tunneled through the sewers of a French Riviera town and stole twenty-five million dollars. The mastermind was caught, but he escaped to South America.

In the evening, a rat broke into the dive locker, ate two of my moths, and dragged away Lee's barracuda skull. It must not be eating well.

Only four of us were healthy. Lee had an ear infection and couldn't go in the water for at least four days. He told me he had some bone necrosis in the left shoulder, which bothered him from time to time. He could do anything under water that a twenty-year-old could, but he looked worn out, and I didn't know if it was from the helium, oxygen breathing, or the cold water, but this job eventually broke a man. Lee was scheduled to leave the barge soon, which will give him time to get his health back.

Steve had sinus block, so he was out of the water, too.

My ears were all right. After every dive, I rinsed my ears. My arms were one red mass of welts from wrist to elbow, though, because I had worn a T-shirt on a pontoon check instead of a long-sleeved shirt, and with my luck that was the day the water had to be infested with jellyfish particles. My arms itched like crazy.

During long pipelaying stretches, I had a great deal of time to think. Sometimes, while resting in my bunk, I'd visualize myself at 160 feet, that mind-altering place, three minutes from eternity. You can't leave in a hurry. It's like a Chinese finger trap. If you struggle too hard, you only get more deeply entangled. Keeping a cool head amid the swirling confusion was the secret to success.

Sometimes when I thought too much my doubts grew. Did I pick something out of my league? Time would tell. Five months at sea was nothing. I was still a novice. I had not made many deep-water dives. There were no short cuts. I thought about other divers. Some of them survived more than ten years. You could only wonder how they did it. Ten years of raw experience burned into their brains. If you met them on the street they looked like anybody else. It was those brain connections that made them special. That's what was so amazing about the human animal. Adaptability. What else did they have besides a cool head?

Dickie worked out in the weight room so he could pop four-inch bolts and lift a drift pin with one hand while straddling a pipe. I guess strength helped, but he got hurt anyway.

Lee was slowly wearing out. He looked like he stepped out of an office, but he had been diving longer than anyone, and that thick-skinned son-of-a-bitch could outperform any tender.

Mike, surface clown and underwater demon, never got hurt. I hoped some of his super confidence rubbed off on me. Whenever he went in the water flanges snapped together, clamps wrapped themselves around jacket legs, and L-bends found their place on the sea floor like a 747 coming in to a lighted airstrip, safely guided by radar.

Larry, cool, calm sleepwalker, needed to be alone in complete darkness at 160 feet to wake up. Anxiety? Never heard of it. It's all anticlimactic when you've come up from a thousand feet.

Craig, no nonsense, unemotional iceman, carried around the memories of Nordic adventurers. If you looked behind his ears he probably had gills.

We were all masochists taking the abuse every day, the pain in the ears, the cold water, the 120-degree heat inside the chamber, the current, the marine life, the surge. I guess once you got used to the shock treatment of sleep deprivation, the constant jarring trips from a soft bunk to a pounding sea, the uncertainty of never knowing what to expect on the bottom, the endless waiting on the surface, you could go on for months or years.

✳ ✳ ✳

I awoke at 3 a.m., watched a movie, ate a sandwich, made the morning dive in rough seas, went back to bed at nine, and woke again at four in the afternoon. Larry and I made the five o'clock dive on the pontoon, I stayed up until midnight not able to sleep, got up at three again, and stayed in the theater until six, when I went up on deck and found a beautiful sunrise. The sea was a dark blue peppered with whitecaps. The wind came in from port. The light hurt my eyes so early. I grabbed a wet suit top and dressed for the morning pontoon check.

Larry and I jumped in with scuba gear. The grogginess vanished as soon as the cold water enveloped us, and we kicked hard to escape the surge. A bad current was running to starboard. I took the lead, swam toward the end of the pontoon, and when I reached the third section at a depth of about seventy feet, I stopped and waited for Larry.

Something was not right. I looked at the pipe bouncing in the rollers, and it was fine, but I had a sense that things weren't right. Larry approached in a hurry. I casually grabbed my pressure gauge. The needle was dropping rapidly, perhaps fifty pounds a second. I hung by the pontoon and stared at the gauge, my mind a blank. The needle continued dropping, 1,800; 1,700; 1,600. Larry pointed to the ladder.

My mind clicked in gear. I grabbed the guide wire on the pontoon and pulled myself hand over hand toward the barge. At the back of my mind was that nagging thought. Will I make it? Will I make it? Thirty feet from the ladder, I sucked on a vacuum. The tank was empty. I held my breath, kicked furiously to the ladder, poked my head out of the water, and gasped air. I removed my fins and climbed on deck.

Lee stood there laughing.

"I don't think I ever saw you move that fast," he said. "With all those bubbles coming up, I thought we had another leak in the pontoon."

I caught my breath, checked the tank, and said, "Looks like it blew an O-ring."

"Let me get you another bottle."

Larry came out of the water and left his tank on while I waited for a replacement. "If you lose air, just pop the cartridge on your vest and surface," he explained.

Lee came back from the dive locker with a fresh tank.

"You should have seen him," Larry said to Lee. "He was hanging there watching all the air go out of his tank."

We finished our pontoon check without any further problems.

That night, Lee got drunk and stayed awake until four o'clock in the morning, but a few hours later, I woke him for the morning pontoon check. He said his ears were better, but I felt bad that I had disturbed him.

I saw a four-foot barracuda on the dive, but the water was murky, and the current was so bad we struggled back to the ladder. After the dive, Lee and I played a few games of darts, and he beat me three out of five, as usual. I asked him what he had to show for his years of diving and he said he owned some apartment houses and silver. He said he hadn't planned on being in the business so long, but no job could compare to diving.

I slept all day. Larry woke me for the 6 p.m. pontoon check, because Steve still had sinus block. Visibility was poor, and as we headed back to the ladder it started raining.

The rain increased during the night and a squall stripped the barge clean of rope, metal plates, cable strands, newspapers, paper cups, and anything else loose on deck.

In the morning it looked thoroughly scrubbed.

Barracuda, Tarpon, and Bangsticks

After six days the barge finished the line and set it on the bottom. We stood by for three days and waited for the next job. On the last day of pipelaying, Craig speared a barracuda, but it escaped.

Larry and I made a bottom survey on our pontoon check and found smooth mud at a depth of 117 feet. Lee asked for fourteen days of relief so his ears could recover, and he left on the crew boat in the afternoon. The company sent a diver to replace Lee, instead of promoting Steve.

"My wife's gonna have a baby soon. I could have used the extra pay," Steve grumbled. He looked dejected.

Steve began chewing tobacco. After five months at sea, we were all becoming hardened, but my attitude was slowly deteriorating. I still had my sanity, though. I didn't feel the need to grow a mustache, chew Skoal, or drink Scotch. Still, there was a mystique in sporting a mustache. Mark, Steve, Craig, and Dickie had mustaches. Maybe if I grew one, I'd look more like a diver and I'd get promoted.

✷ ✷ ✷

The barge towed for a day and set anchors in open water.

One morning I came on deck before dawn, sat on the bitt behind the chamber, and stared at a black sky full of stars. The churning black water, lazy and mysterious, slapped and gurgled against the barge. The sky turned purple, and I watched with awe the unfolding of a new day. The wind picked up, the sea threw whitecaps, and the water lost its mystery as it turned from black to silver and blue. The sky turned white, and the fireball peeked above the horizon. I could still look at it without hurting my eyes. The choppy waves acquired edges, and the dark forms on the barge turned gray and familiar. This was the time of day when my egg and bacon sandwich tasted good, in the cool quiet minutes when nobody seemed to be on deck.

We had seven free days while the barge set two heliport decks on new platforms. Five of us went scuba diving on the days we weren't towing around. Steve still had sinus block, so he stayed busy cleaning the dive locker and labeling the shelves. The barge arrived at a platform in the afternoon, but it was the wrong one, so the barge picked up anchors. In the meanwhile, we made a scuba dive.

I sat on a tubular horizontal support at seventy feet and chipped at a spiny oyster with exceptionally long spines. Brilliantly colored coral encrusted the jacket legs and conductor pipes. Red, green, and white patches nudged each other for all available space on the cylindrical structures. The inside of the platform was heavily populated with barracuda, pompano, tarpon, angelfish, and grouper.

Craig and Mark swam below me with their spear guns. Craig accelerated, his spear gun came within two feet of a small grouper, and he fired. The fish struggled for a few seconds, then went limp. Craig stuffed it into his bag.

Craig and Mark filled their bags until they were heavy, then returned to the stern dive ladder, but the barracudas followed. The barracudas wanted those fish badly. One tried to snatch Craig's bag, but he kicked the predator with his fins, and it rocketed behind a platform leg. Another barracuda arrived, then another, until five barracudas eyed Craig's fish. Mark chased one with his spear gun, fired, and missed. The attack seemed to unsettle the predators, and they gave the divers more room, but one brave five-footer still stalked Craig. Craig hung motionless in the water, watched the fish, and it cruised in slowly, slinking like a coyote toward a campsite. Craig poked at it with his spear gun. The fish darted out of range. Mark reached the dive ladder first, took Craig's bag, and climbed out of the water. The barracudas knew they had lost the battle.

I ascended, watching the barracudas closely, but they seemed to know I had only spiny oysters in the bag, and they left me alone as I swam through the open water between the structure and the barge.

✶ ✶ ✶

When the barge reached the second platform, we dived all day and found more spinys and fish. The barge moved again for the second heliport deck, and we dived on a new platform without much growth on the legs. Steve joined us and speared a tarpon, but it bent the shaft. We saw triggerfish, queen angelfish, tarpon, pompano, jacks, and grouper.

In the afternoon the sea foamed and turned purple, so we waited below deck. Craig won 900 dollars playing booray, a card game popular in Cajun country. The game was similar to Spades.

Larry walked the halls in a drunken trance. I liked Larry, a level-headed person who had taught me about the structure of a pontoon. It was awesome thinking about the dives he had made. When he was drunk, though, he caused some trouble at night, when those black days of Vietnam returned to haunt him. His pissing in the trash cans irritated the stewards, and I wondered if he still chewed on glasses and beer mugs, as he had during his motorcycle riding days.

Skies cleared, and the sea, which had scared us away in anger, invited us back with gentle swells. When we stood at the rail, we looked down into clear turquoise water and saw the anchor cables.

In four days, we finished a twenty-inch line three miles long from Abkatum A. We made a horseshoe curve pattern around a proposed new platform. Abkatum was a small complex of two oil-processing platforms, a drilling platform, two satellite platforms, and one flare stack. Walkways connected the drilling platform with the processing platforms on either side, and the flare stack was attached with a walkway to the left platform. A fifty-foot yellow flame roared day and night.

Lee came back with a smile the last week in August, and I carried his bags below. He said his ears were fine and he was ready for work. Larry went into shore for some relief.

We had not heard anything about Dickie, except one day Steve said, "He's just sitting around his house building beer can castles. He'll be back soon."

Seas became rough when we set the line down. Lee went to the bottom, a depth of 130 feet, and unhooked the cable. Steve and I pressurized the pontoon and helped secure it in the davits, but the work was difficult in the choppy seas, and we were out of breath when we came on deck.

A tug almost sank when it was moving anchors, and everybody thought it had caught a sunken wreck, but it pulled free.

✳ ✳ ✳

A tug towed the barge to Akal for a long pipelaying job. The pipe was thirty-six inches in diameter, like most of them in the oilfield. Steve said the job could last three months, but I didn't believe him. The inspectors changed their minds as often as the sea changed its demeanor.

Lee and I had the morning pontoon check. We went to the bottom, a depth of 104 feet, and the water felt very cold past seventy feet. I saw many tarpon. The popular sport fish grows to eight feet and can weigh up to 360 pounds.

I played darts with Lee after the dive, then took a nap.

In the afternoon, I enjoyed the beautiful weather on the stern with Steve and Ed, the substitute diver who lived in Colorado.

"You ought to explore Mexico on your time off," Ed said.

"Yeah? Where?"

"They got some nice spots on the road between Merida and Villahermosa. Pyramid ruins with big slab doors. Inscriptions look like flying saucers. One place has a waterfall with a lake. I think that's a hippie hangout."

Mark came out of the dive locker carrying a new bangstick.

The bangstick was a six-foot-long pole with a shotgun shell in the end.

"I'm going to get a tarpon," he said, putting a scuba tank on his back.

"They're down there," Steve said. "I saw a six-footer."

"You guys giving up on your spear guns?" I asked.

"I have to try out my new toy," Mark said.

"Those tarpon always bend my spears," Steve said.

Tarpon had unbelievably tough scales. I had witnessed Steve firing a spear from only a foot away, and the spear had glanced off the tarpon's armor.

"How close do you have to get with one of those things?" I asked, looking at Mark's bangstick.

"You have to touch them." Mark put on a mask and fins and jumped in.

"Mark doesn't look too happy since he came on board," I said.

"His wife might divorce him," Steve said.

"He told you?"

"Not exactly. My wife is a friend of his wife, so my wife told me. His wife's tired of being alone while he spends all his time offshore."

"Why did he get married? He should know this isn't the kind of business for a family man."

"He's thirty. How long you expect him to wait?"

"I don't know."

I looked out at the water and scanned for Mark's bubbles. It was peaceful on the stern. Some Mexicans chipped paint. Harvey sunbathed on top of the pontoon shack. Martrell, the assistant superintendent, staggered around glassy-eyed. Juan napped in the forklift, and the blue sea burned our eyes with its brilliance.

We waited fifteen minutes, and Mark surfaced.

I tried to help him with his gear, but he said, "Get out of my way, son."

"What's the matter?" Steve asked.

"Shotgun shells won't detonate."

"Maybe they're getting wet," Steve said humorously.

"Yeah. Why don't you waterproof them?" I asked. "There's some Black Magic on the bench." Black Magic was the stuff we used to repair wetsuits. It was like rubber cement.

Mark left the scuba tank by the ladder and walked in the dive locker.

He returned, put the scuba tank on, and said, "These should work." He jumped in again.

"Why does he want to kill tarpon?" I asked.

"Maybe he wants to hang one on his wall," Steve said.

The struggle to catch a tarpon could be rewarding, but I didn't see any point to killing one. People didn't usually eat tarpon, but sharks did.

Steve looked down at the water. "He probably won't get any. He won't come close enough."

Mark came out of the water again, and Steve said, "Well?"

"Didn't detonate." He threw the bangstick on deck. "I paid a lot of money for that damn thing."

A Brief Interlude on Land

Dickie came aboard on the afternoon crew boat, and Ed left for the *332*, another barge. We were all happy to see Dickie.

In the evening, we sat in the divers' room and watched a movie. Dickie told us of the world outside Mexico, and he gave me a Time Magazine. He seemed to have aged, and his mustache was trimmed and his hair neatly combed.

"It's nice having the family back together," Craig said.

"What did I miss?" Dickie asked.

"We were doing an SBM tie-in near Abkatum. They picked up the line and buckled it. Chink was hot."

"I speared a seven-foot grouper," Mark said.

"Where?"

"Akal J. You should have seen it."

"Yeah," Craig said. "We got sick on grouper that week."

"How's your thumb?" I asked.

"It was fractured in five places. I can't bend the last joint." Dickie held up his hand for all to see.

"Taylor offer you anything?"

"My lawyer's talking with them."

"When are they going to break me out?" Steve asked.

"Not yet," Dickie said. "There are only fourteen divers working in the Gulf. Howie was arrested for cocaine. He'll probably get five to ten years. Pugliese was fired for carrying a can of Mace in the London airport. Mexico is the only place working."

"What about the North Sea?" Mark asked.

"We might be going back up there. My buddy at 2W said another crew of English welder-divers got run off a job. They can't do anything right. Guess what? Singapore wasn't happy with 2W or Hydro, so they asked for people from New Orleans."

2W was a British diving company. Norsk Hydro was a Norwegian oil company.

"I'm not going overseas to work," Steve said. "I've got a family."

"You have to take what they give you, but it looks good here. Comex just got run off a job. The *279* will do it. They're doing tie in after tie in. Of course that's saturation."

The *279* was a Brown and Root barge equipped with a saturation diving system that specialized in underwater welding.

"I'm not going to tend for six years," Steve said.

"I don't know what to tell you, Steve. Mexico's the place. Vail said they're forming a new company. They're going to call it Taylor International."

"A lot of divers are going to Mexican or Norwegian companies," Dickie said. "Pay is better."

"I heard that."

"Protexa is paying eight fifty for sat work," Dickie said.

"Not bad," Mark said.

"Even Divex pays better than Taylor," Dickie said.

"What do they make there?" Steve asked.

"Two hundred a day plus depth."

The boom years were finished, I sadly realized. The golden years of commercial diving were the 1960s and 1970s. Oil prices were about to plunge, grinding worldwide oilfield construction to a halt.

✳ ✳ ✳

The crew boat left the barge at noon. I sat on a padded bench behind the galley with my suitcase between my legs. I closed my eyes, but couldn't close my ears to the whining high speed cadence of the diesel engines as we bounced over choppy seas toward Ciudad del Carmen, the port of call for the oilfield. Once a sleepy little town, del Carmen boomed. Crew boats arrived from the oilfield every hour. Tugs loaded supplies. Workers departed crew boats and headed for their homes in Oaxaca, Veracruz, Mexico City, Chiapas, and Quintana Roo.

I felt strange leaving the floating world where the work was, where my life was. I was leaving my life behind, going to have a quiet interlude, ten days, where I would remember how to be a landlubber again. Ambition can take you places, can't it? How'd you like to get up every morning not knowing where you are, eating breakfast at noon and eating dinner twice a day? How'd you like to work for some boss who never told you his schedule? Report to work, it's cancelled, then up thirty-six hours, sleep four, up again, then a storm and you're down for three days rolling with the barge, drinking, sleeping, watching movies, and then on deck again, then under water for thirty-eight minutes but it feels much longer, then under pressure in the chamber.

Working offshore was like working in a paradox, uncertain, unpredictable, not to mention the Mexican inspectors who couldn't make up their minds. They were like the sea. The sea. It took the form the wind gave it. We raced to finish a job before the next storm came, then waited, waited, waited. Whatever happened to day and night? Out of sequence, stretched, folded, stuffed in a suitcase. I guess it's a tolerable place for some, a stepping stone for others, and hell for the rest. If you miss your family and kids and spacious home and color TV and stereo, that's too bad, because you're making plenty of money, but if twenty years got behind you, you deadened the pain with alcohol. When your wife started bitching, you better call it a year.

I looked at my watch. The big hand was a pipe joint and the little hand was a bolt studded with hex nuts. For me there was surface time, chamber time, and bottom time. Bottom time was intense, unforgettable. I could still hear boat bumpers tangling with chains from my bunk.

What had I given up? A neat, Monday-to-Friday clockwork life for unpredictable days ruled by the sea. An air-conditioned office for wind, salt, sun, rain, and water. An alarm clock for anchor cables unwinding. A spiffy suit for ragged jeans. Daily mail delivery for the hope it might come in six days. A night of sex for dreaming about it. A comfortable house for a ten by ten cubicle shared by four. Dropping money into a sieve for letting it pile up, never spent. Diversions and entertainment for a chance to commune with fish.

I had no wife or children or home, though, so the world on land didn't pull hard on me. It was a time to relax. I felt so relaxed when I stepped off the boat. The ax fell in one great chop, and all anxieties, troubles, and fears fell away. My ears were still ringing from the crew boat engines, but I was absolutely at ease, with a clear mind and conscience. As I walked past sleepy Mexican restaurants I knew I had entered a different world. People sat at curbside tables and chattered in a strange tongue. Vehicles, buildings, roads, stores, and trees my eyes had not seen in half a year seemed new and fascinating, as if I were Robinson Crusoe returning to civilization. Had the world changed much? No, not in Ciudad del Carmen.

Many people lingered in the town square. I looked for a taxi, because I wanted to get to Merida for the morning flight to the States.

A taxi stopped, let out a passenger, and I asked, "*Quanta dinero a la Merida?*" I was still swaying with the sea.

"No."

I found another five minutes later. "*A la Merida?*"

"No." He hesitated. I stood and waited, not knowing about the bus. Then he said, "Okay. Seven thousand pesos." I quickly calculated the amount, 120 dollars. Pocket change.

The driver drove to his house to tell his wife. I heard them talking, and she looked out the window to see what kind of a gringo could afford a taxi to Merida. He returned and we started the journey. He called his dispatcher, and I heard an excited voice on the speaker say, "Is that a millionaire?" The taxi driver didn't say anything. To me, the eight-hour trip was not unusual. It was costing me less than a days' work in the floating world, but in Mexico, the land of the sinking peso, it was many months' work for him.

The journey took us through dry, hilly land. In the middle of the night the driver stopped at the side of the road and slept a few hours until dawn. My knees pressed against the front seat of the tiny car and I couldn't sleep, but I didn't want to complain and tell him to drive on, so after an hour I managed to reach a comfortable position and slept for a short time. We continued through a quiet town where men slept with their sombreros over their eyes, and later in the morning we reached the airport. I gave the driver 3,400 pesos and sixty American dollars. He thanked me and I walked into the departure area. I didn't have to make any complicated decisions. There were only two gates.

✳ ✳ ✳

I arrived in New Orleans late in the afternoon and bargained for half an hour with an airport official to get my car back. In my haste when first departing the States, I had parked my car in a restricted area. Airport officials had towed it away. The banks were closed, and all I had was about $350, so I offered him $300, and he took it. The car started easily.

I drove along the highway past the bread factory, where I could smell the bread baking; past the Superdome; LSU Medical Center; Shell Square, that clean white marble tower; then up the bridge. I saw the Hilton by the river and a big rusty ship was making the turn at Algiers Point.

Everybody zipped by me as I drove to the West Bank. They seemed to be rushing somewhere. I didn't know what their hurry was. The air was warm and humid. People were washing their cars, shopping, coming out of restaurants and movies, fueling up their cars, and when I drove near Danny and Clyde's, I thought of their delicious shrimp po-boys I hadn't eaten in such a long time. It made me hungry, so I stopped in, bought one, then drove on and checked into the Holiday Inn. The room was a palace compared to what I had been used to. It had a TV with a remote control.

I called my dentist the next day, because I had a loose filling. "Could I make an appointment with Dr. Cohen?" I asked the secretary.

"I'm sorry. He doesn't work here."

"Is this Dr. Cohen's office?"

"No. This is Dr. Weller's office."

"I thought this was Dr. Cohen's office." I was sure I had the correct number.

"He passed away two months ago. Dr. Weller is seeing all of his patients."

"What happened?"

"A diving accident in Florida."

I was shocked. "I'm sorry."

"The doctor said it was the worst case of embolism he had ever seen. He passed out near the surface and never regained consciousness."

"He wasn't that old, was he?"

"Only thirty-six."

"That's really unusual."

"I know. It didn't make sense. He was always a health fanatic. Never drank or smoked. Ran every day. It was his certification dive, and he was being extra careful, but you know how he was. He had a bad cold, but went anyway."

"Gosh! I can't believe it."

What kind of cruel irony was this? A young dentist gets killed on his certification dive, while I have done far more dangerous things and suffered only a few cuts and bruises.

I thought about the last time I had sat in his chair. He had seemed impressed with my diving stories. Perhaps he had been so enraptured on his first open-water dive that he had forgotten to exhale on ascent. That was the only explanation I could think of. I didn't think he'd try to be smart and hold his breath on purpose, to see what it felt like. Some of those one-day scuba courses were bullshit, pushing people through before they were ready. People didn't die on their certification dive because of a cold, did they?

Late next morning, I drove to the mini-storage on Whitney Avenue. A cop stopped me, because my auto tag had expired. I told him the car hadn't been driven in six months, but he gave me a ticket anyway. I rented a larger storage space so I could park my car in it and spent all day transferring everything from one unit to another.

I spent three more days in New Orleans, but couldn't relax. It was moving too fast. I wanted to get back to Merida, where the pace was slower, more sensible. I saw an old friend who was once in the diving business, but now sold real estate. Like so many other young men who had wanted to be divers, he had abandoned hope after five years. He struggled to make a living. He and his partner had an office in a converted duplex in Gretna.

After the new dentist put a filling in my bottom right molar, I parked my car in storage and took a cab to the airport on a sunny afternoon. I left without regrets. While America was rushing off to meet the future, I flew to Merida September 8, 1981, and in one hour I went back in time. Things changed slowly down there. It might have been a corrupt town, but the people hadn't sold their souls to the technological juggernaut to the north, yet. More proud of its past, Merida didn't care about the future. In another hundred years the Zocalo, the town square, would probably look the same as it does now. The streets needed work and the houses looked old, but the people were warm and friendly and the girls were beautiful.

I checked into the Hacienda and explored the shops. I was glad to be back. It's always more fun when everything around you is unfamiliar.

Walking along the avenue toward the center of town I passed a residence, an empty lot overgrown with trees and tall grass, a garage, an open-air doctor's waiting room, a small business with typewriters for rent, more empty lots divided by crumbling concrete walls, and a long stretch of houses, all painted white. A policeman directed traffic where five streets intersected. The park along Avenue Itzaes had a zoo, a place for horseback riding, a miniature train that circled the perimeter, and a circular roller-skating path. The public buses smoked badly and they looked like American school buses painted white. Four out of five cars were Volkswagens. Motorbikes buzzed in and out of traffic. The four-hundred-year-old town had succumbed to honking cars, buses, and Coke factories, but the past lived on in the old restaurants, hotels, and narrow streets.

I bought a leather belt near City Hall. People swarmed in the banks exchanging dollars for pesos. The lines extended out the doors. I must have waited forty-five minutes before reaching a teller. One guy came in, went to the front of the line, and squeezed in. Nobody seemed to mind.

★ ★ ★

Three nights in Merida passed quickly and I prepared to go to sea. I looked at the old rotary phone in my hotel room. I couldn't make a call if I wanted to. The phones didn't work much of the time. I didn't want to make a call, anyway. I was tired of efficiency, tired of super efficient America with all its rules. A few days there and all I had was hassles. I was glad to be back in Mexico.

The air conditioner didn't work effectively. The room was too humid. I got a cold soft drink from the refrigerator in the room and sipped it. In a few hours I'd hear the whining diesel engines. I was ready. I wondered why Soyla said "I'm not your *Chiquita*" when I walked her to the cab. What's wrong with a little pretended romance? I had only a few days remaining on land, but she didn't know that. She was too *tranquilo*. I'll have to remember that place. Casa Trabajo. Corner of Avenue Itzaes and Calle 90. It looked like a snack bar. I came to the window and a beautiful bronze-skinned Mayan princess named Ana Delia took my order. She was on the menu and her price was two thousand pesos. Casa Andres was strange. A two-story house in a quiet neighborhood, front lawn, iron fence, wooden gate, big wooden door, old man answered, it was bright and cheery inside, like I interrupted a family's evening Scrabble game, two girls on the couch in the dining room with a big carved table, children playing in the room to the right. I paid the old man, Maria and I went into the next room, the man closed the wooden sliding doors, and I still heard the children playing.

My thoughts returned to the present. I looked around my drab room. I sipped on the drink and counted the pesos I had: 4,200. What would I do with all this money? Where I was going I didn't need money. I decided to save it for the next trip.

I got out my logbook and glanced through it. About forty pontoon checks. Salvage pipe joints. Check cable on the bottom at 135 feet. L-bend salvage to 132 feet. That was a good dive. Remove a clamp at 136 feet. Impacting. More than sixty working dives. Was I getting there? How many dives did I have to make before I was considered one of them? My job title was diver/tender, a diver in training, but my pay was only half of a diver's. I still longed for that elusive promotion, when I wouldn't have to do surface work any longer and could experience bottom time every day.

✷ ✷ ✷

I flew to Ciudad del Carmen September 11 and boarded a crew boat at noon. The boat was full of sleeping Mexicans and the toilet overflowed with vomit from men who had consumed too much liquor and couldn't tolerate a bumpy ride. No one said a word. I settled into a padded bench behind the galley, crossed my arms, and closed my eyes. It was going to be a long ride.

The crew boat stopped at each barge in the oilfield and arrived at the *L.B. Meaders* after dark. The ride had taken about eight hours. It was enough time to get my mind in gear for whatever was waiting, but the sea didn't have any pity on the drunken men. They looked pale facing a trip up a boat bumper on a heaving windswept barge. From a distance, the barge looked mysterious and foreboding, floating quietly on a moonlit sea. The halogen lamps exposed parts of the gray machinery against the angular silhouette of the long vessel. The black latticework of the derrick crane rose into the sky, and blue and white lights along its length cast brilliant halos. No men appeared on the barge deck. It could have been a ghost ship. I was back in the floating world.

A Mexican Loses His Hands

Time beat against the barge, and the unpredictable green soup stretched to the horizon. I adjusted my mind to another self-imposed exile. Not much had changed on the barge. Craig had paneled the dive locker door. He had also paneled the walls inside the locker door and burned the wood to bring out the grain. The divers on board were Dickie, Lee, and Larry. Steve was taking time off.

I didn't know where we were, and few platforms stood on the horizon, but we were depositing a pipeline on the sea bottom from one unknown source to an unknown destination. We had crisscrossed the bay with so much pipe, I thought even the Pemex inspectors didn't know where half of it went. We started a line and after a week or two were interrupted, so we put it on the bottom and buoyed the end, but the inevitable storms tore off our buoys, leaving miles of unfinished pipe that may or may not have existed on some engineer's map.

In the afternoon, there was a commotion in the welding area. A group of men carried a Mexican boy in a stretcher to a waiting helicopter.

I asked one of the welders, and he directed me to a welder's helper.

"It was horrible," the man said. "You didn't want to see it. The poor kid."

"What happened?" I asked.

"Wasn't listening when the whistle blew. Had his arm against the pipe. Lost his balance when it started moving, and the tension shoe took his hand in. He screamed and tried to get it out with his good hand, but that got caught, too. Oh, God. Both were just mangled stumps. Made me sick to my stomach."

"Somebody should have pulled him off that pipe before it moved," a welder said.

"There wasn't anybody around."

With a swirl of wind and dust, the noisy chopper took off and careened over the water, and all was quiet again.

The seventeen-year-old boy had not heard the whistle signaling the pipeline was about to move or didn't know what it meant. I wondered if Pemex bothered to train the boys who came to work offshore, or whether the accident was simply the result of a moment's carelessness.

That evening Jack, the senior welder, came into Dickie's cabin and said, "We're starting a collection for the boy. We would appreciate it, if you gave a little something."

"I'll give you a hundred," Dickie said.

"I'll match that," Larry said. He looked around the room and the rest of us agreed to contribute something.

"The boy won't get anything from Pemex," Jack said.

"Figures," Dickie said.

"They said he's of no further use to them. He's a burden to them, now."

"What kind of company is that?" Mark asked.

Jack shook his head. "Those boys don't have any benefits."

Dickie took some bills out of a box in his locker. "He'll never be able to work again."

"That's some company," Mark said.

"You don't understand Mexico," Larry said.

"What do you mean?"

Dickie handed the money to Jack. "The Indians aren't even human beings to the Spanish. They might as well be cattle."

"They have a union. They have rights," Mark said.

Jack shrugged. "Some rights."

"The right to get killed," Larry said.

Wheel Job in Rough Seas

One afternoon we were laying pipe in open water. The sky filled with thick thunderclouds and a squall hit. I stood by the stern rail as an ugly black mass approached. The wind hit my face, and the water became choppy and opaque. The daily crew boat had already stopped at the *Meaders*, picked up some men, and headed for Ciudad del Carmen, but it returned a while later, its propeller entangled with rope and cable.

Problems seemed to come in pairs. We had to set the pipeline on the bottom and clear the fouled propeller before the storm hit.

Steve had worked the previous wheel job, so it was my turn. I dressed in a wetsuit top and jeans. I wore Playtex rubber gloves under my cotton gloves, because I would be doing some cutting with the oxy-arc torch, and the rubber gloves reduced the chance of electrical shock in the water. I also clipped a hacksaw into my rope belt.

The crew boat limped in at sunset and tied off on the port side. The sea kicked the boat around like a toy. Larry was on the radio, and Steve operated the knife switch, which controlled the current flow. The torch cable was connected to a 300-amp welding machine.

I jumped into a swirling sea with the torch cable in my hand. I kicked hard and swam under the stern. Bracing myself between the hull and the propeller shaft, I groped in the darkness. Thick nylon rope intertwined with one-inch steel cable was tightly wrapped around the starboard shaft.

A wave hit. The boat rose five feet and took my breath away. The boat came down, knocked me against the hull, and I gasped for air. I tried to place the electrode on the cable and not cut the shaft in half.

"Make it hot!" I ordered Steve to throw the knife switch and complete the circuit.

"It's hot."

One strand popped. "Make it cold!"

"It's cold."

A wave came through. I sucked air from the regulator and held my breath. With one hand on the end of the steel electrode the other holding the handle, one foot against the port shaft, back against the hull, faceplate six inches from the cable, I tried to see how much had been cut and where to cut next. My stomach muscles cramped. I pressed the trigger. "Make it hot!"

The oxygen stream shot out the end of the hollow electrode, and the electric arc melted the steel. My fingers felt the hot slag jumping out of the cut as they guided the shrinking electrode along the cable. Cables were always hard to cut. Twisted strands made cutting difficult. I didn't want to press too hard and burn the shaft. "Make it cold!"

"It's cold."

The fourteen-inch rod had shrunk to two inches, and I removed it from the torch head. I grabbed another from the quiver hanging from my belt.

Another wave slammed into the boat. I gasped. I consumed the electrode, then another, and the tangled mass separated a little. "That's it. You can pull up the burning gear."

"Roger."

I reached down and groped for the hacksaw. I sawed in quick strokes against the nylon hawser while bouncing up and down, banging my head against the hull, having the breath knocked out of me, straining in the cramped space. Visibility was poor. My fingers told me how much was left to cut. My joints ached.

"How much longer are you going to be? You've been down almost an hour."

"It's almost through. Give me five minutes." My hand traced the tangled mass of cable and hawser.

"You feel sick?"

"No."

"Larry can go down next."

I cut more, and the mass released its choke hold.

"There it goes! The whole mess fell to the bottom of the sea."

"Picking up your slack."

"Roger."

I surfaced, climbed the boat bumper ladder, took the mask off, and said, "What a ride!"

The men watching were happy. They jumped on the crew boat. The engines started, and the boat sped away.

"Let's get the pontoon disconnected before the sea rips it apart," Larry said.

I showered, dressed, and helped Mark move the burning rig to the stern. The barge pulled forward and dropped the pipeline to the bottom. It started to rain heavily. Ten-foot swells rolled through. The wind stung our faces.

Larry came out of the dive locker wearing a wet suit top and said, "It's too rough to blow the tanks on scuba. I'll do it with surface air."

We had to pressurize the front compartments of the pontoon with air; otherwise it would sink.

Larry put the mask on his head and jumped into a raging sea. I tended his umbilical. The umbilical shook like a mad snake every time a wave crashed into the barge. Larry connected the crane line to the pontoon, and the crane swung the pontoon to the port side, where it was calmer. Larry climbed on top of the first section and straddled the tank. He looked like a spaceman riding a giant three-segmented worm.

The waves came from stern to bow, and each section of the pontoon rose in sequence as the mass of water passed under. The hinges groaned, as they extended beyond their usual arcs.

The rain pelted us, stung our eyes, and the deck became slippery. We fed Larry an air hose. One hundred feet of umbilical was in the water, and it dragged across the barnacle-encrusted pontoon with every surge. I was worried that the umbilical would be shredded.

"Don't let too much slack out," Dickie shouted. He was worried. We were all worried. Larry held on tightly with his legs, rode the monster up then down into the valley, and he screwed in the air hose and pressurized the front two tanks on the pontoon in about fifteen minutes. When he was finished, he fell off the pontoon into the foaming sea. I pulled him to safety.

The crane transferred the pontoon to a tug that towed it away, but we weren't finished.

The pipeline rested on the sea floor, and we had to disconnect the pull cable.

"I don't like this at all," Dickie said.

"I'll make the dive," Lee said.

"Be careful."

Lee came to the stern wearing a wetsuit top and jeans. He slipped on a pair of fins. The sea continued to rage.

As I was about to put the mask on his head, the crane block smashed into the pontoon shack. Glass flew everywhere. All of us danced out of the way, but one of the Mexican riggers grimaced and walked away holding a bloody arm.

"Let's get this over with!" Lee shouted.

He put the mask on, I tightened the straps, and Lee disappeared under chaotic waves that boiled and leaped straight up. I tended the hose, Dickie manned the dive station, and Larry stood by wearing his harness and booties, ready to jump in if needed. Chink and the Mexicans fought the crane block, but Dickie ignored them. He stood calmly in front of the dive station and protected the logbook from the rain. Dickie took a depth reading when Lee reached bottom, and the gauge read 110 feet.

I heard Lee on the phone. It didn't sound good. He grunted and gasped for breath. I knew the cable was whipping around with an unpredictable tremendous force.

"Give me some slack!" he shouted.

I lowered ten feet of hose into the water.

"Give me some slack!"

"His hose must be fouled," Dickie said. "See what you can do about it."

"I don't want to drop any more," I said.

"Can you undo the shackle?" Dickie spoke into the phone.

"I'm trying to . . . uhhh . . ."

"What's the matter?"

"Cable almost hit me. I'll try to get it from the other side."

"Forget about it, Lee. Abort the dive."

"I can't get near the thing."

"Stand by to leave bottom."

"Roger."

Dickie pointed to me. "Pick up the diver's slack."

I strained to pull umbilical up. "I'm pulling! It won't move. It's tangled."

Dickie turned to the radio. "Your hose is fouled."

Lee's voice hissed from the speaker. "I know. I'm working on it."

"Can you clear it?" Dickie asked.

"Wait . . ."

"Can you clear your hose?"

"Try it now."

I pulled, and slack came out of the heaving sea.

"I'm leaving bottom," Lee said.

"It's too rough, Chink," Dickie said.

"We'll pull ahead a little and wait."

Dickie stood calmly making notes in the logbook, while everything around him was out of control. A thirty-foot wave could have crashed over the stern, and he still would have crossed every T.

Lee surfaced and looked all right, but the sea had claimed one fin. His wetsuit top showed a long brown stain where the greasy cable had glanced off his upper arm.

"One fifteen," Dickie said.

Lee and I marched across the slippery deck fighting wind and stinging pellets.

"Are you okay?" I asked Lee.

"Just a scrape." He held his arm.

Lee entered the chamber nude and pressed against the hatch while I cracked the intake valve, keeping one eye on the needle of the gauge and the other eye through the porthole. The needle rose, but Lee put his fist up. I stopped the descent. He was having difficulty clearing. I released some of the pressure and brought him up to thirty feet. He held his nose and wiggled his jaw a minute. He gave the thumbs up signal, and I took him down to forty feet and sat in the rain for twenty minutes.

At three in the morning, Lee came out of the chamber, and we stopped diving.

The barge rolled heavily and turned into the wind. Huge ground swells unleashed torrents of salt water over the bow.

We retreated to the quiet below deck.

What a night! Nothing like some rough seas to spice up pipelaying.

Tales from Vietnam

We slept, watched movies, ate, got drunk, and waited for the storm to pass. The barge creaked with the swells, and the tractor tires and chains banged against the sides. Mark secretly took a crew boat to del Carmen to buy liquor for Lee and Larry. He also looked for *mota*, but the *Federales* had been arresting dealers, so Mark returned with only liquor.

While I itched from the ringworm on my arm and crotch, Larry and Harvey drank Scotch and entertained me with their heroic tales of Vietnam. Harvey had been tortured by the Viet Cong and couldn't conceive children anymore. Larry had killed a few of his buddies by injecting them with morphine, to end their suffering. To them nothing was glorious about war. Larry still had nightmares of finding himself in a bomb crater with a big hole in his chest.

Larry had been a Force Recon marine out of Fort Bragg. He had been to language school, learning many dialects of Southeast Asia. In the southern part of the country, Korean and French were spoken, while in the north, Cambodian was mixed with Chinese.

Harvey was an E5 who had been demoted to E1 twice in one year.

Larry and Harvey had killed many men in Vietnam. Harvey boasted about killing a Viet Cong tax collector. I listened innocently. I was in a room of battle-hardened veterans and I had tried to avoid the draft when I was in college.

Larry spoke unemotionally. "We did a lot of recon. During Operation Phoenix we did a lot of neutralizing—"

"Neutralizing. Ha!" Harvey slapped his thigh.

"That's right. We killed a bunch of 'em. Here Harvey. Try some of this." Larry gave him a glass of Scotch.

"All right, I'll take some."

"We'd have a list of names."

"Oh yeah?"

"We killed a guy at his wedding one time. Dropped him at the alter and left." Larry smiled a crooked smile.

"We had orders to kill this psychological warfare major," Harvey said. "That's what he was there for. Strictly psychological warfare. They gave us five photographs and said okay, we'll be flying you in by chopper within forty clicks, and you'll have to go the rest of the way yourself. They dropped us between two mountain ranges in Cambodia. We humped our ass for a day and a half. Couldn't break radio silence. On short rations. We weren't carrying anything heavy. We had just enough ammunition to hit and run. Our mission was to kill him and his five goddamn staff officers. We found the guy, all right. Among 2,000 other troops. Went in under cover of night, garroted him, knifed him. Damn near got our asses shot coming out of there."

Larry looked at Harvey. "We'd take a sniper with our team. Those guys were all business. Like some college professor carrying a 700 Winchester in a fiberglass case all padded and shit—"

"Those snipers could take down two or three men with a bolt action rifle. If they didn't get two men in three and a half seconds they felt like they were messin' up."

Larry took a sip. "One time we was coming out of a tree line and all of a sudden the sniper stopped and fired. Put his rifle back. Half an hour later we found this dead gook sprawled over a rice paddy with his eyeball hanging out."

"That's how good they are," Harvey said. "They'd work as a team. Two of them. They'd joke about it and make bets. Okay I'll bet you five dollars I hit the first three in the front row right between the eyes. And they're talking 1,000 meters away. They'd knock down three men in four to five seconds. They had those big silencers. Smooth as glass. Pop! Pop! Pop!"

"We used to spot for them with seven-fifty binoculars," Larry said. "They'd shoot one in a group. They'd be sitting there yakking, and one of 'em would keel over. They'd still be yakking and shake him, and then all of a sudden they'd look down, and it dawns on them. They see a hole, and they get this look on their face like they just stepped into a pile of dog shit."

Harvey laughed. "Too late."

"They're already zeroed in on the next one. You can see them looking around in sheer terror."

"They know the sniper's hitting them, but don't know where it's coming from. They had a bounty on any Rangers and Special Forces."

"I know," Larry said. "They called us one night and congratulated us on being the most wanted team in the I Corps."

"We used to find wanted posters in the goddamn jungle stuck on trees," Harvey said. "They offered a 50,000 or 200,000 piaster reward, and they'd have a picture of us just as clear and slick, and we'd say where'd they get that? Doesn't that tell you something?"

"They zeroed in on our ass up there. Our logo was the ace of spades with a death head in the middle. . ."

I looked at Larry. His eyes were getting wild. I knew he wasn't on the barge anymore. He had seen much death, and those horrors would stay with him for life, much like the intense experience of bottom time that gets burned into the psyche, so he could relive the past with detail and accuracy in a drunken revelry.

Harvey and I laughed when Larry told us of a time when his patrol encountered an NVA patrol. Along a ridge line, the two groups of soldiers had cursed each other, then gone their separate ways.

"I mean, why kill each other?" Larry said.

Larry sat motionless on his bunk, with his drink balanced precariously on his thigh. "We raced 'em one time in the DMZ getting to a downed spotter pilot. We was in a hell of a firefight, and those spotters was coming in dropping flares for us, and they crashed, and the NVA was going and we was going. We was in a running firefight. I bet we wasn't fifty yards apart. They was trying to get to them and we was trying to get to them, to get the pilots out and blow up the plane—"

"Yeah, before they—" Harvey shifted on his chair.

"We got them. I always used to get stuck with that shit because I was the corpsman."

"I was probably the only medic that carried forty pounds of demolitions on my back. I carried an M-79 grenade launcher and a forty-four-magnum pistol."

"After we got that bounty on our heads they decided to put us on a recon relay. They was gonna take us out of action for a month. We'd stay up on a hill. We took cases of Coke, stationery, suntan oil—" Larry emphasized each syllable. He was being sarcastic.

"You weren't gonna do shit," Harvey nodded.

"We got up that hill, sat down, called in, and got hit that afternoon. But first was a platoon rush come up and we hit the first gook with an M-79 in the chest. All you could see was a helmet and a pair of boots go flying across the top of the hill. They started rushing us, and we was gonna wait until we saw the whites of their eyes and then blow the shit out of 'em. Some asshole had put the piston in backwards in the M-60s. Fired one round, and it jammed."

Harvey snorted. "Oh shit."

"Couldn't get a helicopter up there. It was a saddle. An old infantry position on 881, where they had Hamburger Hill. So we had little bunkers and stuff. We couldn't get our dead out, because we were having to pull back, and they'd send in air strikes. If they was breathing we'd drag 'em by the collar, drop 'em, regroup, and charge again."

I stayed quiet and sober. I looked at my tape recorder. I was taping the conversation.

Harvey bent over and scratched his leg. "Thousands died up there."

"Took the hill and then gave it back to them."

"Yeah."

Harvey was getting excited. He waved his hands in the air and spilled some Scotch on his shirt. "I was in the whorehouse when Quang Tri was getting hit. I'd hear a crak! crak! crak! crak! crak! You know. What's going on? Then crak! crak! They were getting closer. You can always tell when somebody shoots an RPG. Shit, I couldn't get my pants on—"

Larry finished his glass and poured another. "We were in camp one night getting ready for a seven-day patrol next morning. We had this new guy. Real jumpy. He couldn't get to sleep. His knees was shaking. We had a battery near us. We was laughing at him. Lay down and go to sleep. Finally he got to sleep, and we heard a different boom and looked around and heard another boom and was looking at the stars, and I don't even remember what happened, but the hootch was gone and I was sitting in a trench the next minute, and I didn't even know how I got there. They just blew the whole thing off its stanchions."

"Here. Have some more." Larry gave Harvey the bottle.

"Yeah. When you're a medic you get some jobs."

"What was the worst job you ever had?" Larry asked.

"I don't know. Probably the time I had to take a leech off the balls of a scout dog."

We laughed.

"After that he wouldn't let me near his cage. He'd growl and try to attack me."

"I think the worst job I ever had was when they brought a boy in whose head looked like raw eggs. I couldn't treat him, but we were near the DMZ so I took him to an NVA hospital. I just walked in and told them, "Look I'm at your mercy. Just treat the boy." They did, too. Lanced the blisters and cleaned them, but my driver in the jeep he must have had a heart attack seeing all those North Vietnamese.

"Lost my first wife from that shit. Right after we moved to Texas there was a thunderstorm. I was sitting naked on my hands and knees looking through the slat in the window, and she jumped up and said, 'Larry, what's the matter?' and I said, 'Get your head down! They're walking the rounds in on us!' She thought I was wacko. Another time I had jumped up and stuffed her between the bed and the wall. She was hollering and crying. I was still functioning, but I kicked her off in the corner and slapped her and said, 'Keep firing! Keep firing you sonofabitch! They've broken through the lines!' and she's sitting there going, 'What?'"

We laughed.

Larry continued. "In Old Tucson, I took my wife and her friend down in the dirt when some cowboys staged a shootout."

We laughed again.

"Man, you feel like an asshole. There's tourists from all over the world, and you're in the middle of the street with your wife by one collar and your friend in the other. I looked up and said, 'I'm with the cowboys, ma'am.'"

Harvey nodded. "Yeah that shit stays with you."

"All of my routine dreams have quit now. Mine are kinda symbolic. They say you can't get killed in your dreams, but I did. I died once on the side of a hill rappelling. I got the shit blow'd out of me coming off the ropes. One time I was watching them pull bodies out of a river, and they turned one over and it was me, shot through the head."

"That freaks you out don't it?"

"Scared the shit out of my wife. I'd dream about my partner who was shot in the throat Thanksgiving '66. I don't even celebrate Thanksgiving any more. He lived about three hours. I'd see him in a fog. He would come up to me, and I'd tell him, 'Don't look at me like that! I've done everything I could!' and then blood would gush out of his throat, and I'd give him one more shot of morphine."

"Yeah. I overdosed a lot of 'em on morphine."

Harvey grew somber. "They did some bad things to people—"

"We did some shit, too. Force Recon had free kills. Anything that moved. We shot anything— people on bicycles, on garbage dumps. One time we whacked an Army platoon. They used to give us six clicks— a free-fire zone for recon— anything that moved. They were told not to go in there. An Army second lieutenant took his platoon down there because he didn't think there was any action where they were. They told him it was a recon, and you know, we lived on our nerves anyway, six-man team and—"

"You don't have time to guess who's out there in the dark," Harvey said.

"They went in and set up an ambush. Well, we walked into it, and one guy—it must have been the machine gunner— was on safety. When he threw it off safety it made a click, and when you live in the jungle—"

"That's a trigger," Harvey said.

"There's nothing in the jungle makes a sound like that. We dropped out and fired 200 rounds into the platoon, and I don't know how many M-79s in a split second, you know, each man working. And we heard Americans. Some of them was screaming and crying. We killed a few and shot a bunch of 'em."

"It can go both ways, though."

Larry sat closer to the edge of his bunk. "I'll tell you what. We had an Army tank run our ass one day. We was pissing blood. I ain't shitting you. You try humping, and we was in the bush. I mean we didn't dress like normal people anyway, camis, painted, soft cover—"

"Lot of guys killed over there because of friendly fire," Harvey said.

"What a term. Friendly fire."

Harvey looked down at his feet. "I got shot one time. In the ankle. A nine-year-old kid shot me before I could shoot him."

"I don't have any feeling in some of my fingers. Can't smell things either. Maybe it was the Agent Orange. One of my girl's ears is folded over." Larry held up his glass. "Drink up, Harvey. Tomorrow's a rumor." Larry filled his glass for the third time, then stood and walked behind the door and urinated in the trash can.

"Those stewards aren't going to like you for that."

Larry cursed the stewards.

"Hey, are you taping this?" Harvey asked me.

I smiled and nodded my head.

"A lot of good men died over there. I don't think it's funny."

I quickly turned off the tape recorder.

"It's over," said Larry. "What's the big deal?"

"I don't think it's funny, that's all."

"Have another drink and cool off."

"Dream, my ass. I can't have kids anymore because of that shit. They tortured me, and he thinks it's funny."

"I don't think it's funny," I said.

"What do you know?"

"Take it easy," Larry said.

"Yeah. I need to get out of here. Think I'm gonna grab some chow. I'll see you later." Harvey left the cabin. He was a big man, and I didn't want to tangle with him.

Larry settled in his bunk, finished the glass, and poured another one.

A Panic Attack

In my bunk, blue curtain closed, hearing the water outside, thinking about a soft bed at the Hacienda, quiet, no machinery running, the peaceful tropical quiet with only a bird in a palm tree, lying next to smooth skin of Soyla, not knowing where she came from or why, knowing nothing about the work far away, the bed on firm ground, feeling mellow from the beer, not knowing or caring about two hours later, not caring about anything except the smoothness, the stretched-out moment, unhurried; now in the bunk holding the moment, reliving it before it slips away, while outside a chain clanks as a reminder, and the comfortable bunk, thoughts clinging to it, is warm. The light comes on, a voice says, "Time to go to work," and suddenly the portal shuts and everything is hard as ice. Still numb on the halfdeck before sunrise where the air, fresh and cool, rushes by, still unthinking, shocked into awareness by the whine of an air starter, then the rumble of compressors, drowning out the other, and the drifting, dreamy, edgeless space is closed by a rivet gun. A skinned knuckle on sheet metal, a hard wooden deck rolling on a cold sea, a heavy tank on the back, a weight belt, a wet suit top tight at the wrists, a metal zipper hard to close, cotton gloves, a rubber mask over the face, teeth clamping down on a regulator, fins on the feet, and then another shock, the plunge in the water, as I, absolutely awake, flood the pontoon tanks at 6 a.m. with Dickie, and we fight a strong current.

Later, we installed the pontoon, and Mark guided the line in. Dickie felt tired, because Lee had kept him up all night. The pontoon looked like it had taken some punishment the past few days. I noticed a crack on the second section and a leaking control hose on the T-2 remote header.

We finished the line after two days and set it down on a calm evening.

Nobody knew what the next job would be.

✶ ✶ ✶

Usually I am calm under water, but one day I almost panicked. We had set a Z-bend next to a structure, and I jumped in to take some measurements and check the position of the Z-bend.

Tired from a sleepless night, I reached the thermocline at 100 feet and grew anxious.

Craig's voice came through the speakers. "Give me a pneumo on the top of the flange."

"Okay."

Uncomfortable in the cold water, I hung on the side of the pipe for an unbearable amount of time before bubbles came out of the pneumo hose. The dive had just begun, and already I felt miserable.

"Give me natural bottom."

"Roger." I dropped to the mud. A strong current ran from port to starboard. Getting to the bottom sapped my strength.

"A hundred and twenty-two feet."

"It's cold down here."

"Take a measurement from the flange to the jacket leg."

I swam up ten feet, tied a quarter-inch rope to one of the flange holes, then swam to the structure. Where the rope met the platform leg, I inserted a small welding rod between the strands and twisted the rod to keep it in place. "I have it."

"Good. Where's the clamp?"

"The top of the clamp is—" I took a few breaths. I was out of breath. "The top of the clamp is about three feet above the flange."

"That clamp will have to come down."

"The clamp door is open."

"Go over to the far leg."

"The far leg?"

"They want some measurements there."

"Going over to the other leg." I untied the rope, stuffed it down my wetsuit top, and pulled myself along a horizontal. The jacket leg loomed in the distance. It was a phantom in the speckled, syrupy water. The horizontal was heavily encrusted with spiny oysters.

Halfway across, I stopped. I didn't know why I was out of breath. I couldn't get enough air to my lungs. I concentrated on my breathing. What was wrong with me? Was I working too hard?

The oral-nasal bib of the mask had leaked, and I breathed in a small amount of saltwater, which made things worse. I coughed. I had to slow down and get my breathing under control. I looked up. I considered aborting the dive, but that would be quitting. I couldn't stand the thought of being ridiculed.

I rested on the horizontal support. I opened the free-flow valve, and a blast of air hit my face. My heart was racing. How much longer? What am I going to do? Am I going to freak out? There are worse things than freaking out at 120 feet. Relax. Relax. Relax. I turned the free-flow valve to a trickle and kept going. I reached the jacket leg. "I'm here." I spoke in a whisper. My head was on fire.

"Any clamps?"

"No."

"Give me a pneumo."

"Take it."

"What's wrong? You're coughing."

"Breathed in a little salt water—"

"Got the pneumo. Give me the circumference of the leg."

I took the rope out, swam around the leg, and inserted another welding rod where the ropes met. I still didn't have my normal breath. My face felt hot. My mind was like mush. All I thought about was breathing. Controlled breaths. In-out-in-out-in-out. Like meditating. "I have it."

"Stand by to leave bottom."

That sounded good, but I was a long way from the down line. I swam to the line. The current helped. "Ready to leave bottom."

"Leave bottom."

I came up, fighting the urge to panic. Don't, don't, don't— it was only a hundred feet, but it had to be a controlled ascent, or I might as well stay down. One foot a second, but the barge was in the next county. I felt the panic attack coming— I have to get the hell out of here! I'm going to freak out, I'm going to freak out, No! No! No! No! You'll make it, it's close now; it's better, hand over hand, there it is— the bottom rung. I'm back. The fear subsided. I was okay. I grabbed the ladder, took off my fins, and climbed on deck. I stumbled before Craig.

"You all right?"

"I'm out of breath."

"Two fifteens."

I crawled in the chamber and couldn't stop coughing. I closed my eyes and breathed oxygen. I gradually relaxed and felt better. I don't know why it happened, but I never wanted to go in the water again without enough sleep. I needed plenty of sleep.

I came out, and Mark said, "You had me worried."

"I'm all right."

"You can go below. We're picking up anchors."

"Where are we going?"

"Back to that place where they drove a piling into a line. We're going to disconnect the SBM."

I showered and changed. The coughing stopped. I couldn't expect every dive to go smoothly. I couldn't let it bother me. They were a few bad moments, that's all. I shrugged it off, went below, and ate dinner.

I went to my room. Lee was packing his bags.

"How long you gonna stay on the beach?" I said.

"Three weeks."

He looked worn out and tired. His face was unshaven.

* * *

Craig came into my cabin one morning and led me down the hall. He wanted to show me the electrician's new toy, an Apple computer.

"Ever seen one of those things?"

"No."

I looked at the strange machine. Aaron explained how to operate it. In a few minutes, I learned what the Return key was for and what a floppy disk was. He loaded a chess program, and I battled the machine. Craig left the room. I played the Najdorf Variation of the Sicilian Defense and beat the program in less than an hour with a simple back rank mate with a rook.

I went to the divers' room and Craig asked, "Did you fry the thing's circuits?"

"Yeah. On level four. Maybe level nine is harder, but you have to wait forever for it to make a move."

"Aaron says he can never beat it except on level one. Even then he has a tough time."

"Aaron just needs a few chess lessons from me."

I was a pretty good chess player. I had learned in college.

Craig Finds a Horse Conch

Months passed, but the weather remained warm, and the sea never changed. The passage of time could not be measured by the change in seasons. My calendar said it was October, but it felt like July.

Our pipelaying was interrupted by something new. We were going to disconnect a mooring buoy and install it in deep water near Cayos Arcas, a remote place north of the oilfield. A single-buoy mooring system, or SBM, allowed tankers to fill their holds with oil without taking the risk of going into shallow water.

We towed all night, and I slept soundly. We arrived at the SBM at 6 a.m. to overcast skies and began diving.

The buoy looked like a big orange can, forty-five feet in diameter, and it bobbed slowly in a dark, green sea. Three thick, flexible hoses ran from the bottom of the can to the sea floor where they tied into a pipeline. The top was covered with walkways, pipes, ladders, and hoses. Below the water, a ring encircled the can and held the chains that stretched to the bottom at a forty-five degree angle. Each link was about a foot long. Around the can, sections of rubber served as boat bumpers.

By midnight, we had disconnected four chains on the top. We also had to remove the three flanges that held the hoses below the buoy. Twenty-four nuts held each flange together.

I dived under the buoy with scuba gear and a three-foot-long crescent wrench. I removed a nut, so we could put the right socket on the hydraulic impact wrench. I must have worked more than an hour trying to get that huge nut off, and I consumed most of my air. The job was worse than trying to change the oil on a moving tank. I hung upside down, legs straddling a flange, stomach tensed, with no leverage. I gasped for breath from the regulator in darkness, bouncing up and down with the swells. It would have been a messy job cleaning vomit out of a scuba regulator, so I didn't get sick until I climbed on deck.

Craig said, "Get some sleep. We'll finish it."

When I awoke, I learned Mark had loosened most of the nuts with the impact wrench. He had come up nauseated, too, and vomited on deck.

Craig had finished the job before dawn and had gone to sleep. He didn't get sick. His steel gut could take anything, even working upside down under a bobbing can for two hours.

When I saw him later, he said, "It's not so bad with a helmet."

Larry disconnected the last two chains, and the tug moved the buoy out of the way by late morning. We slept most of the afternoon, waiting for a material barge to arrive. In the evening, we cut two chains at their pilings on the bottom, but then Pemex decided to let *Sarita* finish the job, and the barge towed near Ixtoc to stand by.

We rested for a day while the riggers worked on the buoy, which sat on a barge tied alongside.

We stood by for another day while the inspectors decided what to do with us.

Craig paneled the rest of the dive locker with plywood. He took an acetylene torch and lightly burned it to expose the grain. If he had enough time he could probably panel all the living quarters. He got bored quickly, like the rest of us. We didn't like waiting. We worked at such a high level of energy that after we recouped our sleep, we needed to do something productive.

At night I won fifty-five dollars from Harvey playing darts. Poor Harvey lost money everywhere, first to me, then playing poker and booray.

I sat in the galley and watched Ray, the senior welder, win a pile of money on a good poker hand.

He said, "You heard Anwar Sadat was assassinated?"

"No, I didn't," a welder said.

"Anything that happens over there can affect the whole world," another welder said.

"What could it mean?" I asked.

"I don't know. Maybe a lot. Maybe nothing, but when those Arabs start disagreeing with each other, you can bet oil prices will move one way or another."

I had no idea how much oil controlled our lives. I didn't know what was happening in the world outside, but our days were numbered, because oil prices would collapse the next year.

We towed to a location nearby, set anchors at 1 p.m., and prepared for a short pipelaying job of only twenty joints. The pontoon arrived, we installed it by evening, and the welders finished late the next day. They had a lot of problems, so we didn't set the pipe down until 10 p.m. All day, fireboats sprayed the deck with water, because hot flares nearby turned the barge into an oven. The barge picked up anchors at 1 a.m.

The barge towed for a day and a half and set anchors in dark blue water with no platforms in sight.

I came to the stern and Craig and Mark were checking their spear guns by the dive ladder.

"You coming?" Craig asked.

"Yeah," I said. "Let me get a tank." I went into the dive locker, changed, grabbed my gear, and hurried out. "You don't waste any time, do you?" I asked.

"Nope." In his jeans, denim shirt, black and red scuba mask on his head, snorkel tucked in the left side of the mask, black fins on his feet, cotton gloves on his hands, spear gun loaded and attached with a lanyard and clip to his rope belt, tank on his back, regulator hanging over his right shoulder, Craig looked like Neptune's son. Any free time we had, Craig was in the water.

"What's the depth here?" I asked.

"Hundred and eighty," Craig said. "Water looks nice."

We jumped in and headed to starboard. The water was so clear, I was floating in the sky. Craig and Mark looked for fish in open water, while I hung on the anchor cable at 160 feet and watched the show. The huge three-dimensional playground belonged to us. In a few minutes, a large tarpon appeared, flashing its large silver scales. Craig and Mark chased it at a depth of about 100 feet. Mark kicked furiously, came to within ten feet of the tarpon, and fired. The spear glanced off. The tarpon disappeared with a few powerful strokes, leaving Mark with a spear bent at almost a right angle. Somebody should have reminded him about those thick scales.

I performed tricks on the cable like some superhuman gymnast. I did somersaults and backward flips. I balanced on the cable with the edge of a fin.

Two more tarpon approached, streamlined ghosts that come out of nowhere. Craig gave chase and fired, but they were out of range. They swam by me not more than fifteen feet away, their armor looking like a feudal knight's chain mail, and I saw their big black eyes and their never changing expression.

In a moment they were gone on their far-ranging journey. I had no other fish to focus on in my private aquarium with unlimited visibility.

I began my ascent up the cable. I caught a glimpse of Craig, heading toward the bottom at 180 feet. He disappeared in a fog, and I saw only his bubbles.

I ascended slowly, because I didn't know how much time I had spent at 160 feet. I knew I had exceeded the limit for no decompression, so I hung on the bottom rung of the ladder for a few minutes.

On deck, Mark showed me his bent spear. He was angry.

Craig surfaced, cradling something large in his arms.

"What did you find?" I asked Craig.

"A horse conch." He held up a two-foot-long brownish orange shell in a perfect symmetrical form, wide in the center, radiating to a sharp point at its apex, with a long siphon canal. He had found one of the largest gastropods in the world, the Florida horse conch (Pleuroploca gigantea).

"That thing must be heavy."

"He didn't want to leave the bottom. I had to kick damn hard to get him up."

"That'll make a nice addition to your collection."

✹ ✹ ✹

We towed to Cayos Arcas, where we will set the mooring buoy. Craig said our paychecks would look better, because the depth was 160 feet. Depth pay would be ninety dollars a day. I could make 250 dollars a day, if I dived.

We arrived on a sunny day and anchored in open water next to a rusty can buoy. Craig told me we had to find six chains on the bottom and determine if they were long enough to reach the surface. Another barge had driven pilings in a circular arrangement into the sea floor and attached the chains that would hold the mooring buoy in place. There were supposed to be can buoys on all the chains, but we saw only two bobbing in the deep blue water.

In the evening Craig made the first dive down one buoy line and connected the crane line to the end of the chain. The crane picked it up, Craig took a depth reading when it was fully extended, and we found that the chain was only fifty feet long. We set it down, and told the inspector. Pemex decided we should disconnect all the chains at the pilings, and bring them to the surface, where lengths could be added.

Larry dived and inspected the shackle at the piling. He succeeded in hammering the pin halfway out. With a depth of 160 feet, our bottom times were limited to thirty-eight minutes. Our decompression consisted of three water stops: three minutes at fifty feet, five minutes at forty feet, and eight minutes at thirty feet. Those were followed by three fifteen-minute oxygen breathing periods in the chamber.

Dickie separated the chain from the piling and shackled it into the crane line. We slept for a few hours while the riggers added lengths of chain.

We made two dives to connect the chain to the piling. Late in the afternoon the barge repositioned itself next to the second can buoy. Steve came aboard in good spirits and bragged about his baby girl. He said he had been in the delivery room and the doctor had asked him if he wanted to cut the umbilical, but he didn't want to. He was afraid of cutting umbilicals. He told the doctor it was something about his job.

At 9 p.m., Craig told me to put on a wetsuit. A night dive to 160 feet worried me, but the job seemed simple. I had to find a chain and shackle it into the crane line.

The stern was deserted, except for the divers and Martrell, the assistant superintendent, who sat on a bitt on the port stern. He seemed to be sober as he watched me put on the weight belt. On this strange and lonely night the barge floated alone on a black sea. No platform lights broke the darkness. The water was calm, though. The water invited me in.

The crane block disappeared into the water off the port stern next to the can buoy.

Craig said, "I'm going to make sure you guys get paid for all these dives. It's risky being underneath all that heavy chain."

"I forgot about the money," I said, "but now that you mention it, it would be nice to get paid."

"After we measure all the chains, they have to sandblast the buoy. That will take days and we can go scuba diving."

The air in the mask smelled cool and fresh. With the left hand holding a flashlight and right hand holding a rope that led to the sling under the crane block, I jumped in with barely a splash and found the buoy cable.

Hanging on the buoy cable, comfortable, ready for the long elevator ride down, checking the mask, breathing calmly, I said, "Come down on the big rig."

I descended. Thirty feet, forty, fifty, swallowing, clearing the ears, floating, sinking into a bottomless well, seventy, eighty, ninety, breathing slowly, listening to the exhaust gurgling out the side of the mask, which was a well-adjusted good piece of equipment, one hundred, one hundred and ten, getting colder, one hundred and thirty, one hundred and fifty, and then in pitch black darkness, my feet touched soft mud.

I said, "All stop."

"All stop on the crane line," Craig repeated. His voice was faint and distant and I had to hold my breath to hear him clearly. The buoy cable angled away, but the rope in my left hand was tight. Which direction do I swing the crane line? I took a guess.

"Swing the big rig to the operator's right."

The rope slackened. I crawled a short distance. I collided with a steel object. I touched the curved shape. "I'm at the piling."

"Good. Is there any chain down there?"

"Yes, there's some chain."

"Go to the end of the chain."

The end of the chain. Where's the end of the chain? I had a clear head a minute before, but I couldn't think anymore. It was bad enough not being able to see, but it was dangerous when you couldn't think. I was under the spell of nitrogen narcosis.

Resistance in the umbilical prevented me from moving freely. What had caught the umbilical? The buoy cable continued around the back of the piling, out of reach. My hands were full, and my umbilical was fouled. I didn't know what to do for a moment. The simplest things can become extraordinary problems under water. I turned on the flashlight. It was useless. The weak arc of light reflected the tangled hoses and cables. Darkness piled on darkness, and even a flashlight had a tough time cutting through it. I grew anxious.

I passed under the buoy cable and around the piling. I pulled on the umbilical, and it seemed to be free.

"The buoy cable is wrapped around the piling. I have to follow it out." I tried to sound as if I had everything under control.

"Roger," crackled a weak voice.

I crawled along the mud. I bumped into a pile of chain about my height some distance from the piling.

"Lot of chain down here . . . still searching."

"Did you find the end yet?"

"No."

I groped around, slid my hands along the strange shapes, and tried to construct a mental picture. I had no sense of direction. Touch was everything. I felt soft mud, smooth metal, and the texture of a braided cable.

"The buoy line should be connected to the end of the chain."

"Oh."

The buoy cable's on the end of the chain. Don't get distracted by all the chain. It's the end you want. Where's the end? My fingers moved along the smooth cable, and it ended at a chain link.

"I found it."

"Good. Shackle the crane line into it."

The crane line was somewhere above. How do I bring it to me? I looked up into the darkness and took a deep breath. Last time was to the right. Let's try left. "Swing the big rig to the operator's left."

The rope slackened, I pulled it tight, and when it reached a vertical position, I said, "All stop."

Perhaps it was luck, or perhaps my navigational abilities in complete darkness were improving. "Come down on the big rig."

"Roger. Coming down."

The rope descended slowly, and soon my fingers felt the large shackle on the end of the crane line. "All stop." Prone in the mud, I connected the chain link. "The chain is attached. Now what?"

"Go back to the piling. I want you to inspect the shackle there."

"Roger. Do you want to get some of this chain off the bottom first?"

"We can do that."

"Come up on the big rig."

"Coming up."

Carrying on a normal conversation with the man on the surface wasn't easy. I counted the heavy chain links as a sort of mental exercise to fight the narcosis. "There are about ninety-two links."

"Are you at the piling?"

"Roger."

"Does the shackle have a tack weld on the end of the pin?"

I took my glove off and felt the slight lump on one side of the shackle. "Feel's like it."

"We're going to pull the chain up now. You can ride up with it."

"Roger. Let me go back to the end of the chain." I followed the links along the mud and ascended perhaps thirty feet.

"Come up on the big rig."

I rode up with the chain. Soon warm water entered the wetsuit top, and I knew the surface was near. Glimmers of light appeared.

"Come up a little, and you can start your fifty-foot stop."

"Roger. Looks like the chain isn't long enough."

"I think they're all going to be too short."

I hung motionless for the required three minutes, feeling happy to be back. It was a great ego boost to make a successful dive. I spent five minutes at forty feet, eight minutes at thirty feet, then surfaced.

Mark greeted me with a pat on the back. The halogen lights on the stern were a welcome sight.

I spent an hour in the chamber.

✶ ✶ ✶

We searched for the third piling. The last four pilings didn't have buoys. After four unsuccessful dives, we learned that Pemex had the coordinates, so the barge moved, and we found the piling in one dive. On my dive, I found a crescent wrench, a screwdriver, and something that looked like a chicken bone, but otherwise, I went in circles in total darkness for thirty-eight minutes along soft mud.

Craig connected the crane and measured the chain, Mark burned off the tack weld and knocked the pin halfway out, and Dickie removed the pin by 7 p.m., and we retired to our bunks.

In the morning, Craig made the first dive to search for the next piling, but found nothing. Mark dived and found it, but it was buried in the mud. Pemex told us to shackle the chains together.

I made the first attempt, but after thirty-eight futile minutes, I surfaced, having accomplished nothing. The chain hanging vertically was swinging slowly, and I couldn't align it with the heavy links in the mud.

Larry consumed all his bottom time on his dive, but he connected the links.

The fifth piling didn't have any chain on it, and the sixth was difficult to find. We made six dives one day without success. Two divers from another barge helped us.

Steve came up with a foot-long starfish and lots of auger shells, which lived in the soft muddy bottom in holes. We thought the piling was buried in the mud, but in the morning, the survey boat dropped a buoy, and Mark found it quickly. Three more dives, and we were finished with the chains.

The barge would pull test each chain to 270 tons, sandblast and paint the mooring buoy, and connect it to the chains, before we installed the flanges.

When I was feeling good about getting depth pay for seven days, Dickie gave the tenders bad news. The company sent a telex with the instructions that tenders were not to dive deeper than seventy-five feet, unless a supervisor was on board.

Mark and Steve were angry as hell.

Craig said he would talk to the barge superintendent.

Cayos Arcas

While the barge prepared the mooring buoy, we made scuba dives around Cayos Arcas, which was a great way to escape surface time. Cayos Arcas was a group of three coral islets about 125 statue miles north of Ciudad del Carmen, far from the main oilfield, and if you went farther west, Campeche Bay dropped off to 1,000 meters. The largest of the islets, Cayo del Centro, was only about a mile long and a few hundred yards wide with no trees, only a lighthouse and a tower. Some small fishing boats were anchored along the beach. The other islets, Cayo del Este and Cayo del Oeste, were nothing but dry patches where coral had pushed up out of the sea. The coral reef extended around the islets at depths of forty-five to ninety feet, and frigate birds populated Cayo del Centro. A shipwreck lay in the shallow water off Cayo del Este. Somebody said there was a warship buried nearby.

In the morning, we took the Zodiac, a rubber boat, and eight scuba tanks to an area south of the lighthouse island, Cayo del Centro, where the depth was about forty feet. The motor didn't work on the Zodiac, so we paddled it into shallow water and anchored it on a reef. It was a calm, sunny day and I wore jeans and a long-sleeved denim shirt.

We found coral formations and sandy canyons squeezed between cliffs, with numerous caves full of lobster and red snapper. I collected conch shells, whelks, cowries, and other unusual shells, while Craig and Mark hunted with their spear guns. Craig caught a lobster in a coral cave, and the animal ripped his gloves to shreds. At another cave, he poked his spear gun in and fired. Clouds of coral particles and debris poured out of the cave opening. I swam closer, peered inside, and saw a grouper with a spear through its belly, banging its body against the cave walls in a suicidal frenzy. Craig pulled it out and stuffed it into his mesh bag.

When the tanks ran out, we put the fish and shells in the Zodiac. Two of us paddled, while the rest held on to the sides and kicked with fins for about a mile before the tug picked us up and brought us back to the barge. We were all exhausted from the long swim. The first expedition netted us ten grouper, one snapper, two helmet shells, one lobster, one crab, and assorted shells.

One day we explored an area south of Cayo del Este. Larry stayed behind. He felt sick from too much drinking the previous night. The tug dropped us off, and we paddled to the reef. Craig secured the anchor on a ledge.

I descended to the bottom. Huge coral domes twenty feet high surrounded sandy patches littered with dead coral and shells. Sea fans gently swayed with the current. Angelfish floated past my mask. A patch of elkhorn coral grew like a brown garden, and brightly colored fish nibbled at the sprouts. I looked into a cave, and three red snapper stared at me.

Craig and Mark speared snapper and sea bass in the coral domes. I observed a two-foot-long grouper with a worried look, gills moving, mouth open, and it swam slowly, but it accelerated with an incredible burst of speed across my field of vision. Perhaps my presence disturbed it. I found brain coral and a green variety I'd never seen before. It looked like a bush with thick stems that had been clipped cleanly on top, and each stem split into two and ended in a green tip with a radial pattern that resembled a photographic slide carousel with slots. Along the bottom I found a helmet shell and a large conch.

I came up and saw Dickie putting a beautiful piece of elkhorn coral in the Zodiac.

We returned to the barge with about twenty-five snapper and grouper, and I had shells and coral. A pack of barracudas followed us as we paddled to the tug, but I didn't see any sharks. The red snapper in those caves were the biggest I had ever seen. Some were three feet long. I decided to call the place Snapper Mountain.

On the third day, we threw the Zodiac motor in the mechanic's shed, because it never ran. Billy looked at it for fifteen minutes, shrugged his shoulders, and said, "It ought to run. Maybe it doesn't like salt water."

We speared ten fish and six lobster in an area east of Snapper Mountain, and I found a queen conch. We also saw a spotted moray eel about three feet long in its coral cave. I found new varieties of coral every day.

We swam over fields of staghorn and elkhorn coral. We passed between massive spherical boulders, every square inch populated with colorful fish and invertebrates. We poked around sandy clearings surrounded by forests of coral and sea fans, swam through living arches and tunnels, sailed over miniature canyons, peered into crevices and caves, traversed vertical walls so densely packed with life that every hand had to be carefully placed. We turned over dead shells in sunny valleys, rested in the shallows, and watched wave action kick sea fans to and fro. Staghorn coral grew in clumps like shrubs, with narrow brown branches that broke off easily. Fields of staghorn with interlocking branches formed a network of passageways, ideal protection for the fish. Other forms looked like deer, elk, or moose antlers. Brain coral grew in a dome shape with curved serrated folds and grooves. Some varieties produced massive ten-foot-diameter spherical formations. Fire coral grew vertically in brittle plates that looked like the walls of a maze and the edges were lighter in color. It stung when touched. Some coral looked like flowers, with thick stalks ending in radial green designs; some grew toward the surface in huge meandering formations; some remained near the bottom in oval discs etched with thin grooves; some grew in small clumps like lettuce; some grew flat and wide with jagged edges; some grew flat as a pancake. Some coral looked like the surface of the moon.

When we returned to the barge I put my queen conch in the lounge trunk with the other big shells. I had a peruvian conch, king helmet, turnip whelk, West Indian chank, knobbed whelk, and a milk conch. I kept the smaller shells in cigar boxes. Someday I would have a beautiful aquarium and put my coral and shells in it. The lounge was filling up with all sorts of coral. Craig hung purple sea fans on the back wall.

Rough seas forced the barge into shallow water one day, and we dived off the stern. We discovered coral reefs at a depth of sixty-five feet. We dived all day and collected fish and coral and later had a fish fry. We saw moray eels, snapper, queen angelfish, and grouper. A few dead fish lay on the bottom.

I enjoyed the scuba diving, but surface time, the endless waiting, dragged on, like sitting in a bus station for a bus that never came. I watched three movies in a row, snacked, cleaned spinys. I watched *Against a Crooked Sky* starring Richard Boone. I scribbled in my log, counted the days, crossed off the calendar, added up my pay a dozen different ways, and kept dreaming about the day I would be promoted. The barge kept traveling from one place to another, but I was going nowhere. The sea was the same, but I was older and not as healthy. She was weaving some kind of spell, draining the ambition out of me. The only way to enjoy the present was to go under water. That's where I wanted to be. Bottom time was my salvation. I had close to eighty working dives, not to mention the scuba dives. I guess I should have been happy making all those dives. On another barge, tenders hardly got the chance.

✶ ✶ ✶

We expected a storm. The Mexicans secured the equipment with cables, and we brought the dive tree into the enclosed area under the derrick crane. Dickie went in on the crew boat for some relief, and Lee replaced him.

Seas became choppy midmorning, and the wind blew the baseball caps off the deck hands. Lee felt refreshed from his vacation. At night when the barge rolled, he drank a few beers in our cabin, and Larry and I listened to his stories.

"What's happening in the States?" I asked.

"Nothing much. My wife came back from Argentina and said things are bad down there. The way my broker talks the whole world is in a recession."

"Maybe the rest of the world, but not Carmen," Larry said. "That town never had it better."

"I know. The airport's always crowded. Guess who I saw at the flophouse."

"Who?" Larry asked.

"Pete Gomez."

"Who's he?" I asked.

"A supervisor for Taylor."

"Don't think I know him," Larry said.

"He and I had a job one time. About three years ago a ferry sank near Carmen and they asked us to inspect it. It was me and Pete and another diver. The depth was only thirty-eight feet, so we jumped in with scuba. I checked the hull. There was a port bow plate out of whack. The water was dirty, visibility was only two feet. Don and I swam to the bow into the pilot house and found a body floating on the ceiling. It was the Mexican pilot. He was bloated and his mouth was open."

"I hate those kind of jobs," Larry said.

"We dragged the body out and bumped into a ten-foot shark. Don took the pilot's hand and whacked the shark on the nose. Must have scared the shark, because it took off. We surfaced and tried to put the body into a small boat. Pete was in the boat, and I was trying to give the foot to Pete, but he wouldn't take it. He said, 'Get that thing away from me. Put it in some other boat.' There were a lot of Mexicans buzzing around with their little outboards, and finally one guy took the body to shore."

Lee spat a hunk of Skoal into a paper cup and continued. "When the three of us reached Carmen we went to a whorehouse, and Pete brought a girl back to the company flophouse. Don and I came back after an hour, and they were still there. Don wanted to get some sleep, so he took his clothes off, put a mask and fins on, and surprised them in the room upstairs. The girl screamed. He chased her around, and she tried to jump out the window."

"Whatever happened to Don?" Larry asked.

"He got bent real bad and had to retire."

"I was on a job where we had to recover a body," I said. "We picked a welder off a horizontal at sixty feet."

"Yeah. You got to be careful on some of those rigs," said Larry.

"He was on a lower level of the structure doing some work and somebody dropped a piece of steel from above. I guess it hit him on the head. The diver who found the body said the water was full of sharks."

"Yeah, they can smell death," Larry said.

"I don't like to go in the water when there are a lot of sharks around," Lee said.

Later, Larry and I went to sleep. Lee continued drinking in Dickie's cabin. Craig complained about it the next morning and said Lee kept him up the whole night.

The storm passed quickly.

We returned to deep water, but the storm had sunk three buoys. For three days we dived around the clock and searched for chains. Every eight hours we made three dives in rough seas and couldn't find any chains for a day and a night. Finally, the second night, we found two chains and attached new buoys.

Big ground swells were still sweeping in. The barge rolled to port, water poured in and covered the entire stern to a depth of one foot. The barge rolled to starboard, and the water rushed out below the rails, through the chocks and every other free space, and the deck became slippery.

We were still diving on a 160-foot schedule, with thirty-eight-minute bottom times, but the surface was too rough for water stops, so we hauled the diver out of the water and threw him in the chamber as quickly as possible. The swells killed my back when I tended. I was glad Larry was a small man and didn't weigh much. Every time a swell smashed into the stern, the ladder shook, and we had to time the swells carefully, so the diver could climb the ladder without getting hurt. We deviated from the dive schedules sometimes, because a decompression chamber on board was our insurance policy, if anyone got bent. The dive schedules were only a guideline, the result of thousands of trial and error dives, a statistical solution to a nebulous problem. The Taylor schedules were stricter than the U.S. Navy decompression schedules, because commercial divers made so many dives.

***

The weather grew worse, and the crew boat arrived late in the night. The engines roared, the boat leaped out of the water, and deck hands tried to tie off to the barge. The wind howled, and the seas churned. Heavy rain fell, waves crashed over the bow. but the barge remained seaworthy.

We rested in our bunks. In my mind I bounced around between the surface and sixty feet while listening with one ear to the stories Larry and Lee told of the divers who were killed or went crazy. I tried to find where my ambition went, the ambition I brought to the Gulf a long time ago, but I don't care anymore. The food on the barge was starting to stink. I don't belong with the barge rednecks—Steve said some were Ku Klux Klan. I was getting tired of Lee's raunchy jokes, there were only so many places to walk, I'd seen the movie too many times already, and I can only count my money so many ways. I had something saved, but not enough, and I didn't know what I'd do stepping off the barge. In my mind I dropped to sixty feet. It was better there, easy to forget, counting breaths. The moment. A spiny oyster shell snaps shut. The moment. A glance at a pressure gauge. The moment. An exhalation, a glance up, nothing but the essentials. Inhale, exhale. Three minutes, and the brain cells start to die. The moment. A glance at a grouper. The moment. Under water is where I want to be. I'm alive, strapped to the moment. Thirty-eight minutes of bottom time is a whole day.

In my mind I returned to the surface. The sea had hypnotized me. Maybe I'd never get off the barge. It would be nice to have somebody to miss. It took a month or two to get a letter. Maybe I'd never return to a landlubber's life. The barge would travel on and on around the world. When it finished Mexico, it would go to the South China Sea or the Indian Ocean. I'd travel with it, locked in a deadly embrace with the sea. No, something would happen. Nothing lasted.

***

The weather improved, and we went scuba diving while the barge pull-tested chains. We had great visibility, and we found many deep caves and numerous grouper. I brought up lettuce coral, brain coral, and a variety with thick, round stalks that ended in concentric rings with serrated edges. We made a night dive on scuba. We hung a line in the water and tied a green chemical light stick on the end that was visible for a good distance.

With flashlights the sensation of night diving was similar to being at a disco with strobe lights. The water became invisible, so we levitated a few feet off bottom. We appeared to be ghosts floating through space. Our motion was choppy, and the flashlights reflected our bubbles, jellyfish particles, plankton, and silt. The sandy bottom was alive with invertebrates. Two skates glided by, bodies undulating gracefully.

We explored an endless subterranean cavern until our tanks were almost dry, then floated toward the green beacon like moths to a flame. The light was our only clue to a safe return.

Back on the familiar deck, Craig pulled a large sponge from his bag, but the rest of us had been too mesmerized to collect anything. Later that night, the barge towed into shallow water where the depth was sixty feet. We received two new 5120 compressors and sent the old ones in. We hadn't received any mail for six days.

For nine days we dived in the coral reefs around Cayos Arcas while the barge sandblasted and readied the mooring buoy. The barge anchored south of the main islet, bow facing the lighthouse and antenna. The anchors came close to shore, to a depth of thirty feet, and they damaged a lot of coral. We made many trips to the islets, collected lobster and snapper, and became familiar with the terrain on the bottom. We usually took the Zodiac, but always paddled, because the motor never worked.

One morning we jumped in and followed the bow anchor cable toward the islet with the lighthouse. The visibility was not good, and the bottom was smooth with patches of coral. In the afternoon we took the Zodiac to Snapper Mountain and returned with fifteen red snapper and two grouper. The coral formations south of Cayo del Este were huge domes interspersed with sandy patches. The domes were latticework with secret entrances for the snapper. Craig swam around the perimeter and fired into the caves and always brought out a struggling fish. I didn't want to kill anything, so I explored the bottom for shells and watched the other divers wrestle with dying fish that had spears stuck through them.

The following day, we dived on the northern side of the lighthouse islet where we found walls dropping into a sandy channel. The depth at the top of the wall was thirty feet and the bottom was sixty-five. Fields of elkhorn grew in the shallows, along with many fans and other plants. The intense wave action brought everything on the bottom into motion as if swaying in a breeze, and we struggled against the current. We brought back twelve fish and five lobster. I found a large conch. Craig said he saw a big hogfish.

On the western side of Cayo del Este we found a spot with vertical walls dropping to ninety feet. I saw Larry about to spear a crab, when a moray came out of its hole near his leg. It had an all-consuming evil expression on its face that could turn a man to stone. Curious, it extended its body to see what Larry was doing. Larry glanced at it and froze. He turned slowly, ever so slowly, and I thought the eel was going to lock on his leg and drag him into its hole, but Larry poked it with his spear gun, and the monster recoiled so fast it left a cloud of debris.

I walked along the deserted beach after my scuba tank ran out and found a clump of staghorn coral and a worn piece of dead coral that looked like a bird. The water had carved out a small hole where an eye socket could have been, and the piece had a body and a neck but no legs. Further down the beach some fins moved in the shallow water. When I was five feet away, I saw two fish with brilliant green markings near their tails. They were two feet long, bullet shaped with two dorsal fins, the first one long, the second rising sharply to a point. They didn't stay long enough for me to make a closer inspection or identification. The beach ended in a small lagoon. A sea turtle fed on plant growth. As I returned to the Zodiac, a squall came through and pelted us with rain, but when the rain passed, a rainbow appeared on the horizon.

We sat in the Zodiac and drank beer. The barge seemed far away.

Steve came up with a clump of lettuce coral. Lee held up my curved, weatherbeaten coral and said, "This looks like a gun. Crack it open and see what's inside."

"Turn it around, and it's a bird."

"Did you see that moray?" asked Larry.

"I did."

"I thought he was going to grab my leg. Biggest moray I've ever seen. His head must have been six inches across."

"Where's Craig?" I asked.

"Still on the bottom," Larry said.

"That guy doesn't need much air," I said.

For three days we dived on the spot with vertical walls to ninety feet. One day Mark and Craig traveled out the anchor cable, but the rest of us relaxed. I wrote letters. Large ground swells hit the barge, but otherwise we had beautiful weather. The cooks were happy. We were supplying them with fresh seafood all the time. They made lobster salad and fish fillets.

On November 7, we made a trip to a spot south of the lighthouse islet that had a sandy bottom, not much coral, and few fish.

When we returned, Chink greeted us. "Party's over. We're towing to Abkatum."

Our SBM job had been postponed, but I knew we were coming back.

I Escape a Man-Eating Pipe

I made a memorable dive in late November at the Abkatum A platform, where I guided a pipeline and set it close to an L-bend. The twenty-four-inch diameter pipeline hung from six davits that ran the starboard length of the barge. Seas were rough, so the pipeline was swinging back and forth in a wide arc, and when I reached bottom, complete darkness greeted me. Craig wanted me to set the pipeline parallel to and six feet from the L-bend.

I tied a rope to the davit sling at the end of the pipeline and took a position by the L-bend. I sat on the L-bend so I had a point of reference. I kept a strain on the rope and felt it loosen as the pipeline in the davits approached me. I stuck my foot into the darkness and waited for the pipeline to touch it. The pipeline was only a few feet off bottom. I was worried about my umbilical getting caught under the pipeline when I set it on bottom.

I kept a strain on the rope as the pipeline approached, then concrete touched my foot. The pipe pushed me off the L-bend. I regained my balance. The pipe stopped, hesitated, then moved away, and my foot lost touch with it.

The job was going to be tricky. I estimated how far the pipe had swung by the amount of rope left in my hand. The pipe was swinging in a ten-to-fifteen-foot arc. I let the pipe approach one more time, then swing away. I decided to order the barge to drop the line when it approached me again. I held the rope tightly. Without the rope, I would be lost.

The pipe approached again, and I told Craig to lower the davits.

Somewhere out there, a pipeline descended, came toward me. I stuck my foot out again.

The pipe landed in the mud two feet from the L-bend. I had miscalculated. The pipeline had landed too close, but my bottom time had expired, and I ascended.

On the surface, I quickly ditched the gear and crawled in the chamber. Craig spoke to me on the chamber phone. "How far apart are the pipes?"

I was still excited and overwhelmed by the dive.

I took my oxygen bib off and said, "About two feet."

Craig didn't look happy, but there was nothing more I could do. It's not every day I guide a pipeline in complete darkness to a resting place in the mud exactly six feet from an L-bend, while worrying about my umbilical, my air supply. I also didn't want to get crushed between the two pipes.

✳ ✳ ✳

Sometimes divers faced impossible conditions. Only they could make the decision to risk death or walk away. Refusing to dive often meant a crew boat ride home, because some barge foremen didn't respect the risks divers faced. One time Mike told me the barge wanted him to connect davits in three hundred feet of water. Seas were rough, and he heard the davit chains bouncing up and down on top of the pipeline. He said he and his bell partner were scared shitless. They sat in the bell for two hours and pretended to work.

✳ ✳ ✳

We towed to a desolate place called Midpoint, where the air was cool and the sky overcast. A dirty green sea extended to the horizon. One small four-legged platform stood a few miles away.

We spent days setting a tremendous manifold on the sea floor.

The supply barge carrying the manifold tied off on the port side. The manifold covered the entire deck of the supply barge, which was as long as the *L.B. Meaders*. One of the nylon hawsers snapped and broke a Mexican worker's arm.

On a calm day with absolutely flat water, the derrick crane lifted the manifold on seven slings. Dickie made the first dive to try to align the manifold between two pipelines. The depth was ninety-six feet, and the water was cold with little visibility on the bottom. Dickie surfaced after seventy-eight minutes with no success. I imagined the job was like trying to steer a blue whale through the Panama Canal. I knew he could be at only one end at a time, and when the back end pivoted he could have no knowledge of what the front end was doing. I heard him say there wasn't much clearance between the pipelines.

Craig dived and also had much difficulty.

After discussions, Pemex decided to set the manifold outside the pipelines. Lee set the leviathan on the bottom close to the end of one of the pipelines. Steve removed three slings. Mark also removed three slings.

I removed the last sling. The shackle was stuck under the pipe, and I used a four-foot-long crowbar to pry the shackle loose. I felt miserable on the dive, because of the cold and poor visibility. Pride kept me going.

We moved the pipelines closer to the manifold. We worked day and night. After a couple sleepless days, Dickie asked me if I had the energy to make a dive.

I didn't hesitate. "Sure," I said. "What do I have to do?"

"Close two valves and flood a line."

I studied the blueprint. The manifold seemed small on paper. I memorized the position of the cross braces, the gate valves, the flood valves, and the overall shape of the structure, which was as long as a football field.

"Where does the down line go?" I asked.

"On this gate valve."

Lee said, "He'll need a stand-off pipe. I'll go find one."

Dickie said, "We'll send you the stand-off once you move the down line."

"What's it for?"

"So you won't get sucked in when you open the valve."

"Oh."

I jumped in and found the down line covered with slime. As my gloved hand slid along, green phosphorescent particles dislodged and shot off in crazy arcs. The glow of the halogen lamps faded, and my toes soon touched bottom.

The door to the unknown opened again. In dive school, the instructors said if you're afraid of the dark, close your eyes. I landed on the pipe in front of a large wheel. I assumed it was the gate valve. "On the bottom."

"Close the valve."

"Which way do I turn it?"

"Clockwise."

"Roger." The wheel was about my height. I used my thigh muscles. I crouched, grabbed the wheel, and stood. It moved stiffly. After fifty repetitions, the wheel wouldn't turn anymore. "The valve is closed."

"Go to the next one."

"Roger."

Recalling the mental image of the blueprint of the manifold, I crawled along the pipe for perhaps thirty yards, turned right when the pipe forked, and found the other wheel after about ten yards. The second one required eighty deep-knee bends to close.

I crawled back to the down line.

"How do you feel?" Craig asked.

"Pretty good. What's next?"

"Go out to starboard and take the down line with you. You should run into a pipeline."

"Roger." I untied the down line and groped along the mud like an arthritic crab away from the manifold. I was glad to be in an underwater desert, devoid of coral, triggerfish, sting rays, urchins, moray eels, giant clams, and other menaces. The benign mud concealed no threats, and I moved along confidently. I didn't think about the diver who stepped on a sting ray and had to be hospitalized for six weeks or the diver who almost became a meal for a giant grouper. The umbilical hose and down line trailed behind.

After about twenty yards, I touched a familiar man-made object: chicken wire. Apparently the pipeline had been damaged and some of the concrete had crumbled away, leaving only the reinforcing wire. "I'm at the pipeline."

"Good."

"Making a right turn and going down the pipe." The damaged section continued for a few feet, then rough concrete began. I relaxed and breathed normally. Motion through the water was not difficult. The rough concrete on the pipe gave me some leverage, and the mud was firm. The two wheel valves have not drained my energy. For some reason I felt energetic, though I had not slept in two days. The depth was only ninety-six feet, so nitrogen narcosis was minimal.

After perhaps fifty yards, the concrete ended and smooth steel began. My fingers traced various circular and rectangular steel shapes inside a large oval opening along the top of the pipe.

"I'm at the end of the pipeline."

"Tie off the down line, and we'll send you the stand-off pipe and some wrenches."

"Roger."

Where is the valve? Where do I put the stand-off pipe? What are these shapes? A mental image formed from the information coming in through my fingertips. The steel cube coming out of the circular plate was the valve, and it had to be opened by a large crescent wrench. Six inches in front of the valve was an open flange four inches in diameter connected to the pipeline where the water would flow in. The valve and the opening were too close together. If I opened the valve, the force of the seawater rushing in would pull me in with it.

I tied the manila line to a pad eye at the end of the pipe and waited. I felt good and breathed slowly and easily from the regulator, with only thoughts as a companion. My weightless body almost didn't exist. I was in complete darkness at ninety-six feet and felt at home. I must be a fish, I thought. We all came from the sea, anyway. There was nothing frightening down there except what was man-made.

A distant but familiar voice crackled in the mask. "Check your down line. Do you have the stand-off pipe?"

It was nice to talk to somebody. My fingers groped along the manila line. "I have the pipe and two wrenches."

"There should be three bolts on the end of the stand-off. If you need more, let me know."

"Wait . . . I found them."

I bolted the four-foot-long pipe to the flange and tucked the small wrench in my pocket.

"Ready to open the valve."

"Be careful."

Lying prone in the mud four feet below hell's drainpipe, where in a moment water would rush in with tremendous force, I felt humble. I placed the large wrench on the valve stem and said, "Pick up the diver's slack."

The umbilical tightened. I was worried that it might be too close to the top of the stand-off.

"Opening the valve."

I made a quarter turn with the wrench and glanced up into the darkness. I listened. Nothing. I assumed the sea was altering its shape into a whirlpool as it filled the vacuum and flooded the pipeline. I had no desire to confirm my assumption. "Now what?" I asked.

"Untie the down line, bring it back to the manifold, and tie it off somewhere."

"Roger."

Like a submissive subject to an Aztec god, I wormed toward the down line, loosened the half hitches, and put the big wrench in the wet suit. It felt good to come out from under the man-eating pipe. I groped along an empty expanse of mud, found the manifold, and secured the rope on a cross brace. "The down line is tied off. I'm ready to leave bottom."

"Leave bottom."

"Roger. How long was I down?"

"Seventy-eight minutes."

The journey up lasted a few minutes. Soon I stood on deck breathing unfiltered air. The bright lights of the pipe ramp were warm, and I saw colors again. The world came back in crisp, clear detail.

Craig said, "We're picking up anchors and going back to Cayos Arcas."

"Sounds good." I dropped my weight belt.

"We'll be able to do some more scuba diving."

"I'm ready." I smiled.

"I knew you'd like to hear that. Get going. Two fifteens and two tens."

It was almost midnight. I had three hours' sleep in two days, but I felt great. There was nothing better than standing on deck after a trip into the unknown.

Scuba Dive to 160 Feet

The barge towed to Cayos Arcas to finish the mooring buoy installation. I slept for most of the two-day ride.

Early in the morning we found the sea had claimed three buoys, so we searched for chains again. We worked around the clock for two days, and Lee found the last chain late at night.

I went to sleep before sunrise and woke late in the afternoon. I walked around the deck in a daze and stared at the deep blue water fringed with whitecaps. The arduous work at Midpoint had left my mind a blank. After all the sleep deprivation, I resembled a zombie.

Most of the chains were too short, so we waited for a supply barge to bring more links. Someone had miscalculated the depth or didn't had enough chain.

I wrote letters to a few pen pals in the Philippines. They were my only link to the outside world. Chuchi, from Cebu, told me about some beautiful diving spots, Dumaguete and Mactan Island. She told me about life on the other side of the world. She said most people knew English, the language used in schools and businesses, but everyday conversation was in local dialects, which changed from island to island. In Manila they spoke Tagalog, and on Cebu they spoke Cebuano. She said it would probably not be a good time to visit during the rainy season, from July to October, when it rained every day and there were hurricanes. She told me about the many festivals, such as Sinulog in January. She spoke of the beautiful beaches, like Boracay, where the sand was soft as flour, and other sights like the Mayon Volcano, and I knew I would go there someday.

Lee gave me an Ocean Industry magazine to read, and I noticed that someone predicted the price of oil would be $100 a barrel in eight years. I didn't know that oil prices had peaked this year, 1981. In 1972, the price of oil had been $3. Around the time of the Arab oil embargo in 1973, prices reached $12. In 1981, the price of crude oil reached $35, largely because of the Iran-Iraq war. As a result of the Iranian Revolution, oil production dropped by two million barrels a day. Iraqi oil production dropped by two and a half million barrels a day. A worldwide drilling boom ensued, but the frenzy would be short-lived. I cared little about the price of oil, but my life would be shaped by it. The forecast of $100 oil prices would turn out to be spectacularly false.

Steve took the crew boat in to Ciudad del Carmen to settle a lawsuit regarding having hurt his hand on a sink faucet in California.

In the evening, we watched the movie *Zulu*.

The barge added lengths of chain for two days, then stopped for rough weather.

Black seas with terrific swells hit us, the barge rolled heavily, and everyone avoided the wind and rain. Nobody knew how long we would be down. I studied the stock market and read novels to pass the time.

After two days, skies cleared, and the single-buoy mooring system arrived. The Mexicans installed anodes, painted the SBM bright orange, and at 8 p.m., it floated in the water, secured by six chains connected to pilings on the ocean floor.

We connected the three flanges to the bottom surface of the SBM and connected the three flexible hoses that went from the flanges down to the bottom. The hoses tied into a manifold connected to a pipeline. The pipeline ran from the deep water of Cayos Arcas to an oilfield production platform in the main oilfield south of us. Soon the supertankers would be able to park next to the SBM, load their black gold, and make their global deliveries to the nations addicted to oil.

Lee and I made a quick bounce dive with scuba gear to check the hoses. I discovered that nitrogen narcosis had a greater effect on me when I used scuba to great depths, instead of surface-supplied air. By the time I reached the bottom at 160 feet, I was disoriented.

We jumped in on a sunny morning to a choppy turquoise sea and descended along a buoy line attached to the manifold. Lee, the fifteen-year veteran, showed that he could still outperform the young apprentice who wanted his job. He descended quickly and was soon thirty feet ahead of me. I stopped at sixty feet to clear my ears. The orange buoy bobbed in the frothy turbulence on the surface, and the yellow snakelike hoses undulated in the clear water. The buoy looked like a giant jellyfish with its tentacles reaching the bottom.

Lee's bubbles floated past and made their lazy ascent toward the sunlight, but I couldn't see him. I continued down, and the water became chilly past a hundred feet. When I reached bottom at 160 feet, Lee was crouched in the mud, inspecting a manifold.

The view was murky. I was afraid to leave the down line. I had no peripheral vision, and my brain wasn't working. The air from the regulator felt cold and dry at the back of my throat. I hung on the down line and stared at Lee.

Lee didn't waste any time. He finished the inspection and rocketed to the surface. Again I was left behind. I scrambled up the rope, overwhelmed.

When I climbed on deck, Lee had already disappeared into the dive locker. Craig asked me a question I didn't understand, and I mumbled something incoherently.

Lee made me feel like a novice. Perhaps it was true that those who drank liquor regularly had more tolerance to nitrogen narcosis.

A Taste of Singapore

We stood by for six days under a gloomy sky while eight-foot swells with whitecaps rolled past. We were prisoners again, passing the time below deck. While the barge towed in circles, we played darts, cleaned the dive locker, and learned of the world beyond the sea. It was 1981, a time of skyrocketing oil prices, war between Iran and Iraq, and martial law in Poland. President Reagan survived an assassination attempt, Pope John Paul II survived an assassination attempt, Prince Charles married Lady Diana, and the Iran hostage crisis ended. The Space Shuttle made its first flight, IBM introduced the personal computer, Bill Gates licensed MS-DOS, and Israel destroyed Iraq's nuclear plant. The weekly paper featured two economists' opinions on the future. One predicted a recession more severe than 1973. The other predicted the economy would recover by the next year. I wanted to know who would win the Super Bowl. Somewhere else I read that 650 beagles in Utah were injected with radium and plutonium to predict human tolerance to the radioactive substances. They said at least one human life had been saved from their experiment, but all the dogs had to be euthanized when their pain became apparent. That type of experiment was one of the reasons I never became a biologist. Some of the sick things they do in the name of science, that's not science. All the pressure to publish something, anything, so they can keep their grant money. Can't they do something decent to make a living?

✳ ✳ ✳

One night I watched a movie in the divers' cabin with Dickie, Craig, Steve, Mark, and Lee. After the movie, Craig talked about where he had worked before Mexico. He had spent a season off the coast of Borneo.

"What did you do?" I asked.

"Similar to what we got here. Pipelaying. Risers. Single-buoy mooring systems."

"Where'd you go on your time off?"

"Singapore and Indonesia. Bali was nice."

"Tell us about Singapore," I said.

"It was a modern city."

"What was it like?" I asked.

"What do you want to know?"

"Everything." I knew Craig wasn't exactly eloquent, but I was going to squeeze him like toothpaste.

Craig planted his feet on the floor and sat by the edge of his bunk. "The airport was the cleanest in the world. When I got in the street, I looked for a cab, and they were all black and yellow Mercedes. I thought this must be a rich city to have all those Mercedes."

"Where'd you stay?" Steve asked.

"The Hilton. The company paid for it. You should have seen the doorman. He was dressed in some fancy costume like Genghis Khan."

"What language do they speak there?" I asked.

"Everybody knew English. Most of the dudes I saw walking around were Chinamen. Some Indians and Malaysians. A few Brits, too. All the street signs had four languages on them."

"It's a duty-free port, isn't it?" Lee asked.

"Yeah. You can get a good deal on Japanese electronics. I bought a Canon AE-1 at Peter's Department Store on Orchard Road."

"What else did you do?" I asked.

"My buddy Bob and I walked to Chinatown one night."

"How was that?" Dickie asked.

"Weird. There were barefoot coolies riding around on trishaws."

"What's a trishaw?" Steve asked.

"A bicycle with a side car."

"What kind of grub they got over there?" Steve asked.

"Anything you want. I had this stuffed pancake once called 'murtabak.' It was full of onions, eggs, and minced meat. You dip it in curry sauce. Pretty good."

"If I ever get off this barge, I'm going to the Far East," I said.

"You ought to go to Bali," Craig said. "That place is full of legends. I heard a story once about an evil witch who stole a princess and they had a battle in the sky between monkey armies. I forgot how the rest of the story goes."

★ ★ ★

Winter brought perpetual storms. While I dreamed about traveling to Singapore, the barge towed to Midpoint to set a 380-ton manifold. Weather turned bad again, and we towed in circles.

The standby time was depressing. Lee looked like he hadn't shaved in four days. Mark was gloomy. He stayed in the divers' lounge and listened to Moody Blues tapes. Steve stayed busy assembling and disassembling masks. I suffered from a fungal infection in my crotch.

The sky became black as charcoal, and eight-foot waves marched through for two days. Then skies cleared, but six-foot swells continued to rock the barge. The tugs, like black galloping seahorses, supplied propulsion, and the tow ropes stretched tightly, soaked in saltwater. When the ropes strained, the water dripped back into the sea. The rusty, dented, spherical anchor buoys, taller than a man, lay about the deck like misplaced red and white balloons. The anchors hanging from the sides made a dull clunk every time they hit the barge.

When the swells receded in size to four feet, we prepared to dive. At three a.m., the manifold hung over the water in a spiderweb of slings and tugger cables illuminated by crane lights.

Dickie guided the manifold to the bottom at 102 feet. Larry moved it to within Pemex specifications. Lee removed one sling; Mark removed six slings; Steve removed four; and I removed two. My bottom time was sixty-eight minutes followed by forty-five minutes in the chamber.

We moved two pipelines closer to the manifold, which took a day, a night, and another day of hooking and unhooking davits.

Accidents happened with no warning. I tended Larry on a windy afternoon on the starboard side. I stood on a boat bumper and admired the view. Three flying fish jumped out of the water, sailed fifty yards, and disappeared under the waves. I fished my diver periodically and listened to his breathing on the phone.

Larry said, "I have the sling connected. Get up on davit number three."

"Roger. Coming up on number three."

Chink spoke into his walkie-talkie. A few seconds later the davit chains moved with their usual hollow clanking sound.

"How far do you want to come up?" Dickie asked Chink.

"About four or five feet off bottom."

Suddenly, in a chain reaction, davit number three shook violently, followed by davit two, then davit one.

"What happened?" Dickie asked.

Chink ran to the pipe ramp opening and looked out. "Holy shit!"

"Pick up the diver's slack!" Dickie shouted. "Sonofabitch is falling—get him out of there!"

I yanked five feet out of the water. I waited a few seconds in tense silence.

Larry's voice came through the speaker as unemotional as before. "The pipe fell to the bottom. I guess the slings broke. Lucky I was out of the way. Did you ever hear a sling pop? It's a weird sound."

"Are you okay?" Dickie asked.

"Yeah."

"Those boys should have used heavier slings," Chink said.

"Leave bottom, Larry," Dickie said. "Nothing we can do until they make some new slings."

Larry surfaced, and I helped him remove his gear.

"We'll use five davits," said Chink. He looked embarrassed.

Dickie frowned. "I thought we lost the Troll for a second."

Larry had the look of doom, but he smiled, and I followed him to the chamber.

After that, we didn't have any more problems. We moved the lines to within four feet of the manifold.

Coatzacoalcos

On the Veracruz coast, a small port named Coatzacoalcos processed the crude oil that came from the offshore fields in the Yucatan. A major pipeline ran hundreds of miles along the sea floor from the production platforms to land.

The pipeline had been damaged when a boat anchor had caught it. Oil flow stopped, and Pemex contracted the *L.B. Meaders* to repair the pipeline.

The *Meaders* set anchors in shallow water only forty feet deep.

I looked across a milky blue sea under a cloudless sky. Cold air stung my face. Off the port side, jagged silhouettes rose from the horizon out of a mist. I had not seen land in months. The distant mountains reminded me that something else existed besides the watery world. It was mysterious and strange, being so close to land yet unable to walk on it.

When the sun pierced the haze, the light reflected off the snow on a distant mountain peak, but below the peak everything melted to the horizon in a bluish gray shadow, like a wash in a watercolor painting. A dozen gulls played around the barge. They dived, circled, and soared on currents, their black wingtips angled back in efficient design. It must have been feeding time. A half mile away, the tugboat *Robin One* bounced over the waves and looked for a place to set an anchor. On the horizon, a row of tankers waited for the oil to flow again.

The job would be the most difficult we had faced all year, because the thirty-six-inch-diameter pipeline was buried under six feet of fine sand. We called it sugar sand. Dickie told me another ship, *Stena Inspector*, had tried to repair the line and failed.

We couldn't start, because rough weather brought nine-foot seas, so the barge picked up anchors and headed into deeper water.

The barge returned in two days, and we prepared to dive. I saw a few houses under palm trees where the sea met the earth, and the town of Coatzacoalcos was a few miles down the coast.

We started diving at 10 p.m., and spent four hours looking for the pipeline, because there were no buoys. Finally, after probing, we found it buried under the sand.

Steve hand-jetted around the buckled area followed by Dickie and

Mark. A hand jet was a high-pressure water hose with a nozzle shaped like a T to eliminate torque.

The depth was forty-eight feet, which gave us long bottom times of two and a half hours. The water was very cold.

Larry cut the buckled section with the oxy-arc torch, hooked up two slings, and the crane picked it up and set it on the center deck. A ship anchor had bent the pipe and crimped it almost at a right angle, and it had leaked oil.

Another storm approached. The barge secured the deck. Juan got into an argument with the barge captain for no apparent reason.. Everybody was edgy this time of year. To the landlubbers, December was a festive time. To us, it meant nothing. The only difference was the cold water. It felt like winter.

The storm hit us with rain for two days, and we did not attempt any work. We watched a silent Buster Keaton movie about a man who would get seven million dollars if he married a girl by seven o'clock.

The crew boat came late again, because we were far from the main oilfield, but I received letters and annual reports from companies I invested in. I received an invitation to my high-school reunion. I read the names and addresses of my classmates. Some entries included a few lines describing my former classmates' jobs or families, or a few words of hello to friends they had not seen in a long time. Out of a class of 360 students from a small suburban school, eighty percent had settled within fifty miles of the school. The other twenty percent were scattered across the whole country, in practically every state, with diverse careers.

Many classmates had changed completely. A former athlete taught finance in Ohio, long-haired radicals had become medical doctors. Some folks had stayed in the family business. A brainy friend of mine had picked grapes in the south of France and hitchhiked across the Sahara Desert. The top student in the class was a doctor in Arkansas. Some had moved to Denver. A cute cheerleader had ended up in Los Angeles selling jewelry. A friend in my scout troop was a chemist in Florida. Susan was dancing in New York. Rick was behind an auto parts counter in Lansdale. Some had married their high school sweethearts and settled in nearby communities. Lance had a recording studio. Linda was still in school preparing for a Ph.D. in clinical psychology. Steve was in Austin studying law. Some girls weren't married yet. Diana was teaching physical education at a local high school. Harry was building office towers in New Mexico. The editor of our radical newspaper had become a doctor who practiced in West

Virginia. I don't know what became of my old friend Larry, whose entry in the booklet just showed his parents' address.

Four were dead. I remember sitting behind Dean in Algebra class. He smelled of cow manure, because he lived on a farm. I'm sure as soon as he came home he had to shovel hay and drive the tractor. I think they told me he died in a motorcycle accident. I don't know the circumstances of the others. Most of the names in the booklet didn't include any descriptive entries. I wondered what became of them. Most of the addresses showed they had settled in nearby towns, and I can't imagine what they're doing. Much had changed since those idyllic high school days. If one thing had been different in high school, my whole life would have been different. If I had talked to Diana when I stood behind her in the lunchroom we might have gone on a date, and who knows? I might have married her, and I would never have gone diving in Campeche Bay.

The barge returned to shallow water the third day, and we began diving on a bright morning. We hand-jetted through the day and night and connected five davits, but the pipe still lay firmly under tons of sand.

We used an airlift to remove much of the sand, but the work was time consuming. The airlift was a simple, yet efficient tool. Air entered the bottom, expanded, and rose in the pipe, creating a vacuum that lifted the sand and silt up into shallow water, where it floated away with the current.

Steve airlifted between davits two and three, which loosened the pipe enough to lift it out of the water.

We rested while the welders added two joints on the end and set the pipe on the bottom.

The Night Before Christmas

The barge turned around, and we airlifted the end of the line that headed out to sea. It was also buried in six feet of sand, and the ditch kept caving in, so we made hardly any progress as we worked through the night and the next day.

The Pemex inspector became impatient.

"What can I tell you?" Dickie said to Chink. "We're airlifting and hand-jetting."

"We have to show those clowns in del Carmen we're doing something," Chink said.

"I don't think they understand," Dickie said. "We have to clear a three-hundred-foot ditch in both directions to a depth of six to eight feet and the bottom is sugar sand. We're working round the clock while everyone else sleeps."

Some of the Mexicans got drunk the previous night, and we almost had a rebellion. A crowd gathered by the Pemex inspector's door. One drunken man pounded on the door.

Ignacio opened the door. "What do you want?"

"We are homesick!" the drunk shouted. "We want to go home and see our families."

The crowd murmured in agreement.

"You cannot leave this barge. You have work to do. You signed a contract," Ignacio snorted.

"But this is Christmas," a man in the crowd protested.

Ignacio stared down the drunken men. "I don't care. Make an altar in the pipe ramp and pray to the Virgin of Guadalupe you all don't get fired! Go to your cabins!" Ignacio slammed the door in their faces.

The crowd dispersed with men cursing.

The next night we were still airlifting. It didn't seem like the night before Christmas. We were the only ones on deck working, and the rest of the men on the barge were drunk. Scottish bagpipe music played on the loudspeaker at the stern while we airlifted a pipeline. My turn to dive came near midnight.

"Remember to airlift five feet away from the pipe," Dickie said.

I knew how to use the airlift, but I was more concerned with staying warm during the two and a half hours in the water.

I sank into a ditch, and the airlift hung freely in soupy water. When the airlift had created a hole six feet deep, my toes felt a pipeline. I pushed the airlift away from the pipeline and guided it laterally back and forth as it sculpted the bottom with its invisible knife. The sand shifted, as if it were falling through an egg timer, but fresh sand broke loose from the sides, filled the hole, and trapped my body. My legs were immobilized. I told myself not to panic, but I was alone there. No one could help me. I freed my arms, pulled the airlift closer, and loosened the sand around me. This predicament continued throughout the dive. Trapped for a few minutes, free for a longer time, I struggled in the shifting sand and avoided the suction at the bottom of the pipe. It was dark and cold, but at least I had no narcosis. My mind was clear, and I felt like a child playing in a sandbox. Dickie entertained me by keeping the talk switch pressed, so I heard the bagpipe music. After a long time, Dickie told me to come up.

On deck, sand poured out of my booties and wetsuit. I spent an hour in the chamber, then cleaned the sand out of my ears.

After airlifting countless hours, we shut down at 3 a.m.

Swells increased in size, and the barge raised its anchors and towed away late in the morning on Christmas Day.

It rained all day while we towed within sight of land, and everyone felt mellow. The cooks prepared turkey for dinner, but we were in no mood to celebrate. We slept, tried to regain our energy, and hated to think that the rough seas might be filling the ditches along the pipe.

I woke long enough to read an old newspaper with stories about the world outside. Poland was under martial law, a new science of gene splicing was supposed to revolutionize agriculture, Soviet dissidents were on a hunger strike, and the U.S. won the Davis Cup. I went back to bed.

The barge returned the next afternoon, and we found the pipeline quickly. Some concrete had been knocked off, but the exposed metal had not been damaged.

At night I airlifted between davits two and three and inspected the line for damage. We worked around the clock again. Steve tended for three dives, I tended for three dives, Steve dived, I dived, and we continued the rotation. Mark felt sick and went in to see the doctor in del Carmen. I was getting about four hours of sleep a night.

In the morning we connected davits. Lee took care of number five and dug a hole for number four. Larry connected number four and dug a hole for number three. Steve connected number three, I connected number two, and Dickie connected the first davit. Larry was on the phone and guided me through the job.

We airlifted eighty feet past the first davit to try to loosen the pipe. Ignacio, the Pemex inspector, didn't believe the pipe went in the direction Dickie told him, so I went down and set two milk jug buoys two joints apart. My dive took twenty minutes. I didn't mind the easy dive. Anything was better than two and a half hours of airlifting. I looked at my logbook. I had airlifted every day for seven days.

A squall hit us in the afternoon, and we disconnected the davits but left the slings around the pipe. The barge picked up four anchors, in case we had to leave in a hurry. We worked for a few more hours, then shut down dive operations because of rough seas.

Mark returned on the crew boat. He looked defeated.

Steve jumped on the crew boat and left for a ten-day vacation. He was happy to escape the grueling job. There was no end in sight. If the sea kept playing cat-and-mouse games with the barge, we could be there for months.

A diving supervisor came on board to help us finish the job. He maintained the dive log, handled topside communications, and coordinated the job with the foreman, so the divers could concentrate on the work below the surface. His name was Beyers, and he was an ex-Navy diver with many years of experience.

Dickie said, "He curses a lot, but underneath, he's a nice guy."

The Worst Storm

We resumed work on the last day of the year. We airlifted and connected davits and tried to free the pipeline.

Two days later, the pipe came out of the ditch after we had cleared a hundred feet beyond davit number one. No New Year festivities for us. We walked around deck like zombies with a maniacal purpose. I tended a diver, ran the chamber, tended a diver, ran the chamber, tended another diver, ran the chamber, worked on the bottom for two and a half hours, spent an hour in the chamber, ate, slept for four hours, ate, and tended again, in daylight or darkness, drizzle or sun, and I don't know where I found the energy.

We worked on the pipeline that ran out to sea and moved it to starboard, a few feet from the end that ran to land. We made the first lift twenty feet from the end. We airlifted, connected davits, airlifted between davits, raised the pipeline out of the ditch, disconnected davits, moved farther along the pipeline, airlifted, connected davits, airlifted again, raised this section of pipe out of the ditch, and finally moved the pipelines so they met.

If we didn't have enough problems under water, the Mexican government gave us more things to grumble about. It wanted to tax our salaries fifteen percent. I was considered a diver on the barge, making dives every day, but officially not making diver pay. I received depth pay, but the amount wasn't significant at depths of forty feet.

It was always nice to hear the door open to my cabin and the words, "It's your turn" greet my ears. No matter how tired I was, the promise of bottom time was food to my soul.

Coatzacoalcos was a strange and spooky place. Sometimes a fog rolled in, and the water became smooth as glass. At night, sinister fish appeared, attracted by the barge lights. The fish hung vertically in the water with open mouths showing dagger teeth.

✷ ✷ ✷

Seas became rough again, so the barge picked up anchors and towed away. Twelve-foot waves crashed over the rails and forced us below deck.

The storm passed, we towed into shallow water, and a fog encircled us. When the fog broke in the afternoon, we saw tankers still waiting on the horizon.

Dickie said, "Another storm is coming."

Even he looked tired. I knew winter brought storms and hurricanes, but I didn't think we could endure another month.

Mark decided to go home. The sea had broken him.

What was it about the sea that made men torture themselves, then thank her?

Bottom time was all I cared about. Surface life was something to be tolerated, endured while waiting to slip into a wetsuit. I had become an amphibian. I needed the water, or else I would dry out in the sun, shrivel, and die.

✷ ✷ ✷

When work resumed, we picked up the line running to the beach, welded a flange to the end, and set it on bottom. Later that day, we picked up the other end, welded a flange on, set it on bottom, aligned the two ends, and Lee jumped in at 9 p.m. and inserted the first bolt. He seemed energetic and in good spirits, because we could see the end of the job. Craig returned, and Dickie was happy to get some relief. He went in on the crew boat. Steve was supposed to be back on January 10, and then I'd be able to go in.

We dived through the night, and I slept for three hours.

Seas steadily grew worse for five days, postponing our work, and the barge towed away. The sky remained overcast as ten-foot swells rolled through, and it felt chilly to walk on deck.

I was scheduled to go in after the job was completed, but that date became uncertain.

✷ ✷ ✷

The worst storm of the season erupted. Thirty-foot seas hammered the barge. We stood on the derrick crane walkway and watched the entire stern sink under water. The Mexicans feared that we would capsize. They stood aghast when a big wave came over the pontoon shack on the starboard stern and swallowed the stern rails. We caught the spray ten feet above the main deck. The foaming sea rushed out between the rail posts when the barge came up and the glistening wooden deck planks revealed themselves. The main deck stood ten feet above the water on a calm day. The railing rose another four feet, and the lights on top of the pontoon shack were at least ten feet above the rails, but the sea flooded the lights and tore one from its post. Another wave slammed into the pontoon shack and smothered it with metal-twisting force. The explosion drowned out our thoughts. We watched in fascination as the barge went under again and again, and every time came up, and displaced the sea. On the starboard side white water roared into the enclosed pipe ramp and filled it as if a dam had broken upstream. Lethal davit hooks banged against the walls. The roar echoed through the pipe ramp and became a hiss as water turned to foam and the water receded. The derrick crane rested its boom over the center deck and next to it lay the smaller crane boom. The center deck became a tangled maze of rusty slings, pipes, cans, and hoses. The port side took less punishment, and our decompression chamber stood firmly.

I took pictures with a cheap camera from the crane deck while a group of us stood transfixed. The stern submerged, the water washed over the deck and pounded the base of the crane, the sea retreated, and the deck reappeared. Beyond the barge, a dark green ocean swirled and boiled. Mountains pushed up, crashed over valleys, and disappeared under white foam. Whirlpools pulled the barge, but it resisted. We felt secure on our heavy metal fortress that refused to go down. The barge could take thirty-foot seas, so we towed in circles through the storm. In the North Sea it would have been different. The barge would have returned to shallow water to avoid the fifty-foot seas.

Steve and I went to the divers' lounge and listened to a Moody Blues tape. The lyrics soothed our aching souls. I could see Steve was somewhere far away when they sang "Work away today—work away tomorrow— never comes the day for my love and me—I feel her gently sighing as the evening slips away—if only you knew what's inside of me now—you wouldn't want to know me somehow . . ."

✶ ✶ ✶

Three days later we towed back to the work site under cloudy skies through diminishing seas. Craig came into my cabin and complained. "The supervisor said he wants to finish the job. We all want to finish the job."

"The guy's a hotshot Navy man who wants to look good on paper," Larry said.

After the storm, the sea was a chocolate color, and at dawn the barge set anchors.

We started diving. It felt good to be busy.

Craig found the pipe and the davit cables, connected them, and lifted the pipelines off bottom. Lee aligned the flanges and inserted four bolts. Larry put the O-ring in and the rest of the twenty-four bolts. By the afternoon, we began tightening the bolts with the hydraulic torque machine. The tedious process took all night.

As I stood in line for dinner, Craig introduced me to Joe, Mark's replacement. He extended his right hand in greeting, and I couldn't help staring at it. The first two fingers had been cut off at the first joint below the knuckle.

I shook his hand and said, "Glad to meet you."

He was slim, about my height, with shiny black hair. He had a mustache that didn't extend the full width of his mouth. He wore a faded set of jeans and a T-shirt that had a picture of a drilling rig with the words "Huacabil Delfin" above it. His eyes were blue and set close together and seemed to have a permanent squint. His face and arms were tan, and he wore a silver wristwatch with a black band. We sat in the galley and ate pork chops, peas, and hot rolls.

Joe had been swept into the pipe ramp one season while inspecting the pontoon hitch. A set of rollers had pivoted and crushed his hand. He still dived, though.

"They closed the New Orleans airport because of snow," Joe said.

"That's unusual," Craig said.

"I came in from Houston."

"How long have you been with the company?" I asked.

"Five years. I've been on pipe-lay barges, dredge barges, drilling rigs. You name it, I've been on it. I was over in Bahrain for a year. I hated that place. They didn't deliver any mail for six months."

"You made a lot of dives?"

"Yeah, man. I've made hundreds. I've been to 160 on scuba."

Joe was cocky, but he was a good diver.

✸ ✸ ✸

We tightened bolts into the night. When Pemex was satisfied the flange wouldn't leak, we made a few more dives to disconnect slings.

Some of the crazy things that happened under water could never be predicted. My first mistake was to slip into a wetsuit that was too thin. I thought I would be in the water only thirty minutes, but the dive lasted more than two hours. I jumped into cold water and couldn't see a thing on the bottom. The shackle on the sling I was to disconnect was frozen, so

I had to use the oxy-arc torch to cut the three-inch-thick cable. The worst part of the dive was the waiting. Shivering in darkness, I waited for the deck crew to prepare the oxy-arc torch. I was cold and miserable. When the welding machine was finally ready, I had to return to the ladder, grab a pouch of rods, and return to the bottom. When I cut through the cable, I felt relieved, but the long crawl along the bottom sapped whatever strength I had left. As I headed toward the surface, I became nauseated. I vomited in the mask. I didn't want to drown in my own vomit. I stayed calm and exhaled the rest of the way to the surface. Luckily, I reached the surface quickly and ripped off my mask. I scurried to the chamber and began my two-hour decompression.

✷ ✷ ✷

The fog drifted in over a flat green sea, and the clammy air settled on the deck, the metal walls, the dive hoses, the wooden divers' telephone boxes, and the davit chains. The rubber mask hoods became moist and gritty from the salt.

Joe made the last dive. He disconnected the remaining two slings, checked for more leaks, found none, and surfaced.

Finally, the supertankers could get their oil, and I could get some rest away from the floating world.

In the afternoon, when the sun had burned away the fog, we saw six ships on the horizon. The black gold flowed again.

Somewhere off the coast of Coatzacoalcos, lay a pipeline flanged together. Normally, pipelines were welded together, but the shallow water and sand had forced us to make an unusual repair.

Larry and I took the crew boat to Ciudad del Carmen at midnight, reached the dock at 4 a.m., and flew to Merida later in the morning on a bumpy DC-3. We parted company in Merida.

I flew to Mexico City. The weariness and fatigue vanished when I stepped on land. The body had a tremendous ability to rejuvenate. I had twelve days of complete freedom.

The Geyser at Tecozautla

I arrived in Mexico city Friday afternoon. My flight to New Orleans didn't leave until Monday, so I had two days to kill. I didn't have a care in the world, except for an appointment with the IRS on January 28.

My suitcase came along the conveyor belt in the baggage claim area, but it had been opened and three items trailed behind: a shaving kit, a can of deodorant, and a comb. Irritated, I pulled everything off the belt and ruffled through my clothes, but nothing appeared to have been stolen. One of the latches on the suitcase was broken and had a sharp edge, and I cut my finger closing it.

I wrapped a handkerchief around my finger to stop the bleeding and left the baggage claim area.

A young man in a suit approached and handed me a business card that read: Jorge's Clean Rooms For Rent 1200 p.

He said he was a navigator for Aeromexico who had been laid off. He offered to be a tour guide for a modest fee.

What the hell, I thought. He had an honest face and I had the suggestibility of a child after that herculean task at Coatzacoalcos.

He took me to an apartment in a seedy suburb of Mexico City in his red Camaro convertible.

We came to a small street off the avenue, and the apartment houses reminded me of the Lower East Side of Manhattan. The street ended in a cul-de-sac with an open air grocery stand and an ice cream vendor. Some of the buildings had been disfigured with graffiti, and trash littered the sidewalks. He smiled and waved to a girl who stood outside one of the buildings.

"Come with me," he said. He pulled the suitcase out of the car and led me into a ground floor apartment, where a white dog greeted us. "That's Walker," he said. "And here is your room."

I quickly scanned the living room, kitchen, and narrow hall that led to two bedrooms and a bath. He showed me a small windowless room with a bed, carpeted floor, and dresser.

"Who lives here?" I asked.

"I do." The apartment was too warm and smelled of dog hair. "I give you good deal. Twelve hundred pesos a day including breakfast."

"I'm listening."

"How long you stay?"

"My flight leaves Monday."

"Don't worry. I take care of you. You want to see geyser? We can go tomorrow to my hacienda. I can show you many things. You want to see Xochimilco? Jorge is a good guide."

"I can tell, Jorge. And what's for breakfast?"

"Don't have much, now, but I can buy some eggs, if you like."

"Where do I eat dinner?"

"Jorge will cook for you. Don't worry. You give me some money and I go to the store and buy some steaks. You want a ribeye?" He was trying to impress me with his English. I had not expected to rent a room in someone's apartment.

"I guess I can take it for the weekend, but you have to bring me to the city before Monday."

"No problem." He smiled politely.

"So you're renting a room in your apartment?" I asked.

"Yes." He was still smiling. "I will buy food now. You can give me some money?"

I gave him four hundred pesos, and he left. From looking at his shabby apartment, I guessed that Aeromexico navigators didn't make much money, even when they were employed. My room was cramped, but friendlier than the spartan cubicle on the barge, and I settled in. The place seemed strange, but I adapted. I overcame the culture shock easily, because where I came from there was no culture. Nothing took root on the sea. Nothing stuck to it. It had no permanence. Living in an alien culture was easy.

Jorge came back with the groceries. We ate a tough dry steak with baked potatoes. Afterwards, I told him I was tired from the flight and went to sleep.

In the morning I woke to the sound of eggs frying. I came into the living room.

Jorge said, *"Buenos dias*. I am your guide. Where would you like to go?"

"You said something about a geyser."

"That's near my father's hacienda in Tecozautla. We can stay there and come back tomorrow. You can help pay for gas?"

"Sure. How far is it?"

"About two hours' drive."

"Let's go."

We ate greasy eggs in silence. Jorge took his dog for a walk, then the three of us drove north in the red Camaro. Jorge was proud of his car. Whenever another car came too close he, became angry.

When we reached the periphery of the city, we ran out of gas. Jorge walked a mile to fill his can. He told me the gas gauge didn't work, and he thought he had filled the car three days before.

"Robbers," he said. "They take gas all the time."

We filled the car and resumed our journey. Rolling green hills replaced buildings and stores, and we entered a different Mexico. We drove through mile after mile of farmland and passed a small town that was hosting a bullfight. We stopped for a few minutes and stood with the crowd along the fence. The women were dressed in traditional Spanish clothes. The bull seemed too young and inexperienced for a real fight.

We continued north, and the land became arid and desolate. Rounding a bend, the car headed down into a canyon where the walls were green and intensely alive. At the bottom, a stream flowed, then the road climbed again, and we were on the surface. The barren desert landscape resumed. I looked more intently and saw the green cuts in the land where concealed canyons lay. They were only visible when the road climbed a hill. It was as if the brutal land had to be sliced open to live.

We arrived at a small town with cobblestone streets. There were no cars but the red Camaro, which looked ostentatious. Burros laden with straw baskets walked the streets. We stopped beside a modest fenced property with a brick courtyard. There was a fountain by the gate and further back stood two buildings connected by an angled roof with exposed beams, and between the buildings was a picnic table.

Jorge introduced me to his family. His father and two sisters lived there. His father, a local government clerk, was a widower. Jorge showed me my room in the left building, which could have been a converted garage. A mattress lay on a concrete floor. The building had four rooms separated by plywood walls, and they all faced the courtyard. In the back of the property they had a small yard and some chickens.

Jorge was an efficient guide. He took me across the street to a place with a stone floor, and the bartender fixed us a drink. Colorful bottles lined the wall behind the bar.

Then Jorge took me to a public swimming pool perched halfway down a canyon outside of town, but it was dry and abandoned. Jorge, the dog, and I hiked along a trail that followed a stream. I thought we had gone back in time. Women washed their clothes in the stream. Bright shirts lay on boulders in the clearings. We passed adobe houses where children played in dusty yards and the aroma of wood fires diffused through the motionless air.

When we came to a bridge, Jorge threw Walker over the side. The dog hit the water fifteen feet below, gave a whimper, jumped to the stream bank, shook itself dry, and wagged its tail as if it enjoyed suffering to please its master.

I said, "*Malo hombre*," but Jorge laughed.

We returned to the hacienda before dark, and Jorge's sisters prepared a simple meal of fried liver and corn. They cooked on a wood-burning stove and had no telephone, television, or radio. We ate on the picnic table outside and heard the bray of a burro in the street. Jorge gave me a drink which had an awful taste but I sipped it slowly and tried not to offend my host.

"You like *pulque*?" he asked, filling his glass with the cloudy liquid.

"No more, please. I'm full."

"Tomorrow we go to geyser."

When his sister with the dark hair took my plate I politely practiced my Spanish. "*Gracias por la comida.*"

"*De nada,*" she said.

She was a beautiful girl who could make your heart ache just looking at her. She wore a simple dress and an apron. Our eyes met for a moment. She smiled and probably knew what was on my mind. Did I look like some half-starved escaped convict? I knew the chance of anything happening in this strict Roman Catholic country was about as remote as finding seaweed in the desert. Here I was with twelve free days and I had to be in Mexico where everything was labeled "Look, Don't Touch." I was war-weary, anyway, from the battles at sea and needed to get my strength back, so I went to my mattress and looked forward to spending a few nights in Merida with women who would gladly comfort a lonely sailor in exchange for a little cash. I went to sleep.

In the morning Jorge checked his car. When he approached me, he wasn't smiling.

"Robbers took gas again," he said. "Can you help pay for gas?"

"Why should I pay for stolen gas? It's not my fault."

"Wait a minute." He walked inside the house. I heard some kind of a discussion. When he came out, he was smiling. "We go to geyser now. Don't worry. I take care of you."

He disappeared into town with his gas can and returned twenty minutes later. His sister gave him a basket of food and some towels, and we drove off with Walker in the back seat. We filled the tank at the only station and then followed a narrow paved road that led into the hills. The road became dusty gravel that ended at a steep hill. On the top ridge thick columns of steam shot out horizontally from pipes. People played in and out of the steam and we couldn't hear their voices over the roar. Water flowed down the hill into a wide shallow pool lined with rocks. We removed our shirts and walked through the hot rushing steam and sat in the warm water of the pool. We watched a man and woman working with a falcon in the distance.

Jorge threw sticks that Walker chased. I enjoyed the view of the surrounding hills and was glad to have discovered the real Mexico, which meandered along like a centuries-old horse-drawn cart that didn't care how fast it got to the next town. I looked at the rugged countryside. The rural farmers lived simple lives. I had seen many Indians along the way living in shacks, selling their handicrafts. The Spanish conquerors had not killed them or driven them away to reservations like the white man did in America, but their land had been taken away, and they lived in poverty. I relaxed in the warm water of the pool and saw the falcon return to the arm of its master. I didn't have a care.

After a few hours we left, and Jorge took me to an old Spanish church with huge rotting wooden doors. I admired the stained glass inside, and Jorge laughed when Walker pissed on the floor.

"Should we be going back to Mexico City soon?" I asked.

"Want to stay for dinner? My father bought a goat."

"I want to go now."

He became quiet, but respected my wishes. He drove back to the hacienda, and we prepared our things.

I watched his father skin the goat in the back yard. It hung by its neck and the blood drained into a pan on the grass. We left.

The return trip passed in silence, and by late afternoon we arrived in the densely inhabited city. We settled accounts after some argument over the gas bill, and I asked him to take me to a hotel.

"You've been a very good guide," I said. "I enjoyed the tour."

"Next time I take you anywhere for free." He smiled.

He let me out in a canyon of a different sort, where hundreds of cars belched poisonous smoke and concrete walls blocked the sun. I spent the night in a sterile multistoried hotel and ate breakfast in the morning in a rectangular room full of sulking tourists. I took an Aeromexico jet to New Orleans. Either Jorge's food or something I ate on the plane gave me the worst case of diarrhea in my life, leaving me in bed for two days with cold sweats.

After taking care of business in the States, I flew to Merida and checked into the Hacienda hotel. I had three days before going out to that floating monastery. I had a good time. The cab driver showed me a new place on Calle 80, nothing but a rowhouse with iron bars across the front porch like some prison. It had many dark-skinned Indian girls, which I preferred. They didn't speak English, though. I sat around the pool and drank Cuba Libres, wandered through town, and browsed the shops.

I flew to Ciudad del Carmen and boarded a crew boat to the oilfield. The Detroit diesels kicked in, the boat left the dock, and the fresh salty air hit my face. I knew I was going home. There was no more time for nonsense. When land disappeared, it was as if it had never existed.

The boat reached the *L.B. Meaders* after sundown. The barge was laying pipe near Akal C.

Whale Shark

On board were Dickie, Larry, Lee, Joe, and Steve. We were laying a line four miles long from Akal C to Akal J. The brilliant lavender water hypnotized me. Five-foot swells lapped at the sides of the barge. I made a noon pontoon check on scuba with Dickie, who took me to the bottom at 120 feet.

The smoky emptiness stretched in all directions. Far above, dark silhouettes of the barge and pontoon hovered like toys against the bright surface light. The bottom was barren, except for a few holes where augur shells lived. It felt good to be in the water. Rivalries dissolved in the solitude empty of ambition, peaceful. I floated a few feet off bottom. A clump of bubbles left the regulator and lazily ascended. The most important thing here was a breath. Not happy, not sad, I was one with the sea. Slowly, I ascended into the turbulence above.

Along the pontoon, I passed many sergeant major fish, and by the hitch, was my old friend, the blenny, still guarding her little corner of the universe.

When I came out of the water, I was awed by the Akal platforms off the stern. Four flare stacks shot yellow flames a hundred feet into the sky. Six platforms grew out of the water connected to each other with walkways. Two large work boats were tied off under each of the center platforms. It was an impressive sight.

At night, Akal was even more fantastic. When I tended Joe on the midnight pontoon check, it could have been day on a planet with a weak sun that barely kept out the darkness. The reddish gold water glowed and boiled under the flare stacks, and white and blue lights traced the outlines of the vague and indistinct shapes of the structures and walkways that hung precariously in the sky. The horizontal walkways seemed to float above the water, and when a gale came through, it bent the flames on the towers to one side. Sometimes a flame broke loose from the main body like a solar flare.

In the evanescent orange glow and smoky shadows above the flames, giant frigate birds with six-foot wingspans soared gracefully on the rising heat. The left flare stack wasn't burning cleanly. It belched dark swirling wads that glowed inside and then burst into flames as the smoke dissipated.

The whole scene could have been something out of Edgar Rice Burroughs: an alien city standing high above burning lava on a dark liquid planet, with the flares as burning beacons and us on a ship making a connection to another city.

I wondered what the year would bring.

One day, Steve and Dickie made a spiny dive, while Joe and I stayed behind. I regretted my decision, because Steve said he saw a whale shark, the largest fish in the world.

Steve said, "I didn't know what the hell it was at first. I hugged the jacket leg and pretended to be a barnacle."

"How big was it?" I asked.

"Must have been thirty feet long."

Whale sharks eat plankton, and they are fish, not sharks, but a first encounter with one could be an awesome experience.

Dickie took his Nikonos on the 6 p.m. pontoon check, but the whale shark had returned to the unknown.

The Pemex bosses came on board one day for an inspection tour. Their appearance suggested European descent. There was not a dark-skinned, black-haired person among them. They walked around the deck with nervous frowns like a herd of sheep that had never been at sea before. They watched the pipelaying activity and ate a specially prepared lunch in our humble galley. I didn't know if it was a good or bad omen, the arrival of those decision makers. Were they trying to determine if their money was being well spent? Were they making one last curious visit before canceling our contract? They left by helicopter after two hours.

I paid a visit to the barge medic, who gave me a shot of penicillin to treat the gonorrhea I had brought with me from Merida. I was cured after a few weeks.

A storm sent us below deck for a few days, and Dickie complained that Larry kept him awake all night throwing trash cans in the hall. Larry had a bad dream, and a steward said Larry had almost torn off a lavatory door.

Eventually we came near the Akal J platforms. Their flares burned brightly, and at night they had big halos around them. Seas were choppy, but not too bad. I made a pontoon check at noon. The depth at the end of the pontoon was forty-eight feet and my bottom time was fifteen minutes.

Steve showed us pictures of his baby girl. "I saw her when she was born, and I saw her in January. Now, I won't see her until April," he said.

El Chichon Volcano Erupts

In Mexico, many men exhibited exaggerated masculinity characterized by aggressiveness, intransigence, brutality, and a readiness to fight and kill.

One would think these traits would make a good diver; after all, didn't a person need to be brutal to fight a brutal foe, the sea?

Ironically, machismo was useless under water. Perseverance, stubbornness, and extreme self-confidence helped, but machismo was a liability, because a man had to know his limitations. Nothing could defeat the sea.

I didn't have machismo. Craig didn't have it. He was all business. He was the scientific diver. He could have been buried under a snowdrift, and he'd want to know what temperature it was. Dickie didn't have machismo. He was inscrutable, even-tempered, and modest on deck. Nobody could figure him out. Lee didn't have machismo. Maybe when he was younger he had it, but not anymore. He was too old to care. The Troll had it, but not when he was sober. When he was diving, he was calm and rational. What about Flipper? Mike was more crazy than macho. He was super-human. He didn't need to prove his manhood. What about Steve or Mark? No. They didn't have it. Joe was probably macho before he lost his fingers, but now it surfaced only when he drank.

The thing about diving was that the macho ones were dead or crippled and the ones without it, the ones who admitted their fear, who were too careful at times, who respected the unknown, who didn't have anything to prove, still had all their fingers and made a good living diving. They were the ones you could learn something from, if they wanted to tell you.

I could spot the macho ones. I never wanted to argue with one. They were unpredictable. They might punch you or throw you overboard. You had to give them a wide berth to avoid puncturing their inflated egos. They commanded respect, but you had to pity them when they thought they could break the laws of physics and you saw their mangled hands or swollen eyes. With boxing it's an even fight. You had to be macho to intimidate your opponent and beat him psychologically. Under water, though, you didn't want it. Sure, you needed courage, physical strength, endurance, and stubbornness, but you didn't want machismo. When it's you against a three-inch-thick steel cable bouncing around in rough seas, it's no contest. You approach it carefully, and if it kicks or jumps at you, you leave it alone. To be a good diver you needed to let go of your ego.

✶ ✶ ✶

Rough seas hit us, so the barge towed away from the platform and we went into hibernation. Skies were gloomy for three days, and we became spectators to life. We watched the film *Little Big Man*, played Risk, and slept like cats. We had a darts competition against the British. Larry and I played against Edward White, the pontoon technician, and Mick the warehouseman. We lost pitifully. Edward White threw three triples in a row, and I was demoralized.

✶ ✶ ✶

Through most of March we did some pipelaying from Akal to Abkatum. I made two pontoon checks a day, because Steve had an earache, then the barge ran out of pipe.

Mike returned from his vacation. He had a little flab around the belly; otherwise he was ageless.

One day the barge set a heliport on Echo I platform, then we towed to a place where a boat anchor had buckled a pipeline. The pipeline looked like a letter S.

Pemex got the bright idea to straighten the pipeline by pulling on it.

"I can tell you right now it won't work," Mike said.

"It'll be fun to watch," Larry said. "Whose turn is it to dive?"

"Don't look at me," Mike said. "This whole thing is a joke."

"You're next in the rotation," Craig said.

"I don't care. I'm not hooking up some stupid cable to straighten a line."

"That guy," said Craig, shaking his head. It was the first time I had seen any emotion from Iceman.

"I'll make the dive," Larry said.

Larry connected the stern winch cable to the end of the pipeline using a big shackle. The depth was 102 feet. Optimum bottom time was sixty-eight minutes.

He surfaced. Everybody left the stern.

I sat with Steve by the chamber. We saw the cable stretched over the stern rails as the barge pulled slowly forward with its anchors. After twenty minutes, we heard the sound of steel stretching, then came a loud vicious thunk. The cable parted, gouged a groove in the rail, and fell into the sea.

Pemex wanted us to try again, so Craig dived and connected another cable. The barge pulled ahead. The second cable also snapped.

Pemex wanted us to try one last time with a double cable, so Larry connected it to the line after dark, and the barge started pulling. We went to sleep.

In the morning I learned the cable had broken. We were going to cut the pipe in sections and salvage them.

Mike went down and inspected the buckled line at night. He always played on the bottom. I heard him talking with his friend Mr. Bill. He explained to him why he was on the ocean floor in the middle of the night. He kept rambling on about how cars needed oil and people needed cars and he was doing all this work so some idiot could drive two blocks to a Timesaver instead of walking. I guess he liked talking to himself so he wouldn't get lonely, because he was on the bottom a long time.

Mike buoyed off the buckled area. When he came up he said, "If we cut at the two buckles we can salvage it in three pieces."

I decompressed Mike, then we slept while three divers from the *282*, a pipelaying barge, continued the work into the night.

I woke early in the morning. Steve told me the barge was turning and getting ready to pick up a section of pipe. The three fresh divers from the *282* had made a cut at the first buckle. Beyers was on board again. He wore a crumpled brown Navy uniform with no insignia.

We salvaged one section, then stood by all afternoon while the Pemex inspectors formulated another idea.

I shut down the compressors before dinner and secured the dive station. We did nothing the rest of the night.

✷ ✷ ✷

I walked on deck in the morning and found it covered with a one-inch layer of white powder. The sky was ashen, and the sun glowed dimly, as if we were having an eclipse. The sea was cloudy and shifted lazily. I crouched down and felt the soft powder, which was neither cold nor hot.

I looked up into the sky, and the powder was still falling. The sun barely peeked through the haze. It doesn't snow in Mexico, I thought. The barge was quiet. Two men stood by the coffee machine on the center deck. I walked to the chamber. There was a diver inside. Joe sat on a bitt in front of the controls.

I sat beside him on the other bitt and asked, "What is it?"

"They didn't tell you?"

"I just woke up."

"A volcano erupted a hundred and forty miles southeast of Coatzacoalcos. Ciudad del Carmen is covered with two inches of ash."

"It's strange. Wonder how much will fall." I extended my hand palm up.

"We're a hundred miles out at sea, and it looks like it's snowing. Can you believe it?"

"What about the pipe?"

"Craig said they want to salvage the whole thing."

"The whole thing? How many joints is that?"

"I don't know."

"Are we diving?"

"Standing by. Craig just made another inspection."

There are a number of volcanoes in Mexico, and some are active, including Popocatepetl, Colima, and Pico de Orizaba. El Chichon, in the Chiapas region, was thought to be dormant, but on April 1982, thick columns of ash rained down on Campeche Bay and coastal towns. Lead-colored snow fell on *L.B. Meaders*, but the work didn't stop.

I looked at Joe. He appeared glassy-eyed.

Beyers, the dive supervisor, walked past us. He shot a glance at Joe. "Joe, you better quit the drinking, or I'll run you off." He continued toward the stern.

I went to my room and stayed there most of the day. At 4 p.m. I walked on deck, and the white ash was still falling in a fine mist. The air didn't smell bad, it didn't hurt my eyes or irritate my lungs, but I felt concerned about the dive equipment. The compressors had filters. It shouldn't affect our air supply. What about the dive hoses? Would the ash turn acidic when it mixed with water? Would it corrode parts of the mask? I didn't know. Nobody else appeared on deck, so I went below.

We began salvaging the whole pipeline. Ash still fell throughout the day. We dived in the afternoon when the barge had positioned itself near the platform. We picked up a six-joint section every eight hours.

The procedure to salvage the pipeline was slow. First, we connected the davits, which took two dives. Then we removed the foam from the field joint using crowbars, chisels, hammers, and hydraulic tools. After three or four dives, the bare metal was exposed, and we cut the line with the oxy-arc torch.

We brought the six joints to the surface, the welders cut the section in half, the riggers connected the slings, and the derrick crane lifted the three joint sections on deck where they were cut again and cleaned. We worked without pause for three days, sleeping a few hours here and there, salvaging pipe, cutting pipe, diving continuously, while the white ash continued to fall. The compressors ran hot, the chamber smelled of fermenting seawater, and the mask hoods acquired a salty film, because we didn't have time to rinse them in fresh water.

On the fourth day, the ash stopped.

One of the divers from the other barge came out of the water with numb hands and swollen chest. His skin became crackly, like potato chips. Beyers assumed he was suffering from central nervous system decompression sickness, so he put the diver in the chamber. Joe also crawled in the chamber, in case the diver blacked out or needed first aid.

I pressurized the chamber to sixty feet and stood by the controls.

Beyers gave me a handwritten treatment schedule. It was an extended Table Six, a decompression schedule for severe bends. The total treatment time in the chamber would be 435 minutes.

Beyers couldn't stand still. He walked back and forth around the chamber nervously, cursing and mumbling. "Why can't one damn job go right? Goddamn buckled line. Goddamn volcano. Piss on that volcano. How's he doing in there?" He rushed to the porthole, looked in, saw the diver conscious but in pain, gave me a frightened look, took a container of Skoal from his left shirt pocket, and placed a pinch between his cheek and gum. "Joe has to breathe oxygen too," he said. "There. I marked it on the paper."

I looked through the porthole at the diver who was breathing oxygen, and there was not much we could do except wait.

A group of men gathered around the chamber. The Mexicans and the welders watched curiously as I gave the chamber a vent and everyone wanted to look in the porthole to see the injured diver.

After an hour, seeing that no one was going to die, the crowd dispersed. I looked in the porthole, and the diver seemed to be better. He lay on the cot and breathed oxygen, while Joe sat on the deck plates in the outer lock.

I followed the treatment schedule, which lasted the whole afternoon.

Central nervous system decompression sickness, or CNS, was the most serious kind of bends and sometimes resulted in paralysis or death. The awful responsibility of being a dive supervisor could give a man gray hairs.

Beyers didn't tell me all of the diver's symptoms, but I assumed he knew they were serious enough to consider that CNS was involved. Any neurological symptoms such as loss of sensation or numbness in the extremities, dizziness, or difficulty walking suggested CNS. The crackling of the skin indicated the diver had subcutaneous emphysema, gas under the skin, which was often caused by a collapsed lung.

At 7 p.m., the diver came out of the chamber and climbed into a helicopter. The machine rose and sent a gust of wind across the deck.

"What's going to happen to him?" I asked Craig.

"Could be the end of his career."

"Do you think the volcano had something to do with it?"

"Who knows?"

The diver was slightly overweight; otherwise, I didn't see any reason why he suffered the bends. That's the calculated risk every diver took, never knowing when he would get bent, despite all the precautions, strict adherence to the tables, slow ascents, and lots of oxygen. There was never one-hundred-percent certainty of safety. A diver couldn't worry about the possibility of being bent while working, though. There were too many other things to think about, but the possibility was always there, and nobody knew the susceptibilities and what caused the bends in someone healthy, not overworked, not suffering from old age, obesity, or circulatory problems. The decompression schedules were the result of thousands of trial-and-error dives, and they were safe ninety-nine percent of the time.

That day, though, something happened to a diver, and the reasons for his demise may never be known. The volcanic ash may have affected him, but that possibility was speculation.

✱ ✱ ✱

We finished salvaging the pipe, and I got some rest. I had made a couple dives during the job. I connected a sling to the line and set a buoy on the buckled area. The depth was 107 feet, and my bottom time was fifty-eight minutes. I also removed foam from a field joint with a bottom time of sixty-eight minutes, but I hardly remember what I did, because I was too tired.

The barge picked up anchors and towed toward Akal J, where we resumed our pipelaying job.

Larry decided he'd had enough. He packed his bags. "My wife bitches when I stay out too long," he said. "Sometimes my daughter acts like she doesn't know me. That's the business, I guess."

We shook hands, and I followed him to the crew boat.

Larry shook hands with Craig and Mike, handed his duffel bag to a rigger on the stern of the boat, climbed down, and disappeared into the hatch. He still had a mysterious, invincible aura around him that only a tender saw. To others he was just a troll, but to those of us who aspired to be in his place, he was a living legend.

Land of the Lotus-Eaters

I planned my next vacation. The volcano stopped all flights out of Carmen and Merida, so I waited to go in.

I read a newspaper one day and learned that British warships were racing to the Falkland Islands that had been captured by Argentina; Iran and Iraq were still at war; Russia was fighting guerillas in Afghanistan; Central America was boiling; there were border disputes between Russia and China; and Irish were fighting Irish in Northern Ireland. It seemed only North America was peaceful.

Where could I go for my vacation? I needed to relax, acquire some civilized habits, and eat something besides barge food. I needed to lose the savage for a while. I needed to see something beautiful. I needed to get away from the awful heat.

I flew to Denver, Colorado, to see my friend Rothman who worked as an X-ray technician on the barge, but whose vacation coincided with mine. We had talked about bringing half a ton of marijuana into the States, and we were going to plan the deal. Rothman and I shopped for an airplane. He thought a twin-engine Queen Air would be suitable.

I spent two days at his condo. We planned the route from Oaxaca. He would write me when I got back to the barge.

"When the fat lady sings, we're going," he said. We'd fly in as tourists, make the payoff, and load the airplane at the end of the airstrip, after we cleared customs. I figured I could get off the barge for a few days without getting into trouble.

I flew to New Orleans and checked all the possessions I had in the world in the storage garage on the West Bank. The books, record albums, the car, and clothes were dusty but intact.

After two days, I flew to Cozumel, stayed at the Hotel Aguilar in San Miguel, and explored the ruins of El Castillo.

I took pictures and saw a cruise ship parked south of the Sol Caribe hotel. The water was turquoise, clear, and enticing.

Cozumel was famous for spectacular reefs. The island had the Palancar reef, a U-shaped canyon from sixty-five to eighty-five feet, and Punta Sur, which had a tunnel starting at 100 feet and ending at 130 feet over a vertical wall, but I didn't want to go near the water. It was too much like work.

The whole island was swarming with tourists. I wanted to get the hell out of there. At night a nerd with glasses gave me a dirty look in the cramped elevator when I was bringing a girl up to my room. I felt like picking him up by the neck just to shake him up a little. Probably some self-righteous bigot. What did he know? I left early next morning.

✳ ✳ ✳

A strange kind of melancholy came over me after more than a year at sea. Time ceased to exist. I stared at the water under a spell. I sat on a bitt for hours, listened to the sound of the water, and enjoyed the gentle roll of the barge. I looked down into the turquoise depths and wanted to live there. I recalled my memorable dives. The sea had etched them into my brain.

The underwater sounds, sights, and touch filled my mind. It was easy to slip back in time and relive the tunnel vision under the mooring buoy, feel the sand embrace me in a death grip, hear the hiss of air into my mask, or touch the rough concrete of a pipe. In my mind I could crawl in the mud in complete darkness, experience the feeling that I had no air, rattle my teeth loose with the hydraulic impact wrench, feel the sting of a sea urchin, and feel my eardrums fluttering on ascent. I could shiver to the cold, or bounce in the surface turbulence.

The sea and her many moods hypnotized me. I remembered the warm days, enticing, lazy, clear and calm, with smooth, intoxicating ripples. I recalled other cold and opaque days, repelling and gloomy, with early morning fog hanging over the water. I lived through spooky days, raining white ash, the sun obscured. Some days were choppy and restless, unable to decide which way to go; others brought huge ground swells, rolling on a fixed course, lifting up the barge which stood in the way. Windy days delivered marching whitecaps, tumbling, then stormy days with thirty-foot crashing waves, mountains and valleys in motion, foaming with anger. Lightning storms sliced the sky. Black and mysterious nights glowed under the flare stacks, concealing the depths. Red and gold nights allowed me to watch the birds circling the bright flames. I loved the surface painted green, blue, turquoise, chocolate brown, steely gray, silver, black, red, and any mixture of those. I was ready to be rocked to sleep with her gentle rhythm or be punished by her anger.

✳ ✳ ✳

I salvaged a boat bumper, one day. It rested on the bottom, within the perimeter of a platform. How a boat bumper landed directly under a platform I had no idea, but the barge could always use a spare one, so I gladly jumped in. The dive was pure enjoyment. I dropped to the bottom, a depth of 122 feet, and took the crane line with me.

The bottom was covered in a white mist, about chest height. When I stood, I saw the platform above me, but when I crouched, I saw nothing.

I crawled through the mist. I touched a long wooden object partly buried in the mud. I pressed my faceplate closer, saw the rungs of a ladder, and knew it was the boat bumper. I tied a rope to the boat bumper and found my way out of the mist, back to the corner jacket leg where I had tied off my rope earlier. I ordered the crane line to be lowered and dragged it to the boat bumper.

My activity attracted the attention of two groupers. They hovered above me while I attached the crane line. I was an intruder to their territory. The groupers were about five feet long. I kept working. I enjoyed performing to an audience.

I ordered the crane line to be raised. The ten-foot-long boat bumper emerged from the mist like a prehistoric creature. Mud fell from it. The groupers became excited. Their jaws worked up and down. The boat bumper hung vertically, and the groupers respected its size. They retreated.

The monolith hung quietly, two large wooden planks joined by metal bars, and at the top were four rusty chain links attached to a frame. The boat bumper cleared the platform and disappeared in the bright surface light.

The groupers watched me ascend. I left their world.

✶ ✶ ✶

A new diver boarded. Tony had made a fortune speculating in gold and silver. He had made many saturation dives in the North Sea. He didn't look like a warrior, though. He was average height and wore glasses. He could have been a stockbroker. He seemed proud of the thirteen-thousand-dollar diamond-studded Rolex around his wrist. I learned he owned homes in London and New Orleans.

Tony and I became friends. We always talked about the market. I taught him about high-tech stocks, and he told me about British companies. He was thirty-eight years old and had incredible energy, and like Mike, always complained about the company and worried about what he would do when his career was finished. Commercial diving was for young men, and companies didn't hire any new employees older than thirty-five.

* * *

Tony and I made a trip to another barge, one day, to help with some work, and we had a wild ride in a personnel basket. The tug couldn't tie off to the barge because seas were too rough, so a crane on the barge transferred us. The basket was a circular rubber platform suspended by a thick rope netting that came to a point like a tepee without skin. The basket landed on the stern deck of the tug, but a swell came through, the boat dropped into a trough, and the basket jumped ten feet in the air.

"Hey, man, you'll have to time it just right!" Tony shouted over the howling wind. The basket came down hard again and hit the deck. We jumped and locked our arms through the rope netting. The basket catapulted into the air, and we swung high above the boat. The crane lifted the basket above the control tower and swung around over the barge deck. The barge was rolling, but not as violently as the boat. The basket landed on the barge deck. We quickly jumped off.

We slept four hours, then jumped on the tug when seas had calmed and rode to the Akal platform. Working conditions were terrible. Six-foot seas pounded the deck, oil and water sprayed down on us from the platform, and we couldn't hear ourselves talk over the wind and rumbling compressors. After dark, a hawser broke on the bow, and the tug caught a torque machine hose in its wheel and cut it. Pink hydraulic fluid coated the deck, and made it impossible to walk.

I dived at night and tightened two bolts with the Select-a-torque machine. The depth was 138 feet and my bottom time was thirty-eight minutes. We dived until 11 p.m. the next night, when ten-foot seas forced us to stop.

In the morning we started diving from the tugboat again, but seas steadily increased through the day, and we were miserable. I made another dive in the afternoon, and it felt good to be away from the madness on deck. On the bottom it was calm. I hung on the huge flange and watched the torque machine with its piston arm tighten the bolt a half inch a stroke. I spent thirty-eight minutes on one bolt, took a measurement of the gap around the flange, and surfaced.

After dark, somebody said another ship would finish the job, so we returned to the *Meaders*. We slept for a day and a half.

* * *

Steve smuggled himself into New Orleans, without the company knowing. He took a bus to Merida, flew to Houston, then New Orleans. He desperately wanted to be with his family. He came back in a few days. Joe and I covered for Steve while he was gone.

Dickie arrived on the crew boat, and Tony went in for two weeks. Dickie brought an electronic game called PacMan. It had a six-inch-square screen and a joystick. Everybody wanted to play it. On my first try, I reached a score of 13,780.

I received a letter from Rothman. He told me the volcano had destroyed the marijuana crop in Oaxaca, so we wouldn't be going. Perhaps it was not my karma to engage in dangerous adventures besides diving.

✳ ✳ ✳

On the slack days, when we were laying pipe, I designed a board game similar to Risk, but played on a map of the solar system. Mike helped illustrate it.

I played PacMan. One time, I reached a score of 110,900. It could have been higher, but I started experimenting and went after monsters.

I tracked the price of copper. Tony had said that the metal was due for a rise, once the housing and auto industries recovered. The price was seventy-five cents. I wanted to accumulate more shares of Alaska Interstate and also kept my eye on gambling companies in Atlantic City.

✳ ✳ ✳

The barge towed to the sea buoy near Ciudad del Carmen on August 5. We took a complete inventory of diving equipment. On August 6 the crew took apart the pontoon and set it on the center deck. We knew we were definitely leaving. The barge superintendent couldn't make up his mind whether to go to Tuxpan or Sabine Pass.

We stood by for three days and sat at the edge of our seats wondering if there was a big discussion going on somewhere about how to put the barge to work someplace else in the world. The rumor was we would go to Bahrain. Other boats and barges had also demobilized, such as the *Masagua* and *Tarasco*. I bought another thousand shares of Alaska Interstate. It seemed like the market was bottoming.

The dive crew eventually learned that construction had ceased in Campeche Bay, and almost every barge would be leaving. I packed my things and didn't know how I would get through the airport with my fragile coral, boxes of spinys, suitcase, dive gear, and box of books I had accumulated in a year.

Craig and Dickie watched me empty the locker and Craig said, "This was the Cadillac of diving jobs. There will never be anything like it."

On the crew boat I felt totally relaxed, like I always did coming off the barge, but there was an emptiness, as well. On the barge I at least had a purpose. Now I was thrown into the wind.

Oil prices had collapsed. We were pawns in a financial chess game.

✴ ✴ ✴

The crew boat arrived at the dock in the late afternoon and I stepped on solid ground and it felt strange and new.

Tony said, "Damn it. I forgot my wallet and black book. I have to go back. I'll meet you in Merida." He climbed on the crew boat while we took a taxi to the airport. I thought Tony had lost too many brain cells from all that saturation diving.

The one-room airport in Carmen was full of oilfield workers going home. A company representative gave us our tickets and we boarded a DC-3 after two hours. One hour later we landed in Merida and went to The Hacienda. We stayed a day, relaxed around the pool, and talked with tourists.

Cancun

Joe, Tony, and I flew to the Cancun beach resort, a long sliver of an island crammed with luxury hotels, condominiums, restaurants, and gift shops at the northern edge of the Yucatan Peninsula. Tony rented a car, and we drove down Cancun Boulevard looking for rooms. We stopped at the Sheraton. It was fully booked. We stopped at the Hyatt. It was fully booked. We stopped at the Hotel El Presidente. It was fully booked. Finally, as we were approaching the end of the island, we stopped at the Hotel Calinda.

Tony gave the boy at the desk five hundred pesos and in a quiet tone said, "Hey, *amigo*, find us a room, *por favor*." Within ten minutes we were in front of the Hotel Bojorquez and had two rooms.

We went to Charlie's Restaurant, a notorious meeting place, in the late afternoon. Only a few people were there. I stared at a young girl, seated by herself. She wore a sleeveless top and had long, straight blond hair. Tony bought some marijuana from one of the waiters.

Tony was like a dog that had broken loose from its chain and wanted to overturn every garbage can in the neighborhood. We left the restaurant and explored the area, and Tony found two girls in a swimming pool.

"Hey, man, where are your spinys?" he asked me. "I want to give these girls some spinys."

"I think I left a box in the car."

"They like these things, you know." He gave each girl a spiny oyster and said, "Where are you staying? Do you want to go out dancing tonight?" They giggled and didn't answer.

"He's a rich deep-sea diver. He likes you," said Joe to the tall one.

Tony crouched near the edge of the pool. "Listen. We're staying at the Hotel Bojo—, or whatever you want to call it. Room 311. You want some more spinys? We have boxes full of 'em. Come on over later."

"They're pretty. Where did you get them?" asked the brown-haired girl.

"Diving on the rigs."

"Maybe we'll come by later."

"Great. See you around," Tony said.

Tony was ready to give away all my spinys if he could find a date.

Later we had dinner at Charlie's. Tony and I tried to pick up two teenage girls from Houston. They said they would meet us later at one of the discos, but they never showed up.

I couldn't believe Tony's energy. Joe and I lost him close to midnight. I took a car to a Mexican bar outside of town, got drunk, and brought a fat girl to my room. Tony showed up later carrying my box of spinys. He had carved a hole in the bottom, and there were only two spinys left. I was angry. I wouldn't give him any more spinys.

We slept for a few hours then went scuba diving in the afternoon with some amateurs.

One of the men in our group asked Tony if he had a decompression table, because he wanted to calculate his residual nitrogen time, and Tony said, "Hey, man, what's that?"

"Don't you follow the tables?" he asked.

"When the tank runs dry, I come up, man."

The tourist looked at Tony with contempt and avoided him after that.

Before our Mexican dive master could even explain the gear and dive plan, Tony had jumped in carrying everything in his arms. I quickly followed and watched him descend. Before he hit bottom he had the tank on his back, weight belt snugged up, fins on, mask on, and was waiting for the rest of us in a sandy patch surrounded by coral domes. The Mexican diver, whose name was Umberto, left him alone.

One man in the group couldn't get under the water. He must have had his buoyancy compensator fully inflated and didn't know how to release the air. The man bobbed on the surface while we explored the reefs and saw some huge blue parrotfish.

We stayed down until our tanks were almost empty. Umberto swam around excitedly, read our gauges, and motioned for us to surface, but we ignored him and came up in our own good time.

When we were all back in the boat, Umberto, who was missing a front tooth, said to the floating amateur, "What's your problem?"

I felt sorry for the tourist, and Umberto treated him badly.

Tony and Joe had their swim suits on, but I wore a long-sleeved denim shirt and denim trousers. Tony asked, "What are you wearing all that for? This isn't a pontoon check."

"He's been out there so long he doesn't know the difference any more," Joe said.

In the evening we sat outside at the Café Augustus, drank beer, and ate pizza.

"What will you do now?" I asked Tony.

"I want to retire to the Bahamas, but I need about two million dollars."

"I'd be happy with two hundred thousand," I said.

Tony told me about his plan to attach black boxes under water to the platforms and blackmail Pemex. He would claim he had bombs wired to all the major structures, and would threaten to blow them if he didn't get two million dollars.

I didn't know if Tony was serious, but I didn't think the plan would work.

We spent one more day in Cancun, then flew to New Orleans, and that was the last time I saw Tony.

I went through Customs with my boxes full of spiny oysters and had to open one. The lady behind me said, "Oh, they look like little crabs."

The company I worked for soon went out of business. At least I had a logbook full of memories, and although I was still alone, it seemed insignificant, having faced the unknown so many times. I was in great physical shape, except for ringing in my ears and a scar on my leg. I was happy to be alive.

The pontoon being towed into position in preparation for pipelaying.

The pipeline leaves the barge and enters the first section of the pontoon. Note field joint with smooth section.

The pontoon out of the water. Every inch is covered with barnacles and shells.

A Mexican polishing a riser flange prior to the riser being set by divers.

A riser being lifted off the center deck by the derrick crane.

A riser hanging above the water near the platform where it will be set by a diver. Note drift pins secured with rope above the flange.

Craig prepares for a spearfishing expedition off the stern.

A single buoy mooring system the L.B. Meaders installed at Cayos Arcas.

Rough seas pound the barge.

Rough seas smash into the pontoon shack and cover the stern deck in five feet of water. We watch from the crane deck. On calm days the stern deck is fifteen feet above the waterline.

Recovering a diver after an open-bottom bell dive.

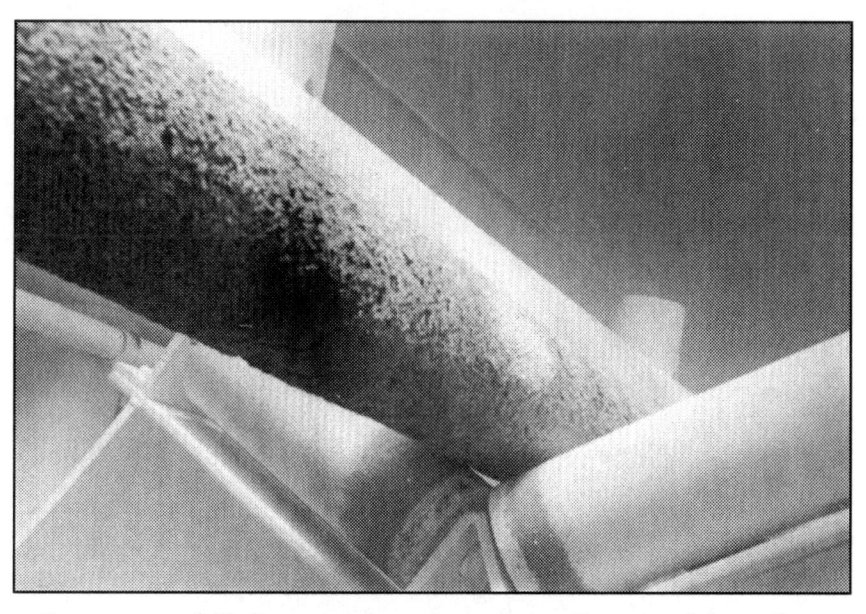

Concrete-coated pipeline going down the pontoon rollers toward the sea floor.

Diver at the end of the pontoon where the pipeline continues its descent to the ocean bottom without support.

A crevalle jack in open water.

Diver descending in an open-bottom bell.

Diver in open-bottom bell. Gas cylinders attached
provide an emergency breathing gas supply.

A school of sargent major fish.

The old and new Bangkok by the Chao Phyra river.

Floating market on the outskirts of Bangkok.

There are 30,000 temples in Thailand. Each one is unique. The Temple of the Reclining Buddha features an 80 meter gold figure with mother-of-pearl on the soles of the feet.

Monks walking in the Grand Palace, one of the most famous tourist destinations in Bangkok.

A temple figure exquisitely decorated with colorful tiles.

A Buddha statue amidst the ruins of the ancient capital Ayutthaya, north of Bangkok. The city was destroyed by the Burmese.

Water buffalo in a small village near Surin in Easter Thailand.

The island of Phuket boasts fabulous beaches.

An underwater habitat near Key Largo, Florida, managed by Craig.

III. Southeast Asia

Train to Bangkok

Oil prices collapsed, and I found myself looking for work in the most unlikely place. I knew construction had ceased in Campeche Bay, so I sensed the Gulf of Mexico would also experience a drought in diving work. I kept my belongings in storage and flew to the other side of the world. I knew Taylor Diving had an office in Singapore, but foolishly, I didn't call on the telephone to inquire if the company was hiring.

Having endured almost eighteen months at sea, I didn't care for life on land. The land was alien to me. I needed to keep moving. I didn't know how to stop. My momentum took me to an island nation at the southern tip of the Malaysian peninsula.

The first thing I noticed was that all the taxis were Mercedes, as Craig had described, and the airport was spotlessly clean. I stayed at a cheap hotel, the Station Hotel, which featured small rooms above the train station. Every morning I heard the toot-toot of a train leaving the station, bound for Malaysia.

I visited most of the diving companies on the island, including Taylor, in Jurong, an industrial park. Nobody offered me work. One manager told me to come back in a month. He said he might have something.

I stayed in Singapore a week and hiked around the city. I visited the modern department stores on Orchard Road, bought souvenirs, and ate fried rice in Chinatown. I mingled with the tourists staying at the higher priced hotels and watched pretty girls in the streets.

Singapore was a mixture of old and new. Chinese junks moored on inland waterways, and skyscrapers rose above modest shanties. Everybody dried their clothes outside the windows of their high-rise apartment buildings. I passed an old Sikh carrying an umbrella. He looked like a holy man, blessing a new construction site. All the street signs were in four languages, English, Tamil, Malay, and Chinese. Although there were distinct ethnic neighborhoods, the city was harmonious proof that people of all religions and races could live together.

What could I do for a month? The hotel rate at the Station was about twenty dollars a day, which would quickly deplete my savings, if I stayed in Singapore for an extended period.

I learned that many divers, while waiting for work, passed the time in

Pattaya, a beach resort in Thailand. I pictured a quiet, remote town with perhaps a few simple bungalows along the beach. I didn't know it was a major tourist destination for Europeans and Middle Easterners.

* * *

I booked a second-class ticket to Bangkok, Thailand.

The train left the station on a warm, moist morning, and within minutes entered the lush, tropical landscape of Malaysia. All the Muslim women wore head scarves, and many of the men wore white shirts. The seats on the train were comfortable, but the toilet was simply a hole in the floor. The train passed modest dwellings of cinder blocks and tin. Everywhere, colorful clothes hung on lines, drying in the sunny air. School children dressed in blue and white uniforms played soccer. Farther north, clouds touched the tops of green hills, and fog lay in the valleys.

After a few stops at small towns, the train arrived at Kuala Lumpur, the capital. The railway station was built in the Moorish style, with horseshoe arches and minarets.

The train continued north, past water buffalo working in rice paddies. A thick tropical forest covered the hillsides.

Night fell, and the train arrived at Penang Station. The train didn't offer sleeper cars, so everyone had to find accommodations in Penang before boarding the train the next morning. I walked into a restaurant at the station, but the menu on the wall was in Bahasa, the Malay language, so I found the cook, who spoke English, and ordered fried rice and a soft drink.

I took the ferry to Penang Island and found a cheap Chinese hotel. The taxi driver was a friendly Muslim boy who spoke with an accent. He kept saying, "You have many sexy omen in your country?" Finally, I understood, but I couldn't understand his fascination with Western women. Perhaps, from watching television and movies, he thought American women had loose morals.

Still hungry, I wandered around town, but the restaurants were closed. I found a beefburger stand by the water. Muslims wouldn't buy anything called hamburger.

Penang used to be a British trading post. Now it was a blend of East and West. The population on the island was composed of Chinese, Malays, Sumatrans, and Indians.

I didn't have time to sightsee. Early in the morning I returned to the train and continued my journey.

The train reached the border of Thailand, and everyone presented their passports. Thai women dressed in T-shirts and sarongs walked through the aisles selling fruits, rice candies, and soft drinks.

Another day and night passed, and I found it difficult to sleep. My eyes grew tired.

At dawn, I peered out the train window, and a new world greeted me.

A saffron-robed monk walked barefoot beside the tracks. He held an alms bowl. A shanty town of rusty tin roofs interrupted the tropical landscape on the outskirts of Bangkok. A man crouched in front of his one-room tin shack and brushed his teeth beside a mud puddle. I looked for a trace of familiarity, but found none. The street signs that passed were in the incomprehensible Thai language, a language that resembled nothing I had ever seen.

The train arrived at the station, but before the cars came to a complete stop, a little man took a seat opposite mine. "You want taxi?" he asked.

I nodded.

He spoke in broken English, and he asked me many questions. Where are you from? Are you from Texas? Are you military man? You want girl friend? He practically offered to be my servant for the day. I told him I had heard of a place called Pattaya, and he said he would take me to the bus station. Pattaya was a two-hour trip south of Bangkok.

Still groggy from lack of sleep, I was suggestible. I didn't know the language, didn't have a street map. Before I could protest, the little man grabbed my suitcase and rushed out the door of the train.

"Hey! Wait a minute—" I followed him.

The man put my suitcase in his taxi. I entered the passenger side, and my knees almost touched the dashboard. The car appeared ready for the junkyard. Most of the fabric and vinyl of the interior had been removed, leaving only bare metal on the floor and doors. None of the instruments on the dashboard worked. The taxi didn't have a meter.

The man called himself Mr. Ong, and he would take me anywhere I wanted to go for 500 Baht. I didn't know the exchange rate.

Mr. Ong took me to the Reno Hotel, where I shaved and washed. Then he took me to a moneychanger, where I exchanged dollars for Baht. The rate was about forty Baht to a dollar. Then he took me to a place called Happy-Happy.

"If girl likes you, she stay with you. You no pay. You take care her," Mr. Ong said.

I understood.

I was introduced to a girl named Sompon. The savage from the deep had never seen such a beautiful creature. With long black hair, delicate hands, and a magical smile, she easily won my starved heart. She moved her hands and walked gracefully, as if schooled in a fine art. Later I learned she had worked as a classical dancer at a resort outside Bangkok. She was from Surin, a town in the rural eastern region of Thailand. She spoke broken English, so we could communicate. She agreed to go with me to Pattaya for a week.

Mr. Ong took us to the bus station. "Next time you come to Bangkok, I take you to meet my family," he said.

Mr. Ong was a friendly man. No doubt he was poor and struggled to survive.

I never saw him again.

Pattaya—The Thai Riviera

I quickly learned that the Thais had the ability to flatter my western ego while taking my money. One time, I took a bus to Phuket in southern Thailand, and a boy had quickly taken my suitcase to a waiting taxi. The ride to the beach was comfortable and air-conditioned, but I spent 500 Baht. I could have taken a three-wheeled taxi for 120 Baht or less.

Pattaya was a small, but crowded resort town with an international clientele. Arabs, Europeans, Orientals, and Americans mingled. Sompon and I stayed at a cheap hotel on the southern part of the beach, amid open-air bars. The northern part of the beach was dominated by expensive hotels, and Japanese tourists stayed there.

I enjoyed paradise for a week. Sompon introduced me to exotic Thai foods. Street vendors everywhere displayed a wide variety of fish, fruits, nuts, and rice snacks. I sampled many dishes, but preferred the basic fried rice and shrimp. Sompon and I enjoyed freshly grilled shrimp and crab on the beach. I also tried dried squid and fried grasshoppers, which tasted good with beer. I dived for cowrie shells with a Thai named Jimmy who owned a boat and took tourists to nearby islands. I jogged up the hill in the mornings to the giant Buddha statue. In the evenings Sompon and I watched Thai kick-boxing competitions and snacked on a wide variety of fruits sold by the street vendors. Rambutan tasted like a soft, sweet pear. My favorite was fried banana. Women, with their portable kitchens in the streets, sliced bananas lengthwise and fried them in woks filled with coconut oil. I took Sompon jet-skiing, but she never wore a bathing suit. She preferred shorts and blouse or T-shirt. She said she couldn't swim. I learned that many people from Isaan, the eastern region, don't swim, especially in the Mekong River, because they believe there is a snake called Phajanak that grabs people and takes them under. In 1973, American soldiers caught a strange twenty-three-foot-long fish in the Mekong River. Perhaps it was the Phajanak the people feared.

Sompon liked the dreamy love songs of Thai pop artists, and I bought her tapes. She taught me to order food from the roadside vendors and how to speak the musical Thai language, where words had various meanings, depending on the tone in which they were spoken. Words could be spoken in a rising tone, falling tone, even tone, high tone, or low tone. Without a good ear for sound, a person could make hilarious mistakes. Instead of saying "How much is that dress in the window?" they might easily say,"How much is that tiger in the window?"

I was glad I had a native friend, because the signs everywhere were the most cryptic I had ever seen. The unique Thai alphabet consisted of forty-four consonants and twenty-eight vowels, and there were no spaces between words. If the indecipherable street signs weren't enough of a challenge, Sompon said that even she couldn't always understand the people of Bangkok, because she spoke an eastern dialect, Isaan. Luckily, the language of instruction in schools was English, so most people could understand ignorant foreigners, which the Thai called Farang.

I quickly learned the most basic phrases for my interactions with taxi drivers, waitresses, and hotel personnel. Fried rice was "cow pot." Fried rice with crab was "cow pat boo." Fried rice with pork was "cow pot moo." How much is the fare? Was "tow lie Baht?" Where is the bathroom? Was "teeny hong nam?"

Sompon had the most alluring smile. She took great delight in smiling at every opportunity. I didn't learn the full implications of the Thai smile until I had lived in Thailand for many months. To maintain harmony, the Thais employ many methods. The people avoid public displays of affection between members of the opposite sex, although it is not unusual to see people of the same sex holding hands. The Thai people rarely show strong emotion in public. To maintain the semblance of a cool heart, they contain their emotions. I have rarely heard a Thai raise his voice in public. Once, in the sweltering Bangkok heat, my taxi driver was involved in a traffic accident. He exchanged a few words under his breath with the driver of the other car, then the men resumed their journeys.

Another way the Thais maintain harmony in their society is creative use of the smile. The Thai smile is used to thank, apologize, show embarrassment, say hello, or smooth tension. If a Thai spills his drink on you in a bar, he may smile. He is not smiling to make fun of you; he is apologizing.

The bringing of the hands together in front of the face, as if in prayer, is called a *wai*. The *wai* may be a greeting, or a show of respect for a superior. The *wai* is always initiated by the inferior party. The superior may or may not return a *wai*. Monks typically don't return a *wai*, but a government official might. Thailand is a stratified society. It is said that making a friend in Thailand is difficult, because only people from the same economic level can be true friends. Most social situations involve an inferior and a superior. The Thai language has many pronouns for addressing people of different economic levels. Royalty and the monks are addressed differently from others. Whenever I went somewhere, one of the first questions I was asked was my income. In the West, this is typically not discussed, but it is a common way to determine a person's economic level in Thailand.

I learned there are appropriate and inappropriate times to *wai*. When I visited Jimmy's mother, I was expected to initiate the *wai*, since she was the older person. In the immigration office, I gave the *wai* to a government official, and he returned it. Giving the *wai* to a host or hostess in a restaurant is not proper, because the customer is the superior.

Bangkok, Venice of the East

In the nineteenth century, many of the people in Bangkok lived in stilt houses near waterways, or *klongs*. Food and other items were sold from boats. Today, the Floating Market is mainly a tourist destination north of Bangkok, but the *klongs* are being used more as an alternative to the crowded streets.

Sompon and I returned to Bangkok, and we stayed at the Grand Palace Hotel, a cheap dormitory along Sukhumvit Road. The incredible contrasts between rich and poor amazed me. Along the street where my hotel was situated, high-rise apartments rose next to tin shacks. Amid glittering temples of gold and jewels, people lived in cardboard houses along railroad tracks. I had never seen such poverty. In the streets, Mercedes, Lexus, Hondas, Toyotas, and the occasional elephant competed with motorcycles, trucks, buses, and *tuk-tuks*, three-wheeled motorbikes that belched smoke and zipped through traffic. I could find a hotel in Bangkok for every taste and budget, from the Oriental Hotel, rated one of the most prestigious in the world, to other luxury hotels that charged up to 1,000 dollars a day or more, to the barely adequate, where rates were only fifteen to twenty dollars a day.

Food also varied greatly in price. In the most expensive hotels, a dinner could cost 400 Baht or more. I ate decent meals of soup or fried rice from the street peddlers and paid only twenty to thirty Baht. One of my favorite soup dishes was *kaeng som*, a sweet and sour mix with fish. I also enjoyed *kuai tiao*, noodle soup with sprouts, meat balls, and spices, such as ginger.

I explored the city for a few weeks. I visited the temples, tasted the night life, and visited a snake farm, where young men taunted cobras and collected their venom. The tourists swarmed to the Patpong area, a privately owned four-acre enclave of bars, massage parlors, discos, and shops between Silom and Surawong Road. Prostitution is illegal in Thailand, but the law is not enforced. Most of the prostitutes in Thailand come from the poor provinces. One of the more modest shows I watched featured a dozen naked girls who danced on stage and dripped hot candle wax on their breasts.

In Bangkok, the massage parlors are the size of department stores. A client walks in, pays 1500 Baht for a two-hour B-course and picks a girl seated behind a large window. She's dressed in an evening gown with a number pinned to her chest. They go to a room upstairs. First comes intercourse in a hot tub, then a round of massage and another round of intercourse, this one on a bed. The client leaves clean, refreshed, and drained.

The tolerant Thais do not consider sex a sin. In a world of suffering, anything that relieves the suffering is good. Sex outside of marriage may be inappropriate, but not a sin; however, anyone engaged in child prostitution can expect a twenty-year prison term.

One visit to Patpong was enough for me. Bangkok was infinitely richer than a few sex shows and massage parlors.

One day Sompon said she was going to see a monk. She returned with a string tied around her wrist. She said it was for good luck, a blessing from the monk. Every day, I learned something new about the incredible richness of Thai culture, a culture unspoiled by the evils of colonialism. Thailand is the only country in southeast Asia never to be colonized.

In front of every house and department store I saw a spirit house. Thais are superstitious. Animism, the belief in ghosts and spirits, permeates Thai culture. People wear amulets to ward off evil spirits, and they build spirit houses to appease the spirits. Daily offerings keep the spirit happy. Food, drinks, or figurines of dancers, servants, and elephants are placed in or beside the spirit house. Garlands are also used in many places to ensure good blessings. Garlands can be found on spirit houses and vehicles or anywhere, to honor seen or unseen people. Malik, Arabic jasmine, is often used, but orchids and other flowers are also used.

In my travels through Thailand, the awe-inspiring temples aroused my curiosity about Buddhism. The architectural gems with their soaring red-tile roofs, sky tassels, elaborately carved gables, colorful doorways, and intricate mosaics showed me that Thais took their religion seriously. Many thousands of hours of painstaking labor produced those temples, which gleamed in the sun and stood in stark contrast to the green tropical countryside or shanty towns of Bangkok.

Whenever I entered temple grounds, the noise and pressures of city life fell away. Temples were tranquil oases, though only footsteps away from the bustle of the street. In a temple complex could be found a main building for worship, modest structures to house monks, a school, food vendors, a catfish pond, a banyan tree (Buddha attained enlightenment under a banyan tree), Buddhist and Thai flags, a dharma wheel, offering bowls, a pavilion for ceremonies, a gong tower, pagodas (*chedis*), a crematorium, and library. Some temples also had a hell garden, with statues depicting what happened to bad people before they went to their next life. Some vendors in the temple grounds sold birds in cages. It was considered a good deed to free a bird from its cage.

Thailand had more than 30,000 temples. I visited only a few, but each one was unique. I took a ferry across the Chao Phyra River, choked with water hyacinth. Near the bank of the river stood Wat Arun, Temple of the Dawn. Built in the Khmer style, with thousands of Chinese porcelain tiles, the temple gleamed in the morning sun. I climbed the steep steps, and photographed schoolchildren in their blue and white uniforms.

Another day I visited the Temple of the Emerald Buddha, the most revered temple, attracting millions of tourists each year. A twenty-four-inch jade figure of Buddha sat in a great hall. The temple grounds reminded me of Disneyland. Mythical figures adorned the courtyard and often supported the foundations of structures. *Yakshas*, guardian giants, protected the gates. *Kinnaris*, graceful half-woman, half-bird creatures, sparkled in blue and gold. *Apsaras*, celestial nymphs, stood frozen in time, and *Naga*, king of serpents, rested on staircase balustrades. The temple was so ornate, it seemed to be made of billions of tiny gems glued together in a fantastic three-dimensional tapestry. Brass bells powered by the wind encircled the temple below the roof, and created music in the courtyard.

Wat Po, the Temple of the Reclining Buddha, invited the visitor to walk around a 150-foot-long statue. Buddha's body was covered in gold leaf, and the soles of his feet were mother of pearl.

Wat Tramitr, Temple of the Golden Buddha, housed a solid gold statue ten feet tall. The statue weighed five and a half tons.

Outside of Bangkok I also visited the Temple of the Black Buddha, an enormous statue that filled an entire room.

Temples were places of refuge for poor people. Anyone could stay for a night. If someone wanted to stay longer than three days, he was expected to shave his head and become a monk. Most young Thai men spent part of their lives as monks.

Buddhism

Siddharta Gautama was born an Indian nobleman. As a young man, he renounced his wealth and position and became a wandering beggar in search of the truth about life. When he finally reached enlightenment, he spent the rest of his life teaching and helping others. Gautama became Buddha, the enlightened one.

Buddha teaches us that there are four noble truths. The first truth acknowledges the existence of suffering. Birth, aging, and sickness are examples of suffering. The second truth tells us that the origin of suffering is attachment. Desire for sense pleasure, desire to become, desire to get rid of are examples of attachment. The idea of self is also a delusion. We are only a part of the ceaseless becoming of the universe. The third truth states that the end of suffering is the renunciation of desire. The fourth truth shows us the path to end suffering. The Eightfold Path is the way out. It consists of right view, right intention, right speech, right action, right livelihood, right effort, right mindfulness, and right concentration. The path can extend beyond many lifetimes. Each rebirth is subject to karma. Life is an endless cycle of birth, death, and rebirth. Actions in the present life determine how we are reborn in the next life, according to the law of karma, the law of cause and effect. In other words, from good will come good, and from evil will come evil.

There are six paths of rebirth: heavenly beings, humans, asuras (beings who appear in heaven or earth as humans or animals who have many good qualities, but like to fight), animals, hungry ghosts, and hell-beings. There are many planes of existence within these groups. There are many categories of heavenly beings. Some are similar to pure energy forms, with life spans of thousands or millions of years.

Ninety percent of the Thai people are Buddhist. The moral leaders are the monks, who also serve as teachers in the rural provinces. The gentle monks, in their orange robes, alms bowls cradled in their arms, can be seen everywhere, walking with expressionless faces. Their life is austere and simple. Monks arise at 3:30 a.m. to meditate and chant. At 5:30, they go on alms rounds, allowing people to give them food. Feeding a monk is a way for an ordinary Thai to gain merit. The monk never thanks the people for the food. After noon, monks are permitted only tea.

The Thai people practice the Theravada form of Buddhism, the older form. Mahayana Buddhism is practiced in China, Vietnam, Korea, and Japan. Theravadins believe in solitary enlightenment and a release from suffering through meditation. They believe Buddha was a man who ceased to exist when he died. Mahayana Buddhists seek not only an end to one's own suffering, but an end to the suffering of all sentient beings. They believe in bodhisattvas, humans or celestial beings who sacrifice their own Buddhahood to help others achieve liberation. Mahayana Buddhists also believe Buddha was a manifestation of a spiritual being. Nirvana becomes a uniting with this universal soul.

I had no religious prejudices. I was not a Christian. The teachings of Buddha appealed to me. Here was a rational religion that didn't require faith. All the teachings could be questioned. All the truths could be discovered with my own eyes. I was a rational person, schooled in the scientific method. It made sense that good deeds and bad deeds were cumulative. A lifetime of bad deeds could not be shrugged off with a simple blessing or prayer.

Buddha said do not dwell in the past, do not dream of the future; concentrate the mind on the present moment. Existence knows only one tense, the present. It is language that creates past and future and a million tensions in the mind. To live in the moment there is no tension. It is wonderfully relaxing. There is no past but a memory. The future is but a wish. How can one live in the moment? Some people clear their minds and meditate; some enter trancelike states; some practice ritualized sex; some go to the bottom of the sea, where only a breath matters. To be fully aware is the essence of the moment.

I found many parallels between living in the present and experiencing bottom time. When I lived on the surface, I always worried about the future. Would I have a job next year? Would I get hurt on the next dive? Would I lose money in the stock market? Would I ever find a wife? Would I ever be promoted? I regretted the past. I wished I would have done better in college and not wasted so many years. I wished I had formulated career goals sooner. I wished I could have enjoyed the boom years of diving. I worried about all these things, yet I wasn't aware of all the things happening in the world. When I was on the bottom, everything changed. I was fully aware of my environment. Past and future dissolved. Breathing became the most important thing. I became conscious of every breath.

Bottom time lasted only a few minutes, though. How could I make bottom time last longer?

I began to practice meditation.

A Visit To Surin

I took a bus to Singapore with the hope of finding some diving work, but the collapse in oil prices had affected that part of the world, too. Company managers told me to try again in a month.

I returned to Bangkok.

I wanted to explore more of Thailand, so one week Sompon and I visited her mother in Surin.

The train ride took most of a day. We arrived in the eastern region of the country on a hot, dry afternoon. Surin was famous for the annual elephant roundup. Elephants were used to haul lumber.

Sompon and I shopped for tangerines and mangos in the town square, then we took a minibus to her mother's house. The bus stopped on a dirt road, and we hiked half a mile to a small village, where Sompon's sister lived. We arrived in the dry season. The rice fields were hard and parched. We hiked into a grove of palm and banana trees, where a few houses stood. Some were made of wood, built above the ground. One was more elaborate, with cinder blocks supporting a frame house with a tin roof. The house had an blue awning, small windows, and a staircase leading to the second-story bedrooms. A bamboo fence encircled the dirt yard around the house. A group of children gathered to see the *farang*, or foreigner, and I handed out tangerines to the children, who were all well-behaved. They crowded around me, smiled, and laughed. I suppose fair-skinned foreigners didn't come to their village often, and I became an object of their curiosity. I greeted Sompon's sister and brother-in-law by giving them a *wai*. I spoke only a few words of Thai, but in Isaan, people spoke a different dialect, so I probably would not have understood the people, even if I had known Thai. Some neighbors joined our group, and we sat on a wooden deck outside the house. I took pictures of the smiling children. Both men and women wore sarongs, large cloths decorated in colorful checkered or batik designs. Some of the men didn't wear shirts, but the women wore western style T-shirts or sport shirts. There was no electricity in the village. Cooking was done with charcoal. I did see a television that never worked in the second-story bedroom, however. It was connected to a car battery. The children didn't seem to have any toys to play with, but they were happy. I helped some of them with their lessons later in the afternoon. I also played soldier in the ditches behind the village, while Sompon and her sister watered the spice garden.

I was sorry I could not communicate better with the people. I wondered what they thought of the outside world. They were simple rice farmers, but they had a rich culture thousands of years old.

Sompon and I walked to a nearby house, where Sompon's mother lived. The old woman lived alone in a one-room wooden hut raised above the ground. Again, crowds of children gathered, and I distributed more tangerines. Sompon said we would spend the night at her sister's, because there were bad men in the village. She thought thieves might find me an easy target, a foreigner. Her sister's husband and his male friends nearby could protect us.

Sompon and I spent the night on a comfortable bed, under a colorful quilt.

At dawn, I opened the door and snapped a picture of Sompon's brother-in-law dressed in a red sarong, leading two water buffalo out his front gate.

A visit to the local temple and a meal of fried rice at a restaurant in town completed the short trip, and we returned to Bangkok by train.

✸ ✸ ✸

I continued to explore the fascinating country. I visited the hill tribes of western Thailand, in Kanchanaburi province. The Mon people, descendants of Burmese, elongated their necks with metal rings, painted their faces white, and wore colorful costumes. I stayed on a river raft for two days, then took the train to the Bridge on the River Kwai, the famous landmark built by captured soldiers.

I took a rice barge up the Chao Phyra River to Ayutthaya, the ruins of an ancient Thai capital that had been sacked by Burmese armies in 1767. The Khmer influence was evident, and huge *chedis*, weathered by time, stood defiantly, proud survivors of a catastrophe. Everywhere, reminders of the city's destruction could be seen. Somber stone faces chopped in half lay amid the ruins.

Phuket

In the Andaman Sea off the coast of southern Thailand lies the island of Phuket (pronounced poo-ket). The island is about forty miles long and has some of the most spectacular scenery and beautiful beaches in the world. A James Bond movie, "The Man With The Golden Gun," was filmed in Phang-nga Bay, north of the island. Huge limestone formations grow out of the sea, and villages built on stilts hug the sides of cliffs. Sea turtles lay their eggs on Surin Beach. The island is a mix of Thais, Muslims, Chinese, and Sea Gypsies. The gypsies differ in language and customs from the other inhabitants, and no one knows where they came from. They make their living fishing.

Divers are attracted to Phuket because of its clear water and coral reefs. A docile leopard shark lives in the waters near the Phi Phi Islands. Hin Daeng features vertical drops to 180 feet. The Similan Islands are considered to be the best dive sites in Thailand. Nine uninhabited islands offer more than twenty-five dive spots. Elephant Head features giant granite boulders, to 120 feet. Christmas Point offers soft corals and white tip sharks, to 105 feet. East of Eden is well suited for slow drift dives, where turtles can be seen. All are accessible by tour operators located in Phuket.

I made two trips to Phuket. On the first trip, I stayed at a bungalow on Karon beach. The bamboo hut had a bed and fan and cost me only 120 Baht a night, which was about six dollars. A small restaurant served American-style breakfast of eggs, toast, ham, and coffee or tea. The beach was about a mile long, a wide arc ending in rocks on either side. The gentle turquoise waters lapped at the sand and filled the crab holes. The beach was relatively undeveloped. Bungalows rose on the hillside at the far end of the beach, and one hotel, Karon Villa, offered luxury air-conditioned bungalows. Otherwise, the south end was dotted by simple one-room bungalows and a few bamboo restaurants. Water buffalo, submerged to their chests, grazed in rice fields behind the palm trees, and green mountains rose in the distance. A mist lay in the valley early in the morning.

Fishermen worked in the bay. They spread a net by boat and pulled both ends to shore. Men and women pulled on the ropes from the beach. Even some tourists joined in the work. As the semicircle became smaller, the water churned. A great mass of writhing fish soon appeared in the shallow water, and women loaded the fish into woven baskets.

I snapped pictures everywhere and swam in the calm water. One morning I hiked along the beach, passed two cats sleeping on the roof of a grass hut, and saw a young girl giving herself a bath. She dropped a plastic bucket into a well, pulled it up by a rope, and poured water over her head.

One day, I witnessed a comic scene, a clash of cultures. A German tourist had his equanimity wrecked by the whimsical nature of the Thai. I was sitting at a table behind a German man and his girlfriend. Apparently, from what I overheard of the conversation, which was spoken in German, the Thai who rented them fins and masks charged different prices every day. He charged whatever he felt. There were no posted prices. This concept was something the German couldn't understand. His orderly brain short-circuited. The man spoke excitedly to his girl friend, waved his hands in the air, and shouted, "They should learn!"

I smiled at his frustration. I had lived in Thailand long enough to know that Thais don't pay attention to details. They're too busy having fun. Order a hot dog, and you might not get a bun. I wanted to tell the German to take it easy, go with the flow, enjoy himself; it doesn't matter.

My second trip to Phuket took me to Patong Beach, a well-developed beach with bars, luxury bungalows, and hotels. Bare-breasted French girls strolled along the sand, to the delight of Thai men who cast quick glances, while they drank their Mekong whiskey. Traditional Thai women don't wear western-style bathing suits or bikinis.

I snorkeled in a lagoon south of Kata Beach and chased squid. I dived in the waters off Patong Beach with some Germans, who brought their Thai girlfriends. Sompon stayed on the beach.

Festivals

There seemed to be a festival in Thailand every month. On the first full moon of the twelfth lunar month (November), everyone celebrates Loy Krathong, the festival honoring the goddess of the waterways. I was in Pattaya at the time, and I followed the custom of the people. I bought a banana leaf boat, lit the candle, and floated it on the water. Thousands of tiny boats drifted out to sea, their candles flickering in the breeze.

In April, people celebrate the Songkran festival, the traditional Thai New Year. People throw water on each other, in the belief that water washes away bad luck. Children sprinkle water on their parents in a gesture of respect, strings are tied around the wrists, and some people coat their face with a white paste to ward off evil.

The king's birthday is in December, another time of celebration. People set off fireworks, and barbers give free haircuts in the parks.

At the beginning of each school year, typically on a Thursday, Wai Kru Day is celebrated. Students pay respect to their teachers by bowing low and offering them flowers.

Kathin, held in October, is a time to offer robes and gifts to the monks. The Vegetarian Festival, held in September, features firewalking, music, dance, and abundant vegetarian dishes. Some participants go into a trance after ten days of meditation and a strict vegetarian diet. They pierce their bodies with hooks and spikes, yet seem unaffected.

Chinese New Year is celebrated, as well as the western New Year's Eve.

May is an especially busy month. The Buddha's birthday is celebrated on the fifteenth day of the fourth lunar month (the first lunar month is February). People bring flowers to the temples, which are decorated with lanterns. Long strips of incense are burned. May also features the Ploughing Ceremony, signifying the beginning of the planting season, and Coronation Day, honoring the coronation of King Rama IX.

If you want to know what day it is in Thailand, consider that the Thai calendar begins in 543 B.C. The year 2004 is 2547 B.E. (Buddhist Era).

Sanuk

There is a Thai saying, "Life is fun. Why so quickly to go?"

My time in the land of smiles had been fun, but came to an end too quickly. I had found no diving work in Singapore, so it was time to return to America.

In six months I had learned many things. The Thai people were perfect teachers who showed me how to approach life from a different perspective.

Sanuk, or fun, was a necessary part of Thai life. If something wasn't fun, Thais wouldn't do it.

Thais were typically not punctual. Their concept of time was refreshingly different from that of most Westerners. Thais didn't watch the clock. There was dawn, usually 6 a.m. Morning lasted until 11 a.m. There was noon, afternoon, and sunset. Two o'clock in the morning to a Thai meant 8 a.m. to a foreigner, because morning started at 6 a.m. Many foreigners become confused when they visit Thailand. I offer them this suggestion. Come with an open mind. Leave all rigid, pre-conceived notions at home. Come to have fun.

I had learned some of the Thai language and learned some customs. Never point a foot at anyone, never touch a person on the head, never walk over someone, never sit on a Buddha statue, never step on currency with a picture of the king on it. Smile often, give superiors a *wai,* and don't shout or wave the hands. Eat food with the right hand, because the left hand is used for wiping the backside and is dirty. Never lose your temper. The one who loses his temper in public loses face. Don't kiss or display affection with the opposite sex in public. Don't be rude.

I knew a few rules, but I was still a foreigner, a *farang,* who knew little about the rich Thai culture.

My time with Sompon had come to an end. We were friends, but a long-lasting relationship was hopeless. She spoke little English and had no education. She said she would give up prostitution and return to classical dance at the Rose Garden. I loved her for her beauty, grace, and smile, but those things were not enough.

The smile of a Thai girl had captured my heart. I left Thailand feeling melancholy, but I could feast on the memories for a lifetime. Traveling through a foreign land was almost as good and as exotic as bottom time.

Dream's End

My ambition to be a commercial diver faded in 1982. Worldwide oilfield construction had virtually ceased. The work yards along Engineer Road in Belle Chase, Louisiana, were deserted.

I had lived at sea long enough to see the deterioration of men's souls. The sea was a cruel mistress. She drove some men to alcohol. She took men away from their wives. The awful monotony of the waves drove some men crazy. Still, there was something about the sea that made me want to stay on the waves forever. Therein lies the addiction of the sea.

I came to America much richer, although I had not earned a cent in the previous six months. My perspective on life changed, which gave me more than money can ever give. My most lasting impression was the sight of monks walking barefoot along a railroad track. I was never religious, but the monks, who owned nothing but the clothes on their backs and alms bowls, were living proof that people can reject materialism and choose a higher life. A wandering beggar is scorned in places like America, but in civilized countries poverty is a virtue. I seriously considered the idea of abandoning my career and possessions when I reached the age of fifty-five, to become a monk and pursue a more spiritual life. Many people did this in the Far East, and it was an honorable act.

In my search for a religion that had meaning, I discovered Buddhism. I always had a difficult time believing the teachings of monotheistic religions. I didn't believe in original sin, heaven or hell, end-of-the-world theories, or that a man returned from the dead. I could not believe that the world was controlled by capricious gods who satisfied their whims by tormenting people. I would rather believe in a rational god than a mysterious one. After all, the laws of the universe can be understood. Science proves this.

I had seen much hypocrisy during my travels. I saw Arabs in Thailand bring a different woman to their hotel rooms every night. They drank beer and smoked cigarettes. Alcohol was forbidden in their countries. What did they say? "Hypocrisy is the price we pay for leading a virtuous life." I had to laugh.

I was never a fatalist. I didn't believe in fate or predetermination. I believed in free will; that's why I readily accepted karma. We have the power to control our destiny in this lifetime. About the only time I believed in fate was when the El Chichon volcano erupted. That was fate telling me not to make any drug deals. I had misgivings about that deal from the start, and I felt relieved when it fell through. I have never again gotten involved in underhanded dealings.

Where would my karma take me next? I settled in Louisiana wondering what to do with myself. My nomadic existence had ended, but I had no social skills. I didn't belong in society. I was a misfit. What could I do?

I knew about the computer revolution, so I enrolled in a technical school and studied computer programming for a year. I found a job with a defense contractor, bought a townhouse in a New Orleans suburb, and joined the throngs of people who fight traffic every day and work under fluorescent lights. I got married, learned how to mow a lawn and navigate an office. I learned how to act civilized. I learned how to use a copy machine and take my clothes to the dry cleaner. I wore a suit and tie, drove an automobile, cut my hair, and learned how to eat properly in a restaurant. I became indistinguishable from the crowd, but the sea was still inside me. I bought a replica of a Mark V diving helmet and placed it in the corner or my living room. I hung a hundred spiny oysters on the wall. My seashells adorned the bookcase and coffee table. The precious, intense moments of bottom time remained baked in my memory.

Sometimes, in my mind, I still drift away from the office and nudge the blenny in the crevice by the pontoon hitch.

About the Author

Norbert Weissinger was born in Germany and grew up in Pennsylvania. He attended Penn State University where he majored in Biology. After college he enrolled in a commercial dive school in Oakland, California. He has logged more than 500 commercial dives in depths ranging from 40 to 200 feet. Diving for work or pleasure has taken him to many parts of the world including Mexico, Central America, Hawaii, the Philippines, Thailand, and Malaysia. He currently lives in Arkansas and works as a database administrator. This is his fourth book.

Printed in the United Kingdom
by Lightning Source UK Ltd.
134678UK00002B/60/A